The National Archaeological
Museum of Naples

Soprintendenza Archeologica
di Napoli e Caserta

Texts by Stefano De Caro

photographs by
Luciano Pedicini

The National Archaeological Museum of Naples

Electa Napoli

Electa Napoli

Editor
Silvia Cassani

Graphic design and layout
Enrica D'Aguanno
Ivana Gaeta

Mark Weir translated the first thirteen
chapters and the entries from pages 15
to 85 and 131 to 200.
Federico Poole translated the five
remaining chapters and the other entries

Contents

Foreword

This small volume is not meant as a companion to accompany the visitor on his or her exploration of the Museum, partly because it would have had to be much more voluminous even to mention the huge number of items on display or being prepared for viewing, but also because we trust that the information provided alongside the exhibits, made increasingly comprehensive as new displays are opened, will serve that end. Our intention is to help the visitor who wanders round the Museum, confronted with splendid images on every side, to adopt a historical perspective that makes sense of the whole, rather than viewing them simply as a collection of «beautiful objects of the ancients».

Since the Museum is rapidly acquiring a new expositional rationale, the structure of this book has had to depart from traditional guides to the various collections, some of which still use 18th and 19th century criteria based on type and material that are no longer acceptable today. In choosing to illustrate the Museum from the historical point of view we have a twofold objective: to reflect the rationale behind the new layouts, and to give this volume a certain autonomy, so that it can be referred to before or after the visit as the stimulus for a voyage of intellectual discovery and a vademecum for an extraordinarily rich cultural experience.

We hope to have accomplished this at least in part by providing a manual written in a style which is readable but not reductive, to help the visitor become familiar with the museum collections and identify their various attributes, whether historical, documentary or aesthetic. In any case we shall be well content if, after dipping into these pages, he or she feels the urge to seek out a more heavyweight book, or go back and have another look at an object which aroused curiosity, or even, why not?, feels driven to ask the Museum director to put on display an item which is not currently visible.

*Transportation of antique sculptures
found in Herculaneum from the
Museum of Portici to Palazzo degli
Studi in Naples, now the Archaeological
Museum, from "Voyage pittoresque ou
description des Royaumes de Naples et
de Sicile" by Jean-Claude Richard,
Abbé de Saint-Non, Paris 1781-86.*

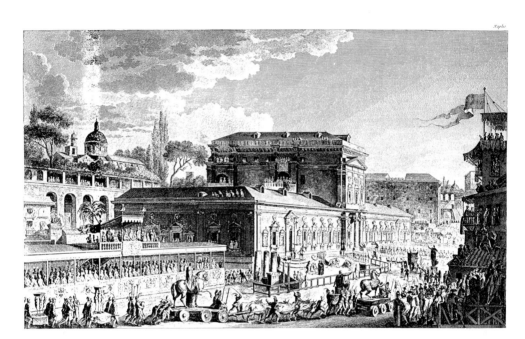

The National Archaeological Museum of Naples: a brief history

«..un juste hommage rendu par une Nation & dans un siècle éclairé à ces beaux arts qui nous ont été transmis, & dont l'éclat a donné un nouveau lustre à l'Italie & à l'Europe moderne»
(Abbé de Saint-Non, *Voyage pittoresque ou description des Royaumes de Naples et de Sicile*, II, Paris 1781-86)

The National Archaeological Museum of Naples is probably the most important museum in the world for classical archaeology. Such a statement naturally begs many questions, for it is impossible to quantify the cultural content of museums in terms of the Guinness Book of Records, but there is no doubt that, quite apart from the extraordinary richness of its collections, the history of this museum represents a fundamental point of reference for the formation of classical culture in Europe.

The origins of the Neapolitan Museum lay in the cultural ferment that led to the first configuration of modern archaeology in the 1700s. By a series of fortunate circumstances the role of the Kingdom of the Two Sicilies in this cultural advance was much more crucial than its status among the other European states would have warranted. In spite of the oppression of the Habsburg viceroys ("the Two Sicilies were Vienna's East Indies..."), which followed two centuries of no less ruthless exploitation by the Spanish, in the first half of the 18th century Naples was undoubtedly one of the most civilised cities in Italy, with a class of gentlemen-scholars who cultivated studies in history and philosophy (as for example Vico or Giannone) and were fine practioners of music and art (Metastasio, Pergolesi, Sanfelice, Vaccaro and Solimena being the most eminent names). What is more, the city had significant precedents for a serious interest in antiquity: one only has to think of the excavations carried out in the Phlegrean Fields during the 17th century by the Viceroy Don Alfonso Pimentel, yielding statues that in 1613 were set up to embellish the Palazzo degli Studi (the future Museum), or those undertaken in 1666 by Cardinal Acquaviva.

However, the decisive impulse for the creation of the Museum came from the dynastic and political conjunctures that brought the Spanish Infanta, Charles III Bourbon, to the throne in Naples in 1734. Both Charles and his wife Maria Amalia of Saxony were from families in which there was a tradition of antique collecting, mainly through purchases in Rome. Charles's mother was born a Farnese, and thus he belonged to the Roman noble family which had built up the foremost collection of antiques in Rome. Then as luck would have it, a few years earlier the rich collection of August of Saxony had been augmented with the statues found in 1711 by the Prince d'Elboeuf in Resina (Herculaneum).

In Charles's project to set up a new kingdom and modernise the city of Naples, culture, and in particular its manifestation in great art collections, had an essential role to play. Thus steps were taken to make Naples a great centre of the arts, transferring from the ancestral duchy of Parma and in part also from Rome the great collections of books, works of art and the antiquities which had been amassed by the Farnese in two centuries of excavations and purchases. The idea of a "Museo Farnesiano" was conceived to embellish the city but also to glorify Charles's dynasty, with a new building, the Royal Villa of Capodimonte, being commissioned for it from the architect Giovanni Antonio Medrano in 1738.

That same year also saw the beginning of another undertaking which was to be decisive in the formation of the Museum. In Resina, on the site of another of the royal residences, the King initiated excavations in exactly the place where thirty years before, during the Austrian domination, Prince d'Elboeuf had discovered the statues which later found their way to the court of Saxony. By great good fortune the dig immediately yielded an extraordinary succession of other statues in marble and bronze and inscriptions which turned out to be the entire decoration, preserved intact, of the proscenium arch of the theatre of Herculaneum. This signalled the start of the exceptional campaign of excavations in the cities at the foot of Vesuvius. Ten years later, in 1748, work was begun at Pompeii, and a year later at Gragnano, to explore the villas of Stabiae. These digs ensured that a constant stream of treasures poured into the royal collection, including statues, many of them in bronze and marble, such as those from the villa of the Pisoni in Herculaneum (1754-58); exceptional finds such as the papyrus scrolls which constituted that villa's library; and an incredible variety of artefacts which could only be found in a whole city "preserved" intact by the volcanic eruption: mosaics, objects in daily use, weapons and precious belongings, glassware. Furthermore there was a staggering quantity of a new class of antique, virtually unknown in collections up to that time: the paintings, which emerged from the ground intact, their colours full of lustre, as beautiful "as if by the hands of the Graces", as Goethe put it.

In order to cope with this treasure trove, the royal villa in Portici was adapted in 1750 as the "Museum Herculanense", which quickly filled up with thousands of finds. It was largely due to these prestigious novelties that Naples, in the new role of capital of a Kingdom with its own importance in the Mediterranean theatre, also became an obligatory port of call on the Grand Tour. Young gentlemen from all over Europe were obliged to complete their education by making a cultural pilgrimage to Italy and drinking at the fountainheads of classicism and good taste in Rome, Florence and Naples.

Faced with such an abundance of archaeological materials, the new Kingdom also had to set up a scientific structure to supervise the excavations and the conservation and administration of what they produced. The staff was composed in part of local scholars and also of experts summoned from further afield, such as the French sculptor Joseph Canart, who was charged with supervising the restoration work, and the Roman Camillo Paderni, in charge of the Museum Herculanense. Besides, the powerful first minister and friend of the King, the Tuscan Marquis Bernardo Tanucci, was quite a proficient antiquarian in his own right, capable of deciding questions of restoration or disposition of materials in the Portici museum in person. Naturally mistakes were made, including some outrageous ones, such as the melting down of fragments of bronze statues which were considered "useless" in order to make modern works, or, for a time, the systematic destruction of all the paintings not considered worthy of the royal collection. Against such errors there was a violent, and largely justified, outcry on the part of learned Italians and foreigners, including the standard-bearer of modern archaeology, J.J. Winckelmann. It must be said that the members of the Accademia Ercolanese, set up in 1755 to publish the royal collections, did nothing to promote mutual understanding by their jealous monopoly of the Vesuvian discoveries. But on the whole, after the initial difficulties, the "Neapolitan approach to antiquities" became more and more reliable. One example can be seen in the varnish which was prepared with melted wax and used to conserve the paintings as they were removed, obtaining much better results than in the case of the paintings left *in situ*. This was no mean technical achievement in those times, and its success is still before our eyes today. Moreover the technique of recording the monuments with plans and drawings of pictures, mosaics and objects, developed by a team of draughtsmen taken on to provide illustrations for the edition of the "Antichità di Ercolano esposte" (1757-1792) reached notable levels of excellence during the second half of the 18th century, as can be seen for example in the records of the rooms of the temple of Isis at Pompeii.

With the departure of Charles to become King of Spain in 1759, work on the projected Museo Farnesiano at Capodimonte slowed down. Over the next few years the shortcomings of the Museum Herculanense became apparent, due in part to lack of space, for it was already filled to overflowing, and more importantly to considerations of safety. There was a real danger that a new eruption of Vesuvius would obliterate it, and there had been a dozen during the previous century. In 1767, following another fearful eruption, pressure mounted to transfer the collections elsewhere. When consulted in Spain, Charles was torn between taking them to Caserta, where the Royal Palace was being finished, or leaving them where they were, in which case, as he commented sardonically, if the worst did happen at least they would be the joy of excavators two thousand years hence!

Thus gradually it was decided to concentrate all the royal art collections, from both Capodimonte and Portici, in a new museum in Naples. The choice fell on the old Palazzo degli Studi (University) at the foot of the hill of Santa Teresa. A building had been erected on this site in 1586, intended as a cavalry barracks for the Spanish troops. Subsequently the Viceroy Don Pedro Fernando de Castro, count of Lemos, commissioned the architect Giulio Cesare Fontana to build new premises for the ancient Neapolitan university, inaugurated in 1615. With few interruptions it was the seat of learning in the city for a century and a half (G.B. Vico taught rhetoric there between 1697 and 1701). In 1777 the building was in a very bad state of repair, and it was decided to move the university to the former Jesuit college of il Salvatore. The old Palazzo was then adapted to house the Portici collections and the royal library. This idea was obviously very much in the air in 1778, when Saint-Non drew the famous view for his volume *Voyage pittoresque* showing the "*transport des Antiquités d'Herculanum, du Musaeum de Portici au Palais des Etudes à Naples*" in the guise of an ancient triumphal procession.

The design by the architect Ferdinando Fuga envisaging the reconversion of the building "for the use of the Royal Museum of Portici, the picture gallery of Capodimonte, the great Public Library, Schools for the three Fine Arts (Painting, Sculpture and Architecture) and Room for study of the Nude" came to nothing. On the death of Fuga the Roman architect Pompeo Schiantarelli was appointed in his place, and the project became even more ambitious, with proposals for a second storey (hitherto the palace had consisted in two wings on one level and a central two storey block) and a great semicircular colonnade to the rear, below the orchards of the Friars of Santa Teresa, "so that altogether it may stand to the greater glory of the Capital and to the delight of the Public" (1780).

12

Charles III had hesitated, in spite of the urgings of Luigi Vanvitelli, about bringing to Naples, along with his other possessions, the very famous sculpture collection which adorned the Roman Palazzo Farnese, his family home, and the other residences where, since the sixteenth century, popes and princes had displayed works which had become universally famous, such as the *Hercules* and *Farnese Bull*. Such a move went contrary to papal legislation and the will of Alexander Farnese, dated 1587, which included a clause stipulating that the statues should remain in Rome *in perpetuum*. Finally, in 1787, in spite of the Pope's protests, Charles's son Ferdinand IV, who had succeeded him in 1759, commissioned Philipp Hackert and Domenico Venuti to supervise the identification, restoration (which was carried out in the Roman workshop of Carlo Albacini) and transportation of the numerous sculptures from the Farnese residences. This operation took several years, and once the statues got to Naples they spent more time scattered between Palazzo Reale and the Real Fabbrica di Porcellane before they were finally installed in the Museum. In 1791 the *Farnese Bull* was set up as the centrepiece of a fountain in the Villa Reale di Chiaia, and only brought to the Museum in 1826.

The plans for the new museum were on the grand scale, and in 1791 it was suggested to add an astronomical observatory, of which the only feature to be installed was the sundial, which still gives its name to the largest of the halls. However, financial difficulties and political upheavals, not to mention the occasional earthquake, made progress difficult. In spite of the turbulent times – one only has to think of the King's two flights to Palermo in 1798 and 1806, both times taking numerous works of art with him (in 1799 the French had actually packed up the *Hercules* to be carted off to Paris!) – it proved possible in 1801 to open to the public the "Royal Library of Naples" and to begin at last to instal in the Museum the material from Portici (1805-1822) and the antiques from Capodimonte and Palazzo Cellamare.

During the ten years of French rule, when first Joseph Bonaparte and then Gioacchino Murat ruled the Kingdom, the Museum was spared the rapacious attentions of Napoleon, and indeed, under its directors Felice Nicolas (1805-1807) and Michele Arditi (1810-1838) it acquired some famous pieces, such as the Carafa head. With the return of the Bourbons and the Restoration it was enlarged once again with the acquisition of such important collections as the Borgia and Vivenzio, as well as the personal collection which Caroline Murat had formed during her time in Naples (known as the Museo Palatino). In 1816 it was renamed the "Royal Bourbon Museum" in a deliberate gesture of dynastic glorification.

The rebuilding of the edifice was finally completed in 1821-1822, under the direction of the architects Maresca, Bonucci and Bianchi. Antonio Canova was summoned to execute a work celebrating Ferdinand IV (following the Restoration styled the First) as protector of the arts, as

Napoleon had been celebrated at Brera. The result, a marble statue of the King as a latterday Athena, was intended to stand at the foot of the great staircase at the end of the entrance hall. However, following the unification of Italy in 1871, it was moved out and its place was taken by the monumental Jove from Cumae.

Thanks to the excavations in Pompeii the museum collections continued to grow. The 1830s and 1840s, for example, saw the arrival of the mosaics from the House of the Faun, of which the most striking example was the mosaic of Alexander (or, as it was called then, simply the "great mosaic"), the "blue glass" from the Villa of the mosaic columns and numerous finds dug up in the various provinces of the Kingdom, above all from the extraordinarily rich necropolises of Puglia. Among the important figures of the period we should mention the director, Francesco Maria Avellino and the young numismatist and epigraphist Giuseppe Fiorelli, whose ideas cost him a brief stay in the Bourbon prisons. It is significant that one of the few actions of the shortlived government of 1848 was the creation of a "Commission for the Reforms of the Royal Bourbon Museum and the excavations of antiquities throughout the Kingdom". Before it was suppressed it managed to produce some interesting considerations on the state of the Museum and of the Bourbon archaeological service, with proposals for their reorganisation.

Although it ended unhappily, the experience of 1848 proved vital for the future of the Museum. After the conquest of Garibaldi, who himself named A. Dumas as an ephemeral Director of the Museum, Fiorelli took over (1863-1875) and in him the innovations of the Commission found an enthusiastic and tireless champion. Now known as the "National Museum", it gained the highly important Santangelo collection and was completely reordered. From the museographical point of view Fiorelli made significant contributions to the history of archaeological research in his work at Pompeii throughout the Bourbon period. His achievements were perfected by his disciples, Giulio De Petra, who took over as Director in 1875, and the architect Michele Ruggiero, who completed the research in the old excavation sites of Herculaneum, Stabiae and in the Terrafirma provinces.

The period around the turn of this century was one of the most turbulent in the history of the Museum. Uncertainties, ambiguities and weakness in the face of pressure exerted by researchers who were primarily collectors and speculators, in the name of a misguided defence of the rights of private property, held up for years the passing of a new law regulating dealings in antiquities. A series of scandals broke out concerning the disappearance of antiques and the granting of export licences, from Rome and Campania in particular (the paintings and silver treasure of Boscoreale, the Capua tile...). The reorganisation of the collections carried out by the historian Ettore Pais (1901-1904) roused violent criticisms of excessive modernism in the Neapolitan milieu. Yet the layout and criteria he introduced, as also the decision to operate according to contexts, the emphasis on the new discipline of prehistory and the markedly historical approach adopted in some of the displays in line with current knowledge (in the Pompeii paintings, the portraits and the Greek sculptures) proved decisive for the Museum in this century and were largely respected by his successors G. Gattini (1906-1910), V. Spinazzola (1910- 1924), A. Maiuri (1925-1961), A. De Franciscis (1961-1977), F. Zevi (1977-1981) and E. Pozzi (1981-1991).

The Museum came through the Second World War unscathed, the building eluding the bombs and the most vulnerable collections being moved first to Cassino and then, just a few days before the destruction of the abbey, to the Vatican Museums. Even the collection of goldware, pilfered by the Nazis, was subsequently found and returned.

With the separation and removal of the picture collection to Capodimonte in 1957 the time was ripe for a general refurbishing of the Museum. There were serious structural problems to be resolved, and also museographical decisions to be taken, since some of the displays were looking decidedly dated (as for example the Secret Cabinet or the Gallery of coloured marbles). The structural problems were aggravated by the 1980-81 earthquake, but since that time the situation has been remedied thanks to a series of impressive works of consolidation. The second aspect is still very much on the agenda, and is highly demanding. The first difficulty is to preserve all the different cultural elements which, as we have seen, went into the history of the Museum (Renaissance collecting, excavations in the Vesuvius area, later extended to the Kingdom of the Two Sicilies and then to Italy, and so on) and ensure that they do not cancel each other out. A second difficulty derives from the fact that, with the creation of many new local museums, this Museum has lost its prime function as the representative institution of the territory.

It has had to rethink its *raison d'être*, and the aspiration now is for it to become the hub of a regional network of museums, finding suitable means of linkage with the local realities and representing the network at the national and international level. This can be achieved if a fruitful collaboration is set up with all the other prestigious cultural and scientific institutions operating in Naples in the field of archaeology, and also if the city itself fulfils its role in the context of the region and of the Italian state. It hardly needs saying that this is one of the thorniest questions in the current political reality.

In the meantime work goes ahead with the reordering of the sculpture collection. Emphasis is placed on the formative and contextual elements of the Farnese collection (the sculptures from the baths of Caracalla, reorganised in 1990, and the precious stones, in 1994, stand as interesting paradigms), the Borgia materials, and the public and private decorative ensembles of the cities of Campania: Pompeii, Herculaneum, Baiae, Cumae, Pozzuoli and Naples itself. The highly important experience of the exposition of the Villa dei Papiri, undertaken by A. De Franciscis in 1973 and based on the recontextualisation of the materials, superseding the arbitrary classification according to types (bronzes large and small, marbles, etc.), was echoed on a more modest scale in the recent (1992) reelaboration of the material from the temple of Isis in Pompeii. Forthcoming are the organisation *ex novo* of the section of epigraphs, the numismatic collection, and the section of prehistory and material from Cumae. The latter will be the first specimen of the sector dedicated to cultures of pre-Roman Campania (Greeks, Etruscans, Italic peoples), which is intended to serve as a general historical introduction, while individual centres are analysed in the more detailed exhibitions which are now to be found in the numerous and richly furnished site museums. While the Museum possesses some exceptional material from Magna Graecia, it does not constitute a complete documentation of this unique phenomenon throughout the various regions, and thus it seems more appropriate to offer a presentation based on the successive phases of archaeological research in this area.

Marble statue of Ferdinand IV
as Minerva

When Ferdinand IV returned from Palermo the greatest sculptor of the age,
Antonio Canova, was commissioned to
celebrate the monarch as Protector of
the Arts, as Napoleon had been celebrated
at Brera. He produced this large marble
statue depicting Ferdinand, now styled
the First, as a latter-day Athena, to be
placed at the foot of the main staircase at
the end of the entrance hall. The Latin
epigraph beneath it reads: *Marble statue
dedicated with this inscription in the
year 1821 to Ferdinand I Bourbon,
pious, fortunate and indomitable ruler
of the Kingdom of the Two Sicilies,
unassailable defender of religion and
the public good; this palace, formerly a
seat of learning, having been liberated
of a garrison of troops and restored to
the Muses by his father the august king
Charles, he completed in a more ample
and worthy form; gave orders that
from all sides should be gathered and
conserved a great number of pictures,
every manner of statue, books and
works of art together with the library of
his forebears and all the treasures
from antiquity of the Farnese family
and those excavated at Pompeii, Herculaneum and other sites, all primarily to the greater glory of the nation
and for the convenience of scholars; to
this venerable Museum he gave the
name of Bourbon; to the same he
added the Bourbon Society of the Sciences
divided into three Academies; and also
the Academy of Herculaneum for
Antiques and the Fine Arts. The work of
Antonio Canova.*
The statue of Ferdinand was moved
from the staircase at the end of the
entrance hall to the side entrance in
1871, whence it is soon to return to the
site for which it was created.

Prehistory and Protohistory
in the Bay of Naples

The museum itinerary dedicated to Prehistory and Protohistory begins in Room 127 and proceeds both horizontally and vertically. In this room and the next one the visitor can follow the succession of the first civilisations to inhabit the Bay of Naples and the immediate hinterland (Capua, *Calatia, Suessula),* up to the beginnings of Greek colonization in the eighth century B.C. (Room 126, Sarno valley, Pre-Hellenic Cuma). Alternatively, by going up the stairs in the middle of Room 127 one goes back in time, viewing on the intermediate floor remains from the Middle and Recent Bronze Age (Grotta di Pertosa, Murgia Timone), and on the top floor still earlier evidence from the Eneolithic, Neolithic, Mesolithic and Palaeolithic times.

This region presents particular difficulties for prehistorical archaeological research. Chief among them are the spectacular volcanic phenomena which ever since the most remote geological eras have represented the principal geomorphological feature of this territory, burying the oldest sites under many metres of lava and debris. Thus it has rarely been possible to carry out scientific investigations on whatever has come to light. In the Phlegrean Fields we lack any evidence of the first Stone Age cultures, the Palaeolithic and Mesolithic, whereas the other side of the Bay of Naples, comprising the Sorrento peninsula and the island of Capri, is not volcanic but made of older, limestone rock and has yielded an abundance of material from those times. Of particular interest are the most ancient remains found on Capri, from the period when the island was still joined to the peninsula. The main site was discovered in 1906 near the Hotel Quisisana (conserved in the Cerio collection on Capri). Above a layer containing fossil remains of wild boar, deer, bears, horses, but also elephants, hippopotami and rhinoceroses, there were stone tools of both the two-faced and flake types from the earlier Palaeolithic with amigdales of the Abbeville and old and evolved Acheleuan varieties and proto-Levallois tools (from between 700,000 and 350,000 years ago).

An additional interest of these Palaeolithic remains from Capri is the fact that they tie in with an observation made by the Roman historian Suetonius. In describing Augusts's insistence on a sober lifestyle, he recounts that the Emperor was not in favour of adorning his villas with statues and paintings, preferring copses and porticoes and "objects of unusual antiquity and rarity, such as the gigantic remains of fearful wild animals discovered on Capri, known as bones of the Giants, and weapons of the heroes".

From the middle Palaeolithic age (350,000-35,000 years ago) we have tools of the Levallois-Muster type found in the grotta dello Scoglione in the bay of Nerano, near the tip of the Sorrento peninsula, together with remains of oxen, ibex and deer, and more Muster tools from other caves in the bay at Punta della Campanella. From the later Palaeolithic (35,000-10,000 years ago) come the products of Epigravettian manufacture, dating from 13-12,000 years ago, found in the grotta La Porta in Positano, while characteristic of the Mesolithic age (10,000-7,000 years ago) is the gathering of sea and land molluscs borne out by animal remains and evidence of stone-working from the same grotta La Porta (8619 +/-200 years ago) and the nearby grotta delle Sopressate or del Mezzogiorno.

The affirmation of the Neolithic Age, an extraordinary phase of innovation in human history known as the "Neolithic revolution" which saw the introduction of agriculture, stamped and painted pottery, settlements and navigation, took place throughout much of the Italian territory about 7,000 years ago with the so-called "second aspect" of impressed pottery (the culture of Masseria La Quercia, near Foggia in Puglia, and Stentinello in Sicily). While some of the characteristics of the Mesolithic persisted, such as the gathering of molluscs, we now find evidence of such typical Neolithic traits as cattle raising, fortified villages and of course agriculture, seen in such finds as millstones, parts of sickles and so on. As well as material from Ariano Irpino, which is analogous to that of Masseria La Quercia, the Museum contains evidence of the entrenched village of Murgia Timone (Matera), a settlement on a plateau surrounded by a ditch which yielded painted and engraved pottery, bones of goat, sheep, ox, pig and dog and a stone industry with examples of blades, axes and machetes.

The grotta delle Felci on Capri revealed material which gave its name to the Capri Culture (about 5,000 years ago), a Neolithic culture which was in fact very widespread throughout Southern Italy, Sicily and the Tyrrhenian basin (it was particularly important in Lipari). The deposits which were investigated, connected with grave furnishings, included magnificent vases made of refined clays polished to a shine and painted fineware pottery with motifs of flames outlined in black, bundles crossed with lines, wide angles, handmills for grinding ochre, blades made of flint and obsidian – a volcanic glass, excellent for making small blades, which was the object of much sea-trading at this time – and bowls painted with schematic human figures.

The subsequent phase of the Eneolithic is very important in the prehistory of Campania and well documented in the Museum. It is characterised by the earliest metal-working cultures in the peninsula, in copper and then bronze. Already visible around 3,000 B.C. in the last neolithic cultures of Diana and Piano Conte (localities in the Aeolian Islands), it received an impulse from the arrival of oriental voyagers who were proficient in metallurgy, moving westwards in the quest for metals. This process appears to have been in full swing by the later Eneolithic, from shortly before 2,500 B.C. The eponymous site for the principle culture known to us in Campania and Lucania is the locality of Gaudo near Paestum. The first necropolises were investigated in 1943 by the Archaeological Unit of the allied troops who had come across it while setting up an airstrip (the so-called Brinson tomb). Many other necropolises with the typical grotto tombs or sporadic material belonging to this culture (circa 2,500 -1,800 B.C.) have been found subsequently at Mirabella Eclano (Avellino), Caiazzo di Caserta, Colle Sannita (Caserta), Piano di Sorrento, Naples in the Materdei quarter, Ischia and Licola, and in the region of Salerno at Buccino, Pontecagnano, Eboli in the grotta di Polla and so on. Recently another settlement may have been identified at Taurasi near Avellino. The materials found seem to denote communities which were predominantly pastoral, since in the remarkable variety of smooth-surface impasto (produced freehand, without a wheel) some of the shapes imitate wineskins made from hides or bladders, although there are also vases based on pumpkins. A few weapons are made of metal, such as triangular daggers and axes, as are some ornamental objects, but still the great majority of arms and tools are in flint. The shape of some vases makes comparisons possible with materials of Troy I and II, and it now seems likely that these peoples originated from that region.

One of the sites for which there is the most comprehensive documentation in the Naples Museum is La Starza at Ariano Irpinia, an opencast site which is important not just as an example of a permanent settlement but also as a transit point on the route from the Tyrrhenian to the Adriatic coasts. The original deposit goes back to the early Neolithic and contains, as we have mentioned, material which can probably be attributed to the culture of Masseria La Quercia in Puglia. Then come strata which can be identified with the late to final Neolithic culture of Serra d'Alto, present in Puglia and Lucania, and the Sicilian cultures of Diana and Piano Conte. This brings us up to the end of the Neolithic and the start of the Eneolithic (3000 B.C.). The permanent settlement dates from the height of the Eneolithic, with the presence of people who had assimilated elements of the northerly culture of Rinaldone in Latium and also had contact with peoples engaged in the trading of obsidian from the Tyrrhenian islands. Various signs point to a mixed economy based above all on grazing and agriculture. Subsequently, all the typical characteristics of the Appenine Bronze Age culture are displayed in strata going up several metres, passing from the earliest to the latest Bronze Age.

This was a typically pastoral culture (whose *floruit* came in about 1400 B.C.), with colander-type vases and other characteristic forms such as the vases used in cheese-making, while objects in stone such as polished axes become rare. The Appenine civilisation naturally recurs in many other sites in the region, from Capri (grotta delle Felci) to Lucania. Among the deposits found in caves we can recall the grotta Nicolucci in Sorrento, which yielded pottery ranging from the Neolithic of Serra d'Alto to the Eneolithic of Gaudo, the Bronze Age and beyond, the grotta dello Zachito near Caggiano (SA), where a sequence of hearths alternating with sterile layers indicates the episodic presence of herdsmen, probably following the seasons, and yielding both Appenine and Subappenine materials. The grotta di Pertosa (SA) at the foot of the Monti Alburni also contained Appenine and Subappenine materials, and is particularly significant for the discovery, in a recess of the rock wall inside the cave, of vases for the treatment of milk and a wooden whisk which confirmed the pastoral vocation of these peoples. The unusual environment, a lake inside a grotto, permitted the exceptional conservation of a series of wooden posts which belonged to a structure raised on piles.

In exploring the village of Palma Campania (NA) in 1972, buried by a prehistoric eruption of Vesuvius, evidence of a new *facies* from the end of the early Bronze Age (1800-1600 B.C.) was identified for the first time, which was subsequently corroborated in sites at Monte Fellino near Nola (NA), Camposauro (BN), on the Monte Taburno (AV) and at Nocera Inferiore (SA) where a tomb had been investigated in the 19th century. The pottery types are undoubtedly those of a pastoral economy, with strong links with the Tyrrhenian environment (Capo Graziano culture in the Aeolian Islands), while the bronze weapons – there were also some in flint – show connections with the metallurgic traditions of central Europe.

The presence in the Appenine region of the first pottery testifying to contacts with the Mycenean world is also very significant. After the discovery of fragments on Ischia going back to the middle Bronze Age (circa 1,300 B.C.) in the opencast site of Castiglione, the excavations carried out on the island of Vivara between Ischia and Procida uncovered the remains of various settlements (middle to late Bronze Age) containing a great abundance of Mycenean material coming from the Peloponnes and possibly also from the Cyclades, in both fine and common ceramic ware. These finds not only gave substance to the mythical journeys of the Greek heroic age (the epic evoked in the Odyssey by Homer when he puts into the mouth of Athena, disguised as Mente, king of Thaphos, the account of one of these voyages), but also indicate the existence of more permanent settlements than mere coastal refuges. In any case we cannot fail to be reminded of those myths, in all likelihood dating back to Mycenean times, which portrayed Ulysses sailing through these waters and founding or worshipping at sanctuaries (Capo Ateneo or Lake Avernus), presented Liparos, the legendary coloniser of the Aeolian Islands, as King of Sorrento, and identified the promontories of the Tyrrhenian, from Licosa to the Sirenusse and Parthenope, as the Syren lands.

The most ancient village on Vivara (16th century B.C.) was at punta Mezzogiorno, comprising elliptical huts made of stakes which measured 10-12 metres at the widest point, had concave floors and, at the back, a hollowed-out hearth protected by a ring of tall sticks. There are very interesting traces of metal-working *in loco* and also of Mycenean pottery of the Late Helladic I style. Another village at Punta d'Alaca, with huts which are roughly rectangular or elliptical and circular semi-interred grain stores, apparently originated in the same period but continued to be inhabited for about a century later (15th century B.C.) and has yielded Mycenean ware from the Late Helladic IIA style. In the Appenine *facies* from the end of the middle Bronze Age (16th century B.C.) can be placed the hamlet at Punta Capitello whose material finds parallels in other sites around the Bay, while evidence of Mycenean importations diminishes or ceases altogether.

A new, highly significant element in the Protohistory of Campania appeared at the end of the Bronze Age (circa 1050- 900 B.C.) with the Protovillanova culture. The funerary rites changed, from burial to cremation in the typical biconical ossuaries. Materials from this culture have been found at La Starza and a tomb with the characteristic ossuary was found at Sant'Angelo in Formis. This was the time in which the great cultural areas of the early Iron Age (900-750 B.C.) were beginning to be defined, on one hand with practitioners of inhumation of the *Fossakultur,* to which can be tentatively linked the names of the indigenous peoples recorded by the Greeks (Opicians in the valley of the Sarno and in pre- Hellenic Cuma, Ausonians in the area of Massico), and on the other practitioners of incineration at Capua, Pontecagnano and Sala Consilina, the progenitors of the Etruscans in the historical era. In the tombs of these peoples we now find (in Cuma, Capua, Pontecagnano and Veio) the first geometric vases brought by merchants from Greece, the harbingers of that colonization which in the first half of the eighth century B.C., with the founding of Pithecusa and then Cuma, marked the beginning of the period in which "history" comes into its own in Southern Italy.

Tomb I from Naples, Materdei
invv. 150473, 150474, 150475, 150476
The two tombs found on the hillside of Materdei in Naples constitute the oldest evidence of human settlement in the area of the city. They were cavities cut out of the tufa of the "oven" type, and both for this characteristic and for the type of material they contained they can be identified with the "Gaudo" style of Eneolithic culture (see above). The grave goods include a large two-handled cinerary urn, a bottle, a cup with a raised handle and a bronze triangular- bladed dagger.

Urn with excised decoration from Ariano Irpino
inv. 241760
In this technique, which produced striking ornamentation, curly and straight patterns were cut into the vase's smooth dark surface and the hollowed out portions were then filled with a white paste, creating a pleasing white on black effect.

The cultures of Preroman Campania:
the Greeks (*Pithekoussai*, Cuma, *Neapolis*)

The shores of the Bay of Naples witnessed the most ancient episodes of Greek colonization of the West. From the middle of the 9th century B.C., in the so-called "precolonization" phase, vases in the Greek geometric style began to appear in early Iron Age tombs in Lazio and Campania, evidence of the first contacts between Greek merchants and the indigenous population. In the first half of the 8th century, about 770 B.C., a body of Greeks from Euboea founded *Pithekoussai* on Monte Vico on the island of Ischia, the first permanent Greek settlement on the Italian peninsula and indeed in the western Mediterranean. The evidence from the tombs excavated by G. Buchner, of which a significant selection is to be displayed in the Museum while the bulk is on view in the site museum of Lacco Ameno, indicates that this was not a *polis* but rather an emporium. It would have been frequented not just by Euboeans but also by Phoenicians and parties of Eastern traders (trading routes linked it to Syria on the opposite shore of the Mediterranean, where emporia gathered goods and know-how from all over Asia). Traders would have been attracted by the enormous commercial potential of this remote outpost near the metalliferous regions of Etruschia, the island of Elba and Amianta. Ischia represented not only a transit point but also a centre of metalworking: remains of forges with scrap metal which certainly originated in Elba have been found in the locality of Mazzola inland from the bay of San Montano, one of the emporium's two ports.

The extraordinary historical importance of *Pithekoussai* lies in the solid cultural links which grew up between the Greeks and the indigenous population on the strength of the trading activity. The inscription on the so-called "cup of Nestor" arouses strong emotions as the most ancient Greek literary text, but the inscription, certainly deriving from *Pithekoussai*, which was discovered recently on a vase dating from about 770 B.C. from the necropoli dell'Osteria dell'Osa, in the territory of the *Gabii*, probably has even greater significance, for Roman myth had it that in this region Romulus and Remus received their knowledge of Greek letters. Thus this is the first documentary evidence we have of the spread of the Greek alphabet from *Pithekoussai* and Cuma outwards until it affected Etruscans, Latins, Opicians and other Italic peoples. After this first phase, based primarily on commercial interests, the Euboeans gained a secure foothold on the mainland itself at Cuma,

on the coast of the Phlegrean Fields opposite Ischia. Here the founding fathers Megasthenes and Hypocles gave rise to a true *polis* which covered a vast area with natural protection from a barrier of swampland and a ridge of high ground running from the crest of Monte Grillo to a volcanic spur. This peak was occupied by an indigenous village which was sacked by the colonizers, who erected the temples of their acropolis on the ruins. A natural harbour and some coastal lagoons offered plenty of shelter for ships and ensured that the trading activity begun in *Pithekoussai* could continue here on a more stable footing. In fact the city expanded rapidly, both round the coast (the whole arc of the Bay of Naples round to Punta della Campanella was known as the Bay of the Cumans, and Cuman fortified ports, or epineia, have been identified at Miseno, Pozzuoli, Pizzofalcone and Capri) and inland for the agricultural resources which were essential to a rapidly growing population.

This expansion led inevitably to conflict with the Etruscans, who were on the move from their bases in the hinterland of Campania (Capua, Calatia, Nola) and the Salernitano (Pontecagnano, Fratte) towards the coast, competing with the Greeks for dominion over the indigenous population. Some episodes of this conflict left traces in the archaeological and documentary sources. The foundation of Pompeii, for example, in the late 7th and early 6th century, represented an attempt by the Etruscans of Nola to break down the hegemony of the Greeks in the coastal region by driving a wedge into their territory at the mouth of the River Sarno. The violent destruction of the town's first ring of walls can be seen as the result of the reaction on the part of the Cumans. They themselves would have lost no opportunity to strengthen their presence with the arrival of new colonizers. In 531 B.C. a group of inhabitants of Samos, who went into exile when the tyrant Polycrates seized power there, took over a Cuman fortress and founded *Dikaiarcheia* (now Pozzuoli) meaning "the city of justice" in contrast to the *adikia* of the home they had left. The origins of Parthenope, another Cuman fortress on the outcrop of Pizzofalcone and the island of Castel dell'Ovo (*Megaris*), must also have been tied up with the struggle between Etruscans and Cumans. The discovery of the Greek necropolis in 1949 gave confirmation to the traditional version of the origins of Naples. This, shrouded in myth, held that the city was founded by seafarers from the island of Rhodes, who were familiar with the westward trading routes well before the founding of *Pithekoussai*. Parthenope was the name of one of the Syrens whose tomb was nearby (another, called Leucosia, was buried at Capo Licosa, while the group of islands called Li Galli off Punta della Campanella were known as le Sirenuse). Other authors ascribe the foundation of Parthenope to a group of exiles from Cuma itself, and its subsequent destruction to the jealousy of the mother city at the success and influence acquired by the new centre. In fact the necropolis of Pizzofalcone indicates the existence of a settlement from the middle of the 7th to the middle of the 6th century, when it was brusquely suppressed, and our reading of the popular tradition would suggest that this was at the hands of the Etruscans together with the vindictive Cumans.

There is no doubt that a few decades later, in 524 B.C., the hostility between Etruscans and Cumans came to a head in a great battle amidst the marshes that surrounded Cuma. The Greeks defeated the Etruscans and were launched on a period of florid expansion which saw them allied with the Latini in a further battle against the Etruscans at Ariccia in 505. This new victory was followed, however, by a period of internal strife at Cuma, in which the oligarchy of cavaliers lost its dominant position. In 492 power was seized by the military leader Aristodemos, who installed a regime of tyranny. He was known as "the Effeminate" (*Malakos),* possibly on account of his pro-Etruscan leanings, one sign of which was the fact that he gave hospitality to Tarquinius the Proud after the defeat of the last of the Kings of Rome in the battle of Lake Regillo. Yet it seems that the power struggle was more a question of alliances of class than a simple opposition of Greeks to Etruscans, because the cavaliers who opposed Aristodemos also had their friends among the Etruscans. They found refuge in the main Etruscan stronghold of Capua, and it was thanks to the support of the latter and groups of Campanian mercenaries that they were finally able to overthrow and kill the tyrant.

Border regions in which interethnic relations are complicated by other ties based on commercial dealings or marriage usually give rise to a hybrid culture which is rich in stimuli and cross-fertilisation, and other archaeological evidence bears this out in the case of ancient Campania. Necropolises in the hinterland (as for example at *Suessula,* preserved in the Spinelli collection) show unmistakeable signs of both Hellenisation, as in banqueting services with vases made in Pithekoussai and Cuma (for example the *oinochoai* of the so-called Cuma-Tarquinia class) and at the same time adherence to Etruscan traditions, such as adorning wooden structures with colourful terracotta facing. In the case of Cuma, however, it was internal strife that eventually sapped the city's strength. The conflict with the Etruscans was decided in a naval battle in the fateful year of 480 B.C. – the same year as the victory of the Athenians over the Persians at Salamanca. The Greeks were victorious, but the brunt of the fighting was borne by the emerging power of Western Greece, Syracuse. As a reward for its part in the victory this Sicilian capital was given the island of Ischia, and in about 475 inhabitants of both Pithekoussai and Cuma came to found *Neapolis,* the new city, as opposed to the old one of Partenope. The new *polis* conserved the ancient Euboic traditions and the heritage of the ancient Cuman cults, but it was also susceptible to the new hegemonous powers, first Syracuse and then Athens. We have documentary evidence of a mission to *Neapolis* by the Athenian strategist Diotymos. At the end of the 5th century he instituted the annual festival of the *Lampadophorai* in honour of the syren Partenope.

When at the close of the 5th century Cuma fell, like its erstwhile Etruscan rival Capua, into the hands of the Campanians, and in the space of a few years the other Greek cities in the South were similarly overrun by Lucanians and other Italic peoples, only Naples (and further south Velia) succeeded in preserving their Greek ascendancy, albeit with frequent compromises. In order to resist the onslaught of the Samnites the city had to incorporate a significant part of Campanian culture which became progressively Hellenised, so that in fact *Neapolis* remained Greek in its language, customs and institutions. In spite of its inevitable involvement in the Samnite wars, which caused it to enter the Roman sphere of influence as an ally of Rome, its excellent location and the tradition it had inherited from Cuma of presiding over important trading routes guaranteed the city's prosperity and ensured its importance as the Roman port for the Greek world.

Here the first silver coin was minted and important artisanal activity grew up (as for example the ceramic ware known as "Campana A"), to be spread throughout the Roman Mediterranean (Gaul, Spain and Africa). When this prosperity too began to decline with the emergence of the port of the new Roman colony of *Puteoli, Neapolis* and its precursor Cuma maintained a certain degree of affluence, and their reputation as repositories of the Greek tradition was gratifying to the Romans. Here on the doorstep of Rome itself the Romans had an image of Greece which they could use as the setting for their myths of the fatherland, with added lustre from the suggestion of Hellenisation, and of course the apogee of this revisionism came in Virgil's Aeneid. In the atmosphere of this latterday Greece they could shake off the suffocating ties of the *mos maiorum* and study Greek philosophy, art and literature; priestesses could be recruited for the cult of Ceres; Silla could dress in the Greek fashion, Augustus founded the "Italici Romani Augusti Isolimpici" games as if he had been the *princeps* in Olympia, and Virgil could study epicurism with Philodemus and Syrus. And as if to bring the wheel full circle, it was in one of the Roman villas on the Bay, built by Lucullus on the ruins of Parthenope (today the site of Castel dell'Ovo), that the last Roman emperor in the West, Romulus Augustulus, expired after being deposed and sent into exile.

Grave goods of tomb 1187 in the necropolis of Pithekoussai, from Lacco Ameno, San Montano invv. 238650-677

This Pithecusan tomb from the first quarter of the 7th century B.C. is likely to have been that of a fisherman, since it contained a bronze fish hook and two weights for holding down a net. The vases can be assigned to the stylistic phase known as Middle Protocorinthian; an oinochoe of Corinthian importation, with the familiar fish motif on the shoulder which was taken up by a large number of local jars exported as far afield as Etruria; another smaller oinochoe, a conical *lekythos* with a snake motif on the shoulder, a *kotyle*, a *skyphos* and no less than eight vases for perfumes (*aryballoi*) in Corinthian, Rhodian and local style. The funeral rite of inhumation denoted, according to the island custom, that the person died young.

Fragment of a female statuette
in terracotta from Cumae,
Stevens collection
inv. 120672

This female figurine dates from the middle of the 7th century B.C. or slightly earlier, in the phase of Greek art known as "Dedalic". It was made in a mould and finished by hand and is of mediocre quality but important in being one of the most ancient pieces of sculpture to have come down to us from the first Euboean colony.

Possibly the image of a goddess, she is portrayed with arms held in to her sides, a small mantle open at the front and the "layered wig" hairstyle typical of this stylistic phase.

Cover from a lekane by the C painter from Cumae

inv. 132615

The so-called C painter (for Corinthianizing, from his style which closely resembles the miniaturism of protocorinthian pottery) was one of the most skilful and productive Attic ceramists from the years 580-570 B.C., and this Cuman vase is the best of his works that we possess. A highly gifted story-teller, he represents here, taking his inspiration from lost epics such as the *Iliou Alosis* by Arctinus of Miletum, the killing of the young Astianax, son of Hector, by Neptolemos on the night of the fall of Troy.

The ferocious son of Achilles has grabbed the child by a leg and is on the point of hurling him off the city walls; with their arms stretched out imploringly Priam and Hecuba, the child's grandparents, approach while the battle rages all around.

Panathenaic style amphora from Cumae

inv. 86333

The name panathenaic is given to the amphorae containing the oil which, according to a reference in Aristotle, was the prize for victorious athletes in the gymnastic and equestrian contests of the Panathenean games. Tradition had it that these games were instituted in Athens by Theseus, and they took on their defini-tive form as a festival held every four years in 566-565 B.C.

The winner of the boxing competition won forty litres of oil (a precious commodity, subject to state monopoly in Athens). The amphorae conformed to a standard shape and decoration, which went on unchanged in the old black figure technique even several decades after this had been superseded by red figure vases.

The images too were unvarying: on one side the figure of the goddess with the inscription *ton Athenethen athlon* (from the games of Athene), and on the other the sport for which the trophy had been won.

This amphora, dating from the end of the 5th century B.C., must have belonged to a discus thrower from Cumae. The design is remarkable for its dynamism and sense of balance.

26

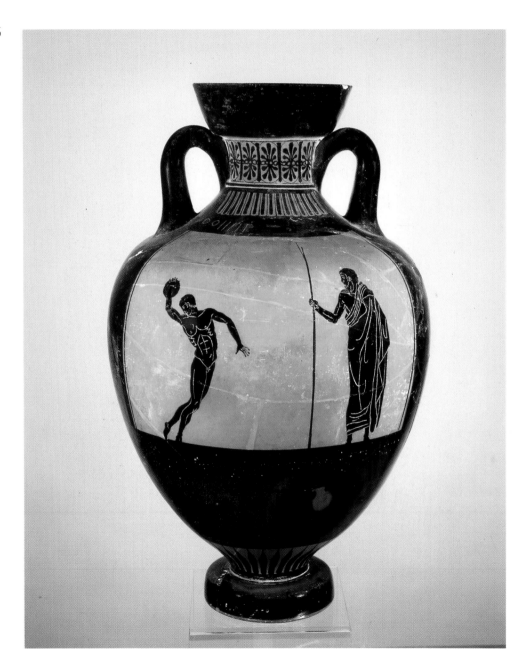

**Attic red figure pelike from Naples,
Via San Tommaso d'Aquino
inv. 151600**
The vase, found in a tomb in 1959, contained the remains of an incineration. The main scene depicted is particularly interesting, showing the birth of Helen from the egg between her brothers, the Dioscuri Castor and Pollux, dressed as hunters and distinguished by two stars over their heads. On either side are their parents, Leda who is making a gesture of surprise, and Tyndarus holding the royal sceptre (in actual fact Helen's father was Zeus, who had possessed Leda in the form of a swan). The vase has been attributed to the so-called Nikia Painter and dated from the last years of the 5th century B.C., subsequent to Euripides's play *Orestes* which this scene seems to evoke.

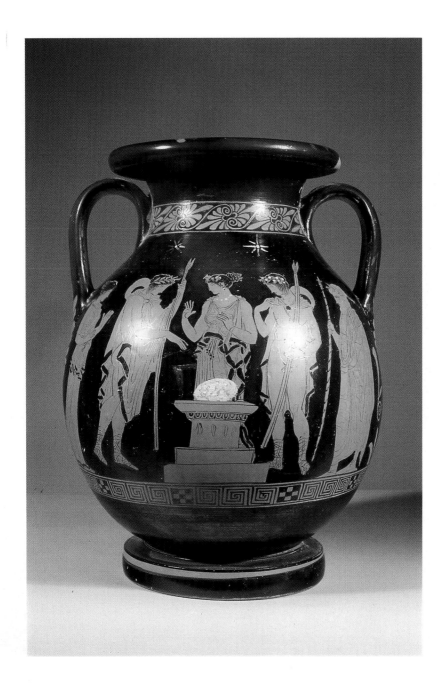

Statuette of a harp player riding a camel, from Cumae, Stevens collection inv. 140137
This figurine of a harp player wearing a short tunic and mounted on a camel (or dromedary) facing backwards is exceptional in the known repertoire of Hellenistic terracotta images. We can imagine that this Oriental musician is beguiling a caravan with his music. Whether this was the case or not, the statuette seems to allude to a Hellenistic fable that we do not know but which must have been very familiar to the citizen of Cumae in whose tomb it was laid.

Terracotta statuette of Aphrodite
in an aedicule, from Cumae, Stevens
collection
inv. 140219
This terracotta representation of a semi-
circular aedicule dates from the 2nd
century B.C. The decoration of the semi-
dome as a shell evokes the marine envi-

ronment of the goddess's birth. She is
seen coming from her bath (*anadiomene*) nude, covering her pubis with
one hand in a pose that vaguely recalls
Praxiteles's Cnydia, while with her other
hand she squeezes the water from her
hair. This is a familiar topos in all centres
of Hellenistic culture.

Torso of Diadumenos from Naples, Castelcapuano
inv. 150361
Found during work carried out in around 1930 in the area of the Castle, this statue is one of the best versions of the famous topos of the athlete binding his hair, created in bronze by Polyclitus of Argos in the 5th century B.C. It was discovered together with another athlete's torso (the so-called Amelung athlete), capitals, columns and other structures, and probably came from the decoration of a public building, quite possibly a palaestra.

On the following page:

Greek marble inscription of the Neapolitan games from Naples, Via Sant'Anna alle Paludi
inv. 2459
The text of the inscription, dating from 161-200 A.D., in the upper panel reads: "Marcus Aurelius Hermagoras, from Magnesia in Sipylus, wrestler (*palaistes*), president of the *xstos* (athletic association) of the Olympics of Ephesus and Smyrna, who won 29 sacred contests and 127 money prizes, achieved a draw in the Olympics of Pisa and drew 18 other times elsewhere". In the wreaths in relief below are inscribed the games at which he was victorious: "Actians, 2 (twice); Nemeans: 3: Aspis (at Argos): 2; Isthmians (on the Corinth isthmus): 2; Panathenians: 2; Panhellenians: 2; Olympics (in Athens?): 1; Hadrianians of Athens: 2; in Pozzuoli, 2; at the Asian *koinon* at Smyrna: 1; Olympics at Smyrna: 1; Olympics at Ephesus: 1; Hadrianians at Ephesus: 1; Balbillians at Ephesus; Augustans at Pergamum: 3; Trajans at Pergamum: 1; Halians at Rhodes: 2". The presence of this and other similar inscriptions erected to honour athletes in Naples is due to the celebration of the local Isolympic Games instituted by Augustus in 2 A.D. and held every five years with competitions of gymnastics, wrestling, boxing, horse and chariot racing, and musical and theatrical contests at which the Emperors often assisted and even on occasions competed. The list of games in the inscription shows that during the year athletes went the rounds of a veritable circuit, taking in Italy, Greece and Asia Minor, in which numerous contests had long been instituted alongside the traditional games from the classical age.

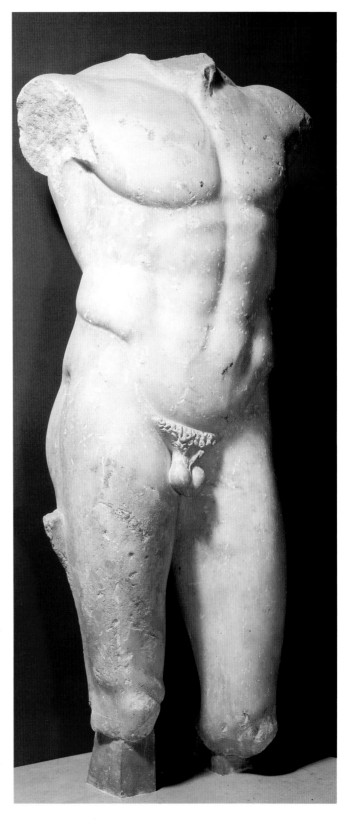

The cultures of Preroman Campania:
the Etruscans, the Italic peoples and their cities

Our knowledge of Etruscan and Italic Campania is primarily the result of research carried out in this century. In the eighteenth century, and for much of the nineteenth, first the necropolises and then the sanctuaries of Nola, Capua, Telesia, *Cales* and Alife were subjected to indiscriminate looting by generations of excavators and merchants, who sold off to the foremost museums and collectors throughout Europe (one example being the collections of Hamilton) painted vases, terracotta ware, jewellery and also – as in the case of the Capua tile – epigraphs. Only a relatively small part of this wealth of material found its way to the Naples Museum, and when it did it was largely lacking in the essential data on provenance and context. Examples of nuclei of material are the Museo Mastrilli, comprising above all painted vases from the Campanian area, which came into the possession first of Mazzocchi and then of the Marchese De Palma, who tried to sell it to Hamilton, at which point it was sequestered by the royal authorities, in 1756; a considerable part of the Santangelo collection; many of the items sold by Gargiulo; or again, in this century, the Spinelli collection of material from *Suessula*. Thus a reconstruction of the sequence of cultures in non-Hellenic Campania has to be based above all on recent excavations and research, which have enabled us to determine the principal phases of the material culture, identifying, locating and dating the main classes of material and giving them for the first time a collocation in history. Thus the Museum will present, alongside the traditional materials from collections, some of the contexts of the more recent excavations, as an essential guide to reconstructing the various cultural manifestations.

When the Greeks landed on the shores of Campania in the eighth century B.C. they found it inhabited by peoples of various languages, customs and degrees of civilisation. Greek historians recorded the names of only two of these peoples, the Ausonians and the Opicians, which on occasions were bracketed together but more often distinguished from each other. The Ausonians were held to be the first inhabitants of the region, probably in the Bronze Age, dominating a very large area including the whole of Southern Italy, Sicily and the Aeolian islands. Their descendants in historic times were identified in the Auruncians, who lived in scattered communities between

the Liri and Volturno rivers and on the Monti Trebulani (between Calvi Risorta and Caiazzo). The Opicians on the other hand, according to some modern-day historians, evoke a later reality connected to the trench tombs (the so-called *Fossakultur)* of the end of the Bronze Age and the early Iron Age. This constitutes an archaeological *facies* which however includes the area of the Auruncians. There is little archaeological evidence of this culture, consisting in the material from the pre-Hellenic necropoli of Cuma, the grave goods from the necropolises of the valle del Sarno (San Marzano, San Valentino Torio, Striano) and a few epigraphic remains such as the pedagogic alphabet of Vico Equense and the Nocera inscription, both engraved on Etruscan bucchero vases in an Italic language and alphabet.

At the end of the Bronze Age (ninth century B.C.) this indigenous stratum of population was overlaid, as it were, with the incinerating culture which we call "Villanovian" (from the burial site near Bologna where it was first identified) and which, in the space of two or three hundred years, evolved into the Etruscan race, which was quite distinct from the indigenous cultures even in its language. We can be absolutely certain about the presence of the Etruscan civilisation in Campania, partly thanks to the historical documentation (the geographer Strabo records that "the Tyrrhenians founded ten cities in the region, calling the capital Capua") and to a notable series of Etruscan inscriptions from Capua (one famous example is the tile with a long sacred text now in Berlin), Nola, Pompeii, Fratte and Pontecagnano. However, the historians of antiquity were divided about how far back to trace this Etruscan presence. Cato placed the foundation of Capua at around 470 B.C., whereas another Latin historian, Velleius Paterculus, set it at around 800 B.C. and thus prior to Cuma and Rome itself. Archaeological research has provided confirmation for this tradition over the last decades in finds of "protovillanovian" material both at Sant'Angelo in Formis (grave goods in the Naples Museum) and at Capua itself.

There is no doubt that Capua quickly took on an urban aspect, as we can tell from the numerous necropolises scattered round the ancient city. The prosperity of Capua, as also of other Etruscan centres such as *Calatia, Nola* and *Nuceria,* derived from the extraordinary fertility of the broad Campanian plain, and also from its excellent situation on the main communication route between the northern territories of the Latians and Etruscans, the south and the interior. This prosperity is manifest in the rich grave goods of the Archaic period with large quantities of imported ceramic ware, especially of Corinthian and Attic manufacture, and of bronze vases, whether imports from Greece or made locally, such as the famous *deinoi* with lids decorated with sculptures of outstanding beauty. A production of black figure vases grew up from the middle of the sixth century in Capua, involving several workshops whose output was heavily influenced by Ionic traits. The Greek, and particularly Attic, influence emanating from *Neapolis* was very potent. Nola imported thousands of painted vases (to such an extent that one form of Attic urn was known in the last century as "Nolan"), and this love-hate relationship between the neighbouring cities gave rise to a legend, which was still alive in Roman times, ascribing a Chalcidian origin (meaning from Cuma/Neapolis) to Nola. It is certainly no coincidence that a local production of red figure vases in strict imitation of the Attic style grew up either in Nola or in one of the other centres no less subject to Greek influence, known as the Group of the Pillar with the Owl, after the scene depicted on two urns in Berlin (most of these vases were found in the 18th and 19th centuries and then dispersed).

Etruscan culture spread throughout the interior of Campania, so that the elite classes of even the more far-flung Italic tribes such as the Samnites eventually adopted Etruscan customs, to judge from the diffusion of the most characteristic Etruscan products such as bucchero and items in bronze. Even the neighbouring Greek colonies such as Cuma and Poseidonia ended up by registering marked Etruscan influence, as for example in the adoption of wooden architectural structures decorated with brightly coloured terracotta facing.

The physiognomy of the region was definitively transformed at the end of the fifth century when, thanks to ever more numerous incursions of people from the remoter Samnite regions, the indigenous peoples of the Campanian plain (now also known as Oscans, a name which conserves traces of the former Opicians) came together to form a political unit. The Greek historian Diodorus mentions this event and recalls that in about 438-437 B.C. "the Campanian people was formed, taking its name from the fertility of the surrounding plains". This process must clearly also be seen as the revolt of the Italic element which hitherto had been subject to Etruscan domination. In the next few years the Samnites took Capua (in 423) and then Cuma and the whole of Campania. The Etruscan element became more and more aleatory, until it finally disappeared altogether. The prevailing language and institutions became those of the Samnites (present in the Museum above all in the material and inscriptions from the important sanctuary of *Bovianum vetus,* near Pietrabbondante in the province of Isernia), with the *touta* and *meddix*. However, the prevailing culture was that of the Campanians, conserving the high degree of Hellenisation which was already a feature of Etruscan Capua. The material culture of Campanian Capua shows clear signs of the adoption of customs in use in the cities of Magna Graecia, and *Neapolis* in particular, but also in the remoter and more venerable centres of the Hellene world, of which the local peoples sometimes gained first-hand experience in their travels as mercenary troops. We can recall the famous Mamertines, troops named after the Samnite Mars *Mamerte,* and Campanians were present on battlefields throughout the Mediterranean world. The scenes depicted on local red figure pottery and tombs reveal, on the one hand, specific elements of national costume, such as the armour (helmets with the double crest, broad belt, and disc chainmail) or the characteristic bonnet and heavy square cloaks of the women, and on the other Greek iconographical features and postures, such as orators or the noblewoman with handmaid, which expressed the penetration of Italic culture by ideologies such as the Orphic-Pythagorean or hero-worship and were typical of the Greek world. Some classes of material reveal more complex interrelations, such as the "mothers of Capua" (in the Museo Provinciale Campano) which certainly imitate the Greek *kourotrophos* but at the same time, by expressing pride in fertility with the numerous children exhibited on their arms, affirm a value and ostentation which are decidedly "barbaric".

By this time Rome was making its presence felt to the north, and war between the two major powers of contemporary Italy was inevitable. In the end the Samnites and Campanians paid the price for being less united and well organised than the Romans in both military and institutional terms.

It was a turbulent period of violent conflicts, and yet notable progress was also made in civic organisation, as for example in urban development: this was the moment in which many cities such as Pompeii, Nocera, *Calatia,* Acerra, *Atella* and probably also Nola were refounded on the lines of the Latin colonies. In the end all the cities of Campania, whatever their origin, came to be incorporated into the Roman state, a process which culminated in the annihilation of any remaining Campanian autonomy in the war against Hannibal of 211 B.C. From that time forward Capua, Titus Livy's *urbs maxima opulentissimaque Italiae* and Cicero's *altera Roma,* was governed by a Roman prefect and definitively renounced any aspirations of autonomy.

Capeduncula with navel from
Suessula, Spinelli collection
inv. 156856
This typical Iron Age vase from the
Campanian hinterland derives from the
water scoops common in the Bronze
Age. It presents an elaborate form of
"lyre-shaped" biphorous handle, pierced
with slits and decorated with half-moon
designs impressed with a vivacious ornamental effect. End of 8th century B.C.

**Trilobe oinochoe from Suessula,
Spinelli collection**
inv. 157-176
The trilobe oinochoe, of which this is a
locally made example with a simple
brown ring decoration, is one of the
characteristic vases of Archaic age grave
furnishings not only in Campania but
all over ancient Italy. It was used to pour
out wine into bowls and was thus the
centrepiece of the social ritual of the
banquet, which had Greek origins but
was adopted by all the upwardly mobile
classes even in Etruscan funerary rites.

Beaded necklace in polychrome glass from Suessula, Spinelli collection inv. 197518
Made by Phoenician or Rhodian glass-blowers and diffused round the coasts through the Greek trading posts, which soon began their own output, polychrome beads exercised a powerful fascination over the "barbarians" of the interior, which in the case of this necklace may have been heightened by the magic eye effect created by the different bands of colour. Glass beads have always been used as currency in trading on the outposts of civilisation: the Romans produced them a thousand years later for the barbarians beyond the *limes*, and the Venetians did the same after another millennium for their overseas markets. 8th-7th century B.C.

Antefix with Maenad's head, from Cales (?)
inv. 21580
The antefix, which was originally Dedalic, then sculpted with a crown of leaves, here reaches a highly ornate form with a palmette and vegetal volutes terminating in a lotus flower. End of 6th century B.C.

Antefix with human head, from Minturno, sanctuary of the Goddess Marica
inv. 176346
The Greek-Peloponnese influence is marked in this antefix with a female face, the hairstyle done in the typical "Dedalic" scheme with large bobs.

Antefix with Gorgon's head from Santa Maria Capua Vetere
inv. 21049
This type of bearded Gorgon is known from a large number of replicas, found also in the various sanctuaries of Latium and southern Etruria. End of 6th century B.C.

Campanian black figure amphora and situla from Suessula, Spinelli collection
invv. 164208, 164277

The decorative themes on Campanian pottery are the common ones of Attic ceramics from the last decades of the 6th century B.C. On the amphora we have the theme of women running, characterised as Etruscan or oriental by the *sakkos* on their heads and the sandals turned-up at the point (*calcei repandi*); on the situla, a typical vase form of the region, there is a Triton, one of the standard monstrous beings in the fantasies of Archaic Greeks. First half of 5th century B.C.

**Attic kylix with Oscan inscription
from Nola**
inv. 80554

Round the outside of the bowl is
scratched from right to left the customary formula of ownership, using the
Etruscan alphabet but in Oscan, as is
seen in the final verb: "I am of Lucio
Nevio" (*luvkies Canaiviies sum*). The
name is that of the renowned Campanian family of the Nevii, of which at a
later date the famous Latin poet was a
member.

A similar Etruscan inscription on another
kylix from Suessula gives us the same
formula in Etruscan: "I am of Velchaie
Pustmina" (*velchaie pustminas mi*).
First half of 5th century B.C.

41

Campanian black figure amphora, from Suessula
inv. 209, Spinelli collection
This amphora showing on both sides a dance scene involving a nude youth and a silenus has been attributed to the Diphros painter, one of the most prolific in the archaic Capuan workshops. The Dionysian theme certainly derives from Attic pottery, but the style and indeed the syntax of the decorative elements, like the pod design on the shoulder and the palmetta on the neck, are not at all local, owing much to oriental and Etruscan models. End of 6th - beginning of 5th century B.C.

42

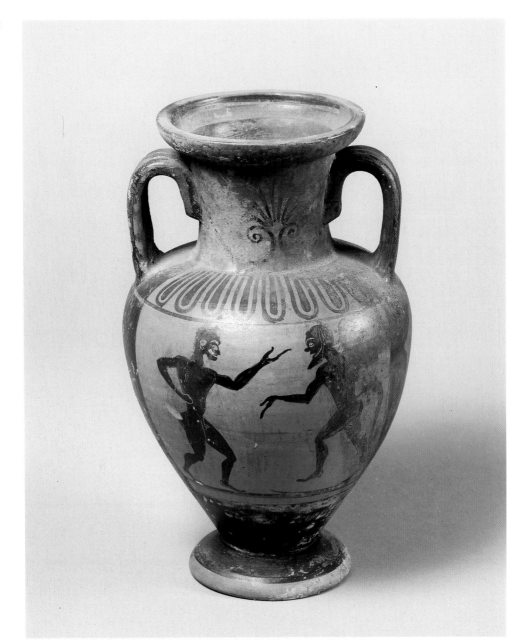

Vivenzio hydria, from Nola
inv. 81669

The Vivenzio brothers were the most famous excavators of tombs at Nola in the 1700s, and supplied Greek figured vases, which at that time were reputed Etruscan or Nolan, to the leading collectors of the period. The ransacking of the necropolis of Nola yielded many masterpieces of Attic ceramic ware, one of which was the famous *hydria* named after Vivenzio.

Fashioned by an outstanding Attic craftsman, known as the *Kleophrades* painter, this vase, which dates from about 480 B.C., presents in the figured band round the shoulder one of the most famous representations of the *Ilioupersis:* on the left Aeneas is seen fleeing with the young Ascanius; in the centre (here on the left) Ajax assaults Cassandra who clings to the statue of Athena; Neoptolemos slays Priam on the altar as he holds in his lap the bleeding corpse of the little Astianax; and finally the Trojan women are seen being taken prisoners by the Greeks.

Attic stamnos by the so-called
Deinos painter, from Nola
inv. 81674
Named after a vase that is in Berlin, the
Attic workman who produced this *stamnos*
favoured Dionysian themes. Of particular interest here, because unusual in the
generally repetitive repertoire connected
with the cult of Dionysus, is the representation of a festival during which some
Maenads adorn a model of the god with
wreaths of flowers. The model comprises
a mask and a belted *chiton* mounted on
a wooden post stuck into the ground.
Stylistically the painter here still favours
formal and stately images, following in
the footsteps of the great "classical"
masters, but in other works he indulges
in the whimsical decoration which
characterises the so-called "flowery style".
425-415 B.C. circa.

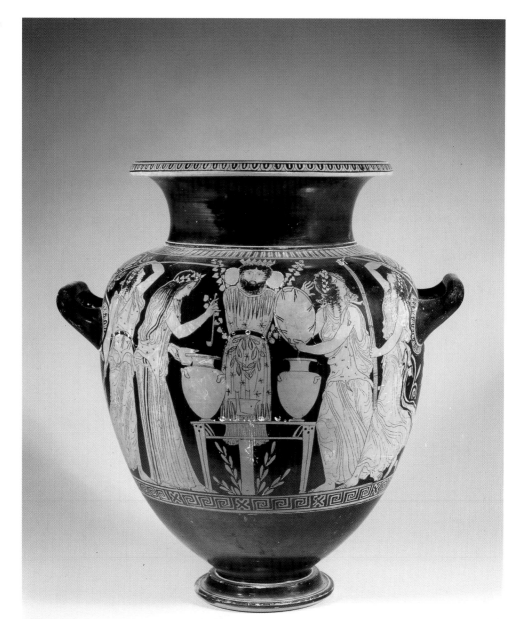

Bronze vases and objects from Nocera

invv. 77594, 77596, 77599, 76350, 73707, 73653, 73651

In 1856 some tombs in the preroman necropolis to the south of Nocera were investigated, and the Royal Bourbon Museum purchased a notable series of bronze vases of Etruscan make, as well as Attic and Campanian figured pottery. The material shown here provides an example of the bronzeware (jugs, basins, wine ladles) used by the nobility of this Etruscan-Campanian centre in the 5th century B.C. in ritual banqueting. The reproduction of this in grave furnishings served to emphasise, in line with a common procedure in funerary ideology, the status of the deceased as a well-born adult male. Some of the objects, such as the strainers of Etruscan make and the grater, recall the custom of drinking wine mixed with various ingredients including grated cheese.

Polygnotos hydria, from Nola
inv. 81398

The potter Polygnotos (not to be confused with the painter of the same name cited in documentary sources) was the pupil of the painter of the Niobides. Together with a vast throng of imitators, he dominated the market of Attic pottery in the second half of the 5th century B.C. Active in the years 440-420 B.C., he introduced into the iconographic repertoire new mythical themes and scenes of everyday life, such as the lively frieze round this *hydria* illustrating with lithe figures the most celebrated dances of the time, from the Pyrrhic to the dance on the swords.

**Aison aryballic lekythos
with Amazzonomachia, from Cumae**
inv. 86496

In 421 B.C. Cumae was occupied by the Samnites, but Attic pottery continued to arrive in the last quarter of the century. This vase is the work of the Attic potter Aison who left his signature on a number of vases in this period. In this representation of an Amazzonomachia, we see his dependence on the tradition of battle scenes which flourished in mid-century when, in the painting of Polygnotos of Thasos and the ceramic ware of the Niobides painter, a new technique for rendering complex scenes in space by placing characters on different levels indicated by base lines had been perfected.

Nonetheless, in his predilection for minute draperies and richly decorated clothing Aison appears as a typical exponent of the so-called "flowery style".

**Amphora from the Group of the
Pillar with the Owl**
inv. 81536

On the front of the vase a warrior and a woman enact the scene of the warrior's departure; on the back are seen two female figures. Even though the execution is summary, this is one of the highest quality vases in the group. Shortly before the middle of the 5th century B.C.

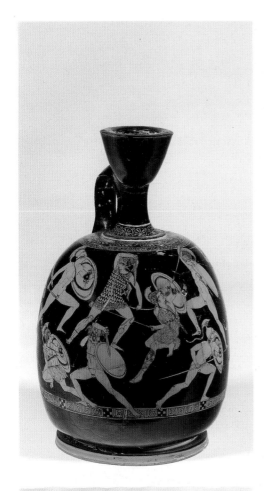

So-called "Italo-Gallic" helmet
from Pietrabbondante (IS)
inv. 5744

This type of helmet was common throughout central Italy, including Rome, and dates from the 4th-3rd century B.C. There are obvious allusions to the Trojan epic in the weapons of Achilles and the Nereids bearing arms on the lateral face guards. The large sanctuary of Pietrabbondante was the religious centre of the Samnite tribe of the Pentrians, who were active in the struggle against first the Greeks and Etruscans and later the Romans. It was dedicated to the goddess of Victory, and thus it comes as no surprise to find *ex voto* offerings in the form of arms.

Funerary painting, from Cumae
inv. 12329

The frieze, found on the Correale property in 1891 and painted on three headstones of a chamber tomb, depicts the scene of a lady's toilette, a frequent subject in female tombs of the aristocratic classes of Campanians and Samnites in the 4th and early 3rd century. The dead woman, clothed in a long white tunic held in at the waist by a gilded belt and a red mantle, her hair gathered up under a red bonnet, is sitting sideways on a throne with armrests sustained by gilt gryphons.In her right hand she holds a gilt mirror up to her face while a servant girl standing on the left hands her a long *alabastron* of perfume and a basket (*kalathos*) containing pomegranates, a fruit often associated with funerary rites and symbolising rebirth. Two other pomegranates are shown in the background, possibly hanging on the wall. The scene takes place in a room decorated in two tiers with a frieze of whorls which, together with the oblique positioning of the figures, shows that the recent spatial innovations in Greek art had reached Campania.

Ring with bezel showing a
Gorgon's head from Cumae, Stevens
collection
inv. 126408
When at the end of the 4th century B.C.
the personality who was wearing this
remarkable ring was buried in the Cumae
necropolis, the city had already been
under Samnite rule for a century. And in
fact while it exhibits a refined technique
which reflects the persistence of the Greek
tradition of the goldsmith's art, the
elaborate taste in ornamentation and the
object's sheer dimensions reveal an
ostentatiousness which is a typical trait of
the Italic nobility of this period.

Gold fibulas terminating in "pomegranates" with a bowed hasp decorated with vegetal motifs, from Teano
invv. 131634, 131712
Found among grave goods in Teano, the two fibulas, on which the highly elaborate filigrane betrays a sense of barbaric *horror vacui,* were designed to be pinned to the funeral robes to proclaim the status of the deceased person. Late 4th-early 3rd century B.C.

Campanian red figure amphora
from the Group with three points
inv. 82744
Datable to the middle of the 4th century
B.C., this amphora depicts, as is often the
case in this production, a Samnite warrior –
the characteristic belt is placed well in
evidence – going into attack on rocky
terrain. On the neck a female head is seen in
profile with hair drawn into a cap (*sakkos*).
The workshop which produced this object
must have been situated in Capua or nearby.

Red figure crater with banqueting
scene, from Cumae
inv. 85873
Assigned to the so-called CA (Cumae A)
painter who was active in the workshop
that produced the figured vases for the
market of Cumae, this crater presents a
lively symposium scene making much
of the richly ornamented hall with
branches, masks, *oscilla,* birds, a cande-
labrum and touches of additional colour.
Circa 340-330 B.C.

Painted tomb, slab with horseman, from Nola
inv. 224929

Found in 1977, this painted tomb, in common with many other tombs from Capua and Paestum, depicts the theme, which was particularly dear to Campanian horsemen, of the return of the warrior. In the main slab we see the dead man, on horseback, wearing a tight-fitting cuirass and helmet with one gold and one silver horn.

The light reflects off them, making this the first example in Campania of that achievement of protohellenistic painting which the ancient sources called *skiagraphia*. In the other slabs, on the left a pair of maidens welcome the dead man with *skyphoi* and wreaths, and on the right a companion of the warrior, also on horseback, is followed by a groom holding up his horse's tail.

On the short slab facing the main one we see the dead man's shield bearer.

The product of a very proficient workshop, this tomb can be dated to between the end of the 4th and the first decades of the 3rd century B.C.

54

Bearded male head from Cales

inv. 22135

This head, datable to the 3rd century B.C., is related to another famous head, found during the 1950s at Triflisco near Tifata, which at the time caused much discussion as to its collocation. The oval face, the hair style and the beard rendered with little tufts arranged with geometrical precision around the face, the eyes with ridges for the brows and an incision for the pupils, the mouth pursed to a slit are all transpositions from Greek models (Zeus, Hercules?) by a workshop deliberately making use of a local language which is intentionally "primitive" and aimed at a specific clientele. It is certainly not a case of mere technical incompetence, for the availability of moulds and the precision of the execution show that the artisan was perfectly capable of modelling more refined figures according to the rules of classical art.

Terracotta relief of girl with a flabellum, from Cales

inv. 20411

The figure has been identified as Aphrodite because the relief, probably votive, was part of a pair with another showing a bust believed to depict Ares. The shape of the relief is quite rare; the figure is based on Hellenistic Aphrodites. 2nd century B.C.

Terracotta head representing Hercules, from Teano
inv. 163593

Teano was an important Ausonian centre, subsequently occupied by the Sabellic tribe of the Sidicians and eventually Romanised as a result of the Samnite wars. Significant remains of the preroman phase have come down to us, above all in the sanctuaries which sprang up all over the territory from the 6th century onwards. In one on fondo Loreto and another important centre of worship on fondo Ruozzo thousands of votive objects were found like this head, telling us much about both the religious rites and contemporary taste, which here tends to the Hellenistic, of the Italic populations of this key region of Campania. 3rd century B.C.

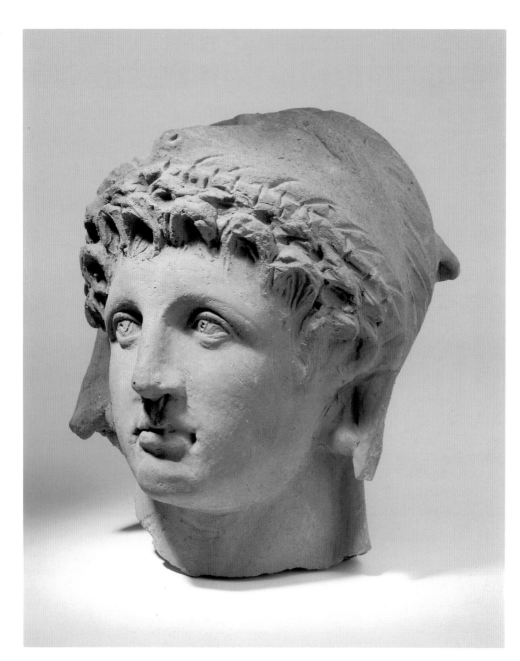

**Signet ring with male portrait
from Santa Maria Capua Vetere
inv. 25085**
Datable to the 1st century B.C., this ring, signed by the goldsmith Erakleidas, seeks its effect in the contrast between red gold and yellow gold and above all in the qualty of the male portrait on the bezel. This fine achievement links Roman realism with the stylistic traits of the Hellenistic tradition, seen quite clearly, for example, in the decorativism of the hair style.

The history of the ancient Etruscan city has finally come to an end, and Capua is now, after enduring wave after wave of Roman colonisers, an important model Roman city.

Evidence of Magna Graecia

The Naples Museum was the centre and dynamo for all the archaeological activity carried on under the Bourbons, and thus for many years, from the end of the eighteenth century until the creation of museums in the major provinces of Southern Italy (Taranto, Reggio Calabria and so on, following the Unification of Italy), it received a large part of the material excavated throughout the territory known in ancient times as Magna Graecia. It should, of course, have received all this material, but some of it, alas, found its way onto the antiquarian market, to the joy of merchants and collectors such as William Hamilton, and now constitutes a significant part of the antique collections of the leading museums in Europe and America. Most of the objects were either purchased by the Museum or donated, because in fact the Bourbon government did not undertake many excavations in the provinces itself. Of the major nuclei we can recall in particular the Santangelo collection, formed between the end of the 18th and the first half of the 19th century by a family which played a very eminent role in the Bourbon administration, and secured on behalf of the Museum following the Unification by G. Fiorelli with municipal funds. The fact that much of the material came from collections, while the centres for which we have significant remains are few and far between, makes it impossible for us to give an organic presentation of the major cities of Magna Graecia. The history of the *poleis* has largely been reconstructed by archaeological research carried out following the Unification of Italy. However, the evidence contained in the Museum remains of great interest, not least for the artistic importance of some of the nuclei, which simply has no equal. Examples are the large *collection of Apulian vases* from Ruvo and Canosa, the *Tarantine goldware* coming from the same tombs, the *figured terracotta ware,* the *weapons,* the *funerary paintings,* which may have been surpassed in terms of quantity by more recent finds but not in quality, the *coins* and the *epigraphs,* the last two being exhibited in specific sections. Another striking feature of the Museum is its documentation of the earliest scientific approach to the history of Magna Graecia, putting an end to a tradition of humanistic studies embodied at the turn of the seventeenth century in the scholars who sought, with generous but blinkered local patriotism, to exalt the illustrious ancient traditions of the cities of Southern Italy, often in contrast with the desolating reality of their times (*magna urbs, magna solitudo*). The rediscovery of the concept of Magna Graecia, by the Dutchman H. Goltz who in 1576 published a numismatical treatise on Magna Graecia and Sicily, gave rise to an outpouring of works of historical topography seeking above all to establish the whereabouts of many of the ancient cities which, in the aftermath of the Dark Ages, had been lost to view under the swamps and dunes of malaria-infested coasts. It was only with the new Bourbon Kingdom that such discoveries were given their just deserts, partly because Charles wished to establish the glory and prestige of his reign in a specific and illustrious past and also thanks to their rapid diffusion throughout civilised Europe by means of the constant presence of foreigners making the Grand Tour.

The new climate found a significant expression in the publication, promoted in 1754 by the clergyman Alessio Simmaco Mazzocchi, of the *Heraclean tables* (see the epigraphic collection), which had an enthusiastic reception all over Europe. The tables contained a general treatise on Magna Graecia and, by underlining the specifically Italiot characteristics of Pythagoras's philosophy, gave considerable credit to the myth of an ancient philosophical culture present in pre-Roman Italy, Vico's *antiquissima Italorum sapientia* which was to be taken up by Vincenzo Cuoco to remind the reemerging Italian nation "that they had once been virtuous, powerful and well content". This same cultural climate favoured the discovery of the temples of Paestum, reported by Bourbon soldiers (Count Felice Gazzola) at work on the new road to Calabria. The immediate publication of drawings and the first eye-witness accounts (Soufflot, Mayor, Paoli, Saint-Non, Piranesi), not to mention the visit of Winckelmann in 1758, not only set the seal on the fame of this ancient city but opened up to the Europe of the Grand Tour the sites of the other temples scattered through Magna Graecia and Sicily and ensured that "fortune of the Doric" that became one of the keystones of Neoclassicism. Evidence of this aspect can be perceived in a particularly curious object in the Museum's collections, the cork model of the so-called basilica of Paestum, made at the end of the eighteenth century.

Figured terracotta

inv. Santangelo collection 106

This fragment of terracotta, undoubtedly an *ex voto,* was part of a female figure made in very low relief and probably deriving from a Sybarite type, since another identical fragment has been found in that region. The decoration of the elaborate robe, with figures in tiers, indicates unmistakeably that the figure was a goddess. The topmost tier shows the heroic scene of Ajax with the corpse of Achilles, while the next two depict girls and boys dancing. Datable to the years 625-600 B.C. and characterised by the persistence of the Dedalic style, this fragment constitutes one of the oldest and most authoritative figured remains to have come down to us from the world of Magna Graecia.

60

Chalcidian skyphos

inv. Santangelo collection 120

The class of vases known as "Chalcidian" is still awaiting a definitive assignation to a specific centre of production, in spite of the large number found and the indications in the numerous inscriptions on them. It was clearly an important source of ceramic ware in Magna Graecia, treating complicated subjects with considerable panache and expressiveness, and on occasions even allowing itself certain liberties with Attic iconography. On one side of the bowl there is the theme, ever popular in Greek Archaism, of the capture of the Delphic tripod by Hercules (on the right, with receding hairline and red tinted hair), opposed by a bearded Apollo, while a Fury stands behind the tripod as if to symbolise the contest. Behind Apollo we see Artemis, winged as in the most ancient representations, while Hermes assists Hercules. The other side shows the equally common scene of a duel between two warriors armed in the Opician manner with two women looking on. Circa 540 B.C.

Bronze hydria, possibly
from Locri
inv. 73144
The *hydria* takes its name from its use for drawing water and is often depicted in scenes of women at wells.

This example is of high quality workmanship with splendid decoration, both in the *gorgoneion* at the end of the ribbon-like handle and in the two male figurines in relief, applied horizontally head to head on the side handles. The distribution of the few similar artefacts suggests that they were produced on the western coast of Greece, perhaps at Dodona or Sikyon. 6th century B.C.

62

Female terracotta statuette, from Locri

inv. 141064

Found by Paolo Orsi in his excavations in Locri, the figurine is certainly an *ex voto* in imitation of a statue of much larger dimensions. The hairstyle in curls on the forehead helps to date it to the first decades of the 5th century B.C.

Terracotta figurine of a casket with sacred objects, from Locri

inv. 20684

This three-dimensional figurine represents a casket for toiletries.

On top of the chest, which has lion's paw feet and is decorated with rosettes, indented borders, wave volutes and two compartments made to resemble doors, there are two more miniature caskets of the same type with two birds below and two cakes on top.

Between them there are three *alabastra,* a large *oinochoe* and a *kalathos.*

Such caskets are often shown in the hands of Persephone in representations of the goddess. 5th century B.C.

Gold necklace, from Ruvo
inv. 24883
The necklace, with a flat braid, is hung with pendents representing silenus protomes, acorns and lotus flowers in lamina with a dusted finish. Probably the work of an Etruscan workshop in Campania, it is excellent evidence of the rich output of this centre of Peucetia in the 6th century B.C.

Gold necklace, from Ruvo,
detail

Glass perfume vases with
gold holders, from Ruvo
invv. 24876-89
The Phoenician-style amphorette *unguentarii* in polychrome glass with their
cylindrical holders in gold decorated with
Gorgon heads and craters comprise a
female cosmetics set of extraordinary
refinement. 5th century B.C.

Attic volute crater by the Niobides painter, from Ruvo
inv. 81673

The name Niobides painter was given to the artist who, working in Athens in the years 470-450 B.C., succeeded in adapting the achievements of the finest classical painting to produce ceramic ware of the highest artistic quality. He drew on that repertoire to decorate large craters with scenes from the famous battles fought by the Greeks and their gods against a series of enemies - Giants, Amazons, Centaurs, Trojans. Here it is customary to identify, although without definitive confirmation, Achilles in the act of slaying Penthesilea at the climax of the Amazzonomachia on the front of the vase. In any case the interest in ethical and psychological themes is characteristic of the period, shown in the exchanges of piercing looks.

Attic volute crater by the Pronomos painter, from Ruvo
inv. 81673

This vase, from the last decade of the 5th century B.C., is extremely interesting for what it tells us about classical theatre and in particular the satyr drama. In the upper tier, flanking the divine couple Dionysus and Ariadne seated in a languid pose, we see various characters, including Laomedes, Hesion and Heracles, each with his mask in his hand, sumptuously dressed in rich stage costumes and the *kothournos,* the typical actors' footwear. The Papposilenus clad in his characteristic shaggy costume is a striking figure. In the lower tier a musician is practising his aulos next to a lyre player and actors dressed as satyrs. This painter was Attic and a pupil of the Deinos painter.

He draws on the tradition of Polygnotos in making a spatial construct on different levels, and also on the output of his contemporary the Medias painter in the decoration of female drapery.

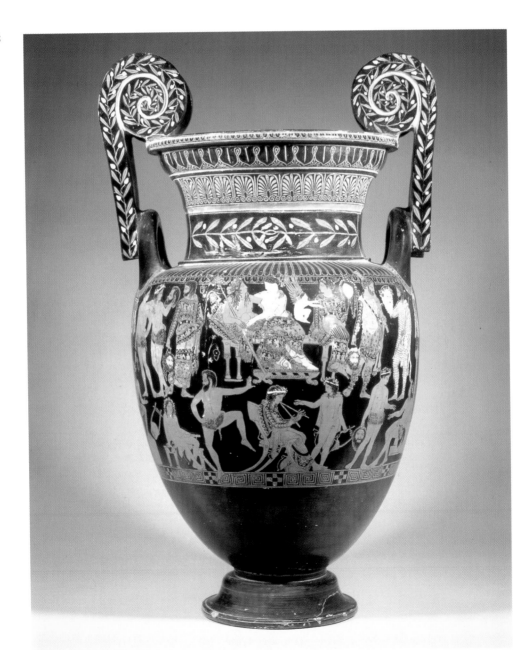

Painted tomb slab with women dancing, from Ruvo
inv. 9357

The decoration of this semi-chamber tomb from Ruvo remains a *unicum* with its scene of a dance by funeral mourners with their hands linked, led by three boys. Its striking effectiveness derives from the rhythmical repetition of lines and gestures, ever so slightly varied in the sombre, earthy colours used. Second half of 4th century B.C.

Tomb with "the warrior's return", from Paestum
inv. 9363

This fine tomb dates from the period 350-325 B.C. The procession of horsemen gives much greater breadth to the familiar iconographic scheme of "the warrior's return" than was usually achieved by painters active in Paestum. The woman on the left offers a *skyphos* to the horseman returning from battle with an escort of two foot soldiers and a shield bearer who holds up the horse's tail. The warriors are wearing the national armour of the Italic peoples (helmets with plumes and crests, wide belts) and display the trophies of their defeated opponents hanging from their lances.

Earrings with pyramidal pendents, from Taranto
invv. 25234-35
The earrings are disc-shaped and bear, as on a shield, the Gorgon head surrounded by a whorly motif. The main pendent has the form of an inverted pyramid with filigrane decorations, and is flanked by two smaller ones with acorn shapes.
This type of earring was very famous in the 4th century B.C. The examples in the Naples Museum date from towards the end of the century.

Pilos helmet, from Paestum

inv. 5691

In Paestum in 1805 a rich suit of
armour was found in a tomb near the
so-called temple of Ceres, with a modelled cuirass and two helmets, one of the
pilos type and the other "Chalcidian".
Like the painted scene of "the warrior's
return", the funerary suit of armour
distinguishes the deceased man as
belonging to the aristocracy. End of 4th
century B.C.

**Red figure lekythos by Assteas,
from Paestum**
inv. 81847

This aryballic lekythos is signed by Assteas (*Assteas egrapse)* and is crucial for a reconstruction of this artist's personality. It shows a scene of the gardens of the Hesperides, with a girl collecting apples for Heracles while another distracts a snake with food offerings. Active between 360 and 330 B.C., Assteas was one of the most original ceramics craftsmen in Magna Graecia and a leading light in the Paestum workshop.

Red figure crater made in
Paestum by Assteas, from Sant'Agata
dei Goti (Saticula)
inv. 82258
The scene from Euripides of Cadmon
advancing with a stone on the dragon
which guarded the Theban spring, symbolised by the amphora on the ground, must have been one of the most popular in the workshop of Assteas, whose signature is also on this crater, and of Python, who decorated a similar crater also found in Sant'Agata dei Goti, now in the Louvre.

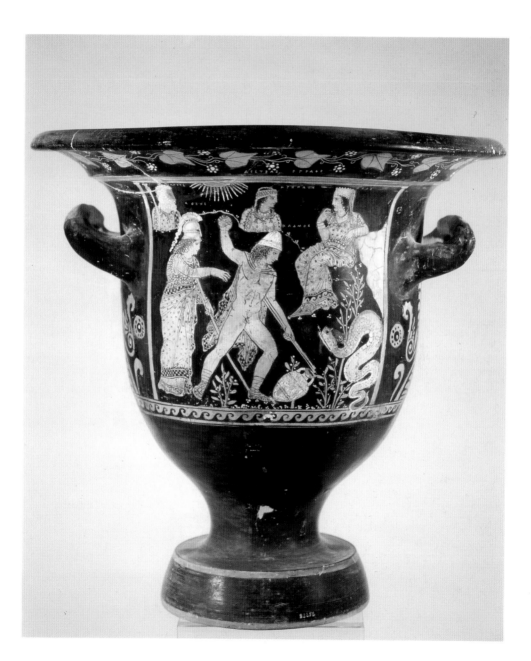

Crater with phliakes
inv. 81925

Painted pottery is our most vivid record of the comedy of the *phliakes*, a theatrical genre which was popular in Magna Graecia in the 4th and 3rd centuries B.C. The *phliakes* were actors who wore a skintight costume with padding on the stomach and behind to give a grotesque effect, heightened by the phallic caricature waving between their legs. Performances took place on a rudimentary stage with steps leading up to it and a simple curtain at the back which also served as the changing room. It was popular entertainment, with themes taken from every-day life or parodies of myths and tragic drama (in this case a heroic theme is being parodied).

The most famous author of the comedy of the *phliakes* was Rinton, a writer who lived in Taranto in the 3rd century B.C. He collected and gave literary form to the vast and confused material of the popular farces.

Red figure crater made in Paestum by Python, from Sant'Agata dei Goti inv. 81417

The scene on the front represents a version for *phliakes* of the myth of Oedipus and the Sphinx. In a Dionysian setting with branches of ivy Oedipus, clad in the hairy costume of a satyr and holding a thyrsus, interrogates a Sphinx sporting polychrome wings and squatting on a tall rock.

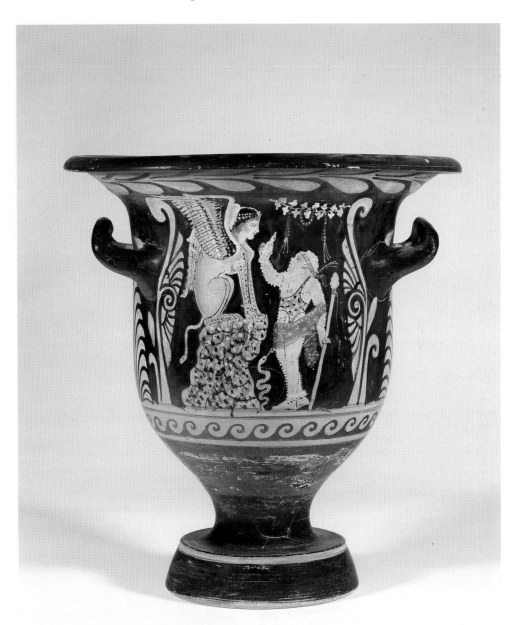

Apulian volute crater, from Ruvo
inv. 82126

The Lycurgus painter, who takes his name from a vase depicting the madness of Lycurgus now in London, worked in a grandiose style. On the right of this crater Jason, protected by an Argonaut, lifts the golden fleece from its branch while on the left Medea offers a sleeping potion to the dragon who stood guard over the tree (the details are very similar to the garden of the Hesperides on the vase by Assteas).

This is the version of the myth which was made definitive by Apollonius of Rhodes.

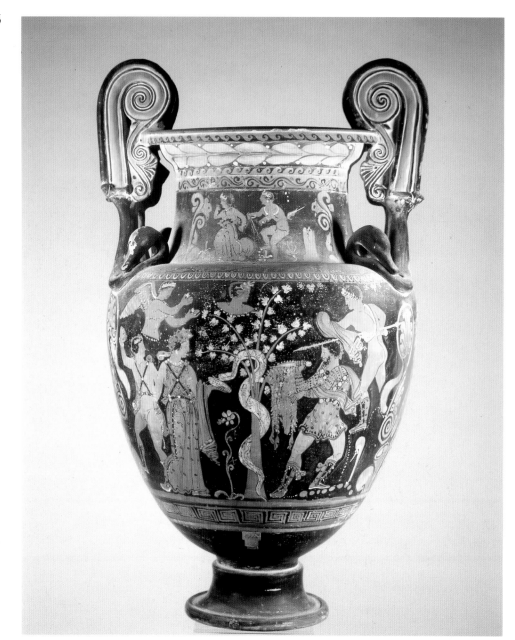

Apulian red figure situla, from Ruvo
inv. 81863
This vase, aslo by the Lycurgus painter, represents an episode from the Illiad (X, 469) which never occurs in Attic ceramic ware and perhaps found its way onto Apulian vases through the Euripidean tragedy *Rhesus*.

In fact the king of the Thracians is caught unawares in camp at night by Ulysses and Diomedes, slain and deprived of his famous horses. The same theme is found on the beautiful crater by the Darius painter which since 1984 has been at the Antikenmuseum in Berlin.

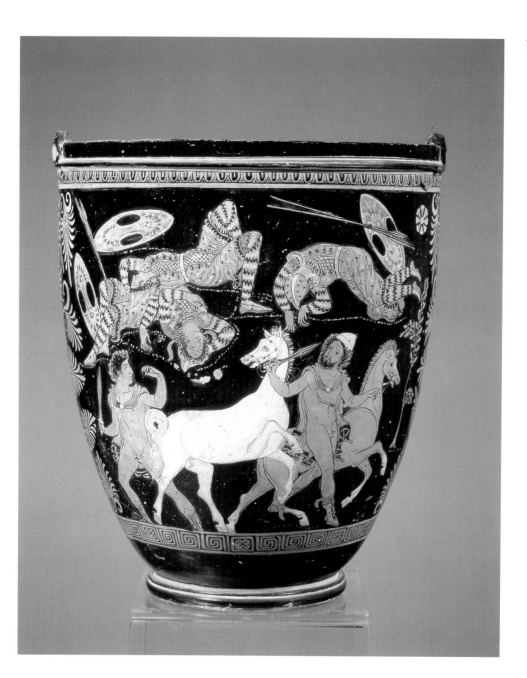

78 The artist, known as the Darius painter on account of this vase, was the last (340-320 B.C.) of the great Apulian vase decorators. This monumental crater with female masks in the handles was found in 1851 at Canosa together with the crater shown next, other vases, two bronze cuirasses, a javelin and a horse's bit in one of the large hypogea, obviously the tomb of a horseman, at the gates of Canosa. On the front the scene is disposed on three levels, with at the centre of the intermediate one, Darius king of Persia (identified by an inscription) seated on a throne and listening to a messenger, surrounded by dignitaries described as *Persai*. The upper level shows the personifications of Hellas and Asia in front of Zeus amidst various deities including Apathes or deception. In the lower level we see Persian subjects presenting themselves to the royal treasurer. The theme, which may derive from a lost tragedy, Phrynicus's *The Persians*, evokes one of the episodes leading up to the war between Darius and the Greeks, possibly the announcement of the treachery of Histios of Miletum. The structure of the scene seems to echo those based on the theatre with different prospects and including allegorical figures used by Apelles, the outstanding painter of the age of Alexander the Great. It must surely have had antecedents in painted pictures. As regards the choice of subject matter, it seems to echo the propaganda disseminated by Macedonians and Epyrotes in the colonies of Magna Graecia at the time of the great conflict between Macedonians and Persians. The depiction of a scene of Andronomachia on the neck goes to confirm the theme of the struggle of the Greeks against the barbarians. On the reverse side Bellerophorous is poised to strike the Chimera in the midst of Amazons. On the neck a Dionysiac scene shows Maenads and Silenes near a *louterion*.

Apulian red figure crater with masks
("vase of Patroclus"), from Canosa
inv. 81954

Found in the same hypogeum as the vase of the Persians, this crater is also the work of the Darius painter and again echoes themes of anti-Persian propaganda, identifying the latter with the Trojans who were defeated by the Greeks. On the front we see the sacrifice of Trojan prisoners by Achilles on the funeral pyre of Patroclus *(Patroklou taphos* is written at the base of the pile of trunks). While Agamemnon performs the ritual libation a prisoner is about to be despatched with a sword while three others in fetters await their turn. On the upper tier Phoenix and Nestor are shown under a canopy amidst groups of deities and heroes and a young girl. In the lower tier Automedon drags the body of Hector behind his chariot. On the neck is a scene with Oedipus and the Sphinx with a Harpy.

On the reverse side the body of the vase is decorated with a funerary ritual scene at a *naiskos* in which a young nude warrior (with servant) is conversing with a seated female figure. On the neck we see a Dionysiac procession.

Apulian red figure loutrophoros with Andromeda, from Canosa
inv. 82266

Also by the Darius painter and from the same hypogeum as the two previous vases, this splendid *loutrophoros* shows Andromeda bound to stakes in the upper tier between Cassiopea and Cephesus, and below Perseus in combat with the marine monster amidst Nereids riding seahorses.

The theme of Andromeda bound reflects the *incipit* of the Euripidean tragedy. The frieze depicting marine creatures is also remarkable. 340-320 B.C.

**Apulian pelike with the death
of Adonis, from Canosa**
inv. Santangelo collection 702
This other celebrated vase by the Darius
painter shows the very handsome young
man lying on his death bed with
Aphrodite and Persephone in attendance
and the implacable Hecate at the foot of
the bed.
The upper tier portrays the contest of
Aphrodite and Persephone for possession
of the youth in front of Zeus. At the
bottom there is a scene from a *gynaikeion*. 340-320 B.C.

Apulian red figure amphora, from Ruvo
inv. 81952

Found in the same hypogeum as the Darius vase and attributed to the same artist, on one side this amphora shows a white bull amidst a group of young girls, possibly the prelude to the abduction of Europa by Zeus in the form of a bull. On the reverse side, the upper tier has a four horse chariot driven by an Erote between Zeus on a throne, to the right, and Hermes, Pan and a satyr to the left.

At the bottom there is a scene from a *gynaikeion*. 346-320 B.C.

Crater in the style of Gnathia from Oria
inv. 80987

With its elegant profile and the ribbing in relief, this crater deliberately imitates metallic models. The decoration, done in the customary technique for this class of vase of overpainting following the firing, consists in objects alluding to the gods: Apollo's lyre, Dionysus's crater, Arthemisia's torches, framed by a trellis of Dionysian vines. It appears as a Hellenising anticipation of the characteristic Hellenistic genre of still lifes. This class of vases is undoubtedly of Apulian origin, although the centre (or centres) of production have still to be identified. Second half of 4th century B.C.

"Pilgrim's flask" from Canosa
inv. 16270
This flask, of which the Museum has three examples (the same decoration appears also on a *pyxis*), has a round body and two handles and (only in this case) a base for support.

On both sides there is the figure of Scylla with the naked breasts of a woman, two dog's heads on either side of the belt and, in stead of legs, two tails of a fish or dolphin.

Below her a darting fish alludes to the sea. There are traces of white and coloured slip.

This is obviously an imitation in modest materials of silver ware which was often decorated with similar figures of marine monsters, like the famous bivalve mirror from Taranto. 3rd century B.C.

Lamb's head rhython
inv. Santangelo collection 975
The decoration presents the figure of a dancing Maenad, head flung back in ecstasy, one breast laid bare. Next to her a young satyr sits immersed in melancholy, his *pedum* abandoned at his side. The shiny yellow varnish which covered it imitated the gilding of the precious versions in metal, a few of which have come down to us.

**Bronze stag's head rhython,
from Herculaneum**
inv. 69174

The provenance of this splendid *rhython* in the form of a stag's head should not mislead us. It is a Hellenistic artefact of notable quality, belonging to a well-known type which was produced in Magna Graecia in both engraved metal and ceramic ware from the 4th century B.C. onwards, in imitation of analogous 5th century Attic products.

Such objects were rarely used in the Roman world. Smooth horns were used for drinking in the symposia, while others, decorated with protomes, appear in cult scenes, for example in the hands of the Lares.

Roman Campania and its artistic production: a brief historical profile

A large part of the collections of the Naples Museum comes from Campania in Roman times, and especially from the towns around Vesuvius, in the Phlegrean area and inland in the Terra di Lavoro. Thus it seems appropriate to recall briefly the stages by which the cultures of preroman Campania became part of the Roman world.

Even in the Archaic period Campania was the traditional source of agricultural produce for Rome, as can be seen from the dealings between the Tarquins and the Cumae of the tyrant Demaratos. Roman interest in the fertile countryside grew at the end of the fifth century B.C. as a result of the ban on trading which was imposed by the Samnites, who had just gained possession of the region. In the first half of the fourth century the Romans were kept busy elsewhere, fighting urgent wars against the Gauls, the Ernicians and the Latins, but the inevitable clash for control of Campania broke out in the first Samnite war in 343-341 B.C. This ended with the concession of Roman citizenship without the right to vote (*civitas sine suffragio)* to Capua, and shortly afterwards to *Calatia* (Maddaloni,CE), *Atella* (Succivo, Orta di Atella,CE), *Suessula* (Acerra, NA), Acerra and Cumae. Thus the political and social reality in this period was characterised by an alliance between Rome and the local oligarchies: this was particularly significant in Capua with its military elite of cavalrymen, the *equites Campani,* who are cited in numerous sources for their deeds of arms in Roman battles throughout the Mediterranean area. In 334 Rome installed the new colony of Cales, near Calvi Risorta (CE), to guard the main road leading to this newly pacified region.

The second conflict with the Samnites, which ended in 304 B.C., marked the transformation of the Campanian centres from allies to subjects of Rome. More Latin colonies were set up, at *Suessa* (Sessa Aurunca,CE) and *Saticula* (Sant'Agata dei Goti, BN), to complete the encirclement of the region. Under the impetus of Rome and the influence of its political organisation, which stimulated urban development, the second half of the fourth century and much of the third were, in spite of the warfare, a period of great prosperity for Campania. The traditional form of settlement in scattered villages *(pagi* and *vici),* which had survived in the areas unaffected by Greek or Etruscan colonisation, was replaced by towns. Artisan activities flourished, with large-scale production of ceramic ware, both with red figures and black varnish in imitation of Attic output. Funerary rites give us some idea of the dignity of the aristocratic classes, for they favoured rich grave furnishings which often reflected the noble Greek custom of the banquet, and the paintings on the burial slabs also often derive from Hellenic models (see tombs from Nola, Cumae, Afragola).

Another indication of the self-confidence and enterprising spirit of the new Campanian-Samnite communities is the minting of their own coinage (probably at the mint in *Neapolis),* in which the iconography is inspired not only by Cuman and Neapolitan issues but also by the major Greek *poleis* which had dealings with Naples. Thus the helmeted head of Athena on Campanian coins is an explicit evocation of the goddess, and there are numerous affinities with coins from Thurii, the Athenian colony built on the site of Sybaris. This new monetary activity undoubtedly reflected the influx of silver brought by returning mercenaries who had been paid off in the Greek fashion. Furthermore Campania, with the mint in *Neapolis,* guided Rome in its production of coinage, providing the model for the first silver coin and actually minting Rome's first bronze coin, with Apollo in profile and a bull with a human head, inscribed *Rhomaion,* appropriately enough in Greek letters.

The fortunate preservation of Pompeii makes it possible to recognise here, better than in other more important centres, the prosperity which flourished under Roman tutelage. An extraordinary rebuilding activity suddenly began in the city. Even at the beginning of the third century it must still have looked a rather seedy late-Archaic town, with its temple to Apollo, the presiding deity, still decorated with old-fashioned terracotta facing in the Etruscan manner. Around the turn of the second century it went through a remarkable metamorphosis, becoming a large modern city complete with all the requisite Hellenistic urban attributes. Surrounded by majestic new walls at the beginning of the third century, it was given a completely new tripartite lay-out which in these same years was also adopted in *Paestum* and Nocera *(Nuceria Alfaterna).* As in Velia, a theatre and baths (the so-called *terme Stabiane)* were the first new facilities introduced to modernise the city. The discovery of architectonic terracotta work and a tufa metope representing the myth of Hyssion indicate the refurbishing of the archaic temple of Athene in the triangular forum, while recent exploratory digs below a house standing behind the temple of Fortuna Augusta have demonstrated the presence, which was quite unexpected in a third century Samnite town, of a public banqueting hall on the lines of a Greek *hestiatorion*.

In spite of the increasing prosperity, the evident disparity between the social classes, visible particularly in the elaborate tombs of the emerging classes, led to growing tension which came to a head in open rebellion against Rome. The occasion for this was the invasion of Hannibal at the close of the third century, when popular factions in all the Campanian towns tried to overthrow the ruling oligarchies. Capua, *Calatia* and *Atella* went over to Hannibal, and Campanian coinage bears witness to the fact in a bronze coin bearing the effigy of an elephant. The Roman reconquest of these towns in 211 B.C. led to severe reprisals against the local rulers, who either took refuge in other Italic centres or fled to the east. The capital of Campania, Capua, was stripped of all political autonomy and placed under the control of a Roman magistrate, the *praefectus Capuam Cumas*. It lost all its territory, which together with that of *Calatia* and *Atella* became part of the *ager publicus populi Romani* to be either assigned to new colonisers or sold off. From this time on Capua lived in symbiosis with its counterpart on the coast *Puteoli,* founded in 194 B.C. as a Roman colony on the site of the former Greek Dikaiarcheia.

This total submission to Rome in political terms must not be taken to imply, however, a "Romanisation" of the material culture and artisan production. It is still too early to speak of a "Roman" output as such with its own artistic language: this emerged only gradually under the influence of the much more advanced Campanian know-how. The inclusion of the whole region in the orbit of Roman influence represented the start of an overall design, symbolised by the opening of the Via Appia in 312 B.C. and the subsequent completion of a great network of roads which favoured the distribution circuits for artisan production. With results which varied in their immediacy and scope according to different circumstances, this design led in the space of a century or so to the complete homogenisation of the region and the formation of a Roman *koine*. This was characterised on the one hand by the political traits of the Latin tradition (consider for example the significance of the official adoption of the Latin language and measurements in Cumae in 180 B.C.) and on the other, in the sphere of aesthetical expression, by the hallmarks of Hellenistic culture.

The section of the Museum dedicated to *Neapolis* illustrates, as an example of what we have outlined above, the phenomenon of the production, first on Ischia and then in Naples, of black varnish pottery, known as *Campana A*. From the point of view of its formal repertory it appears typically Hellenistic, inspired by Greek output and especially the black varnish ware «invented» for the Athenian workshops by Thericles of Corinth, but its extraordinary diffusion throughout the whole of the western Mediterranean between the third and first centuries B.C. was only possible with the backing of the substantial capital investment and distribution network introduced by the Roman conquests. Similar mechanisms must have operated for other classes of artisan activity for which *alas* we do not have many tangible remains, such as fabrics, objects in bronze and metal, and Capua perfumes on sale in the local market, such as the renowned scent *Seplasia*.

The same goes for the production of Calenian pottery, which is well documented in literary sources and by archaeological items in the Museum's collection. This class of black varnish vases showing the Hellenistic tradition and influence mediated by Etruria was produced in the Latin colony of *Cales* and in some other workshops in the region (such as Venafro) and widely exported (or imitated) between the middle of the third century and the beginning of the second. These small vases with relief work, signed by Latin craftsmen, were cheap alternatives to the precious metal vases and derived their formal and above all figurative repertoires, featuring gods and heroes of the Greek myths, from Hellenistic and classical metalworking, engraving, sculpture and painting. Another production of some note which was roughly contemporary (end of 4th – first third of 3rd century) was that of Teano, characterised by a varied and florid decoration which was alternately engraved, stamped and painted on. The so-called *Cups of Arethusa (Arethusaschalen)* are related to this, again with black varnish, and bearing in the base a moulded relief of coins from Syracuse showing the head of the nymph Arethusa, made by the engraver *Euainetos*. Another class of Campanian ceramic ware was destined for more long-lasting fame, even though it had no artistic pretensions, being produced for use in cooking. This was the pottery with internal red varnish, common all over Italy from the end of the third century until the Imperial era. It has recently been possible to establish that this was the style of plate from Cumae *(Cumanae patinae)* immortalised by Apicius in his famous cookery book.

If, as we have seen, ceramic ware in general, and the more refined tableware in particular, showed strong evidence of assimilation and cultural levelling, the sculpture tradition, due in part perhaps to its more complex ideological and religious components, maintains over a longer period interesting aspects of diversification (see the sections of the Museum dedicated to the various cultures of ancient Campania). On the one hand the Hellenising production becomes ever more prevalent, and from the end of the fourth century is standardised according to both the canons of Attic art and the models of Lysippus. The influence of the former is seen, thanks possibly to the mediation of *Neapolis,* in the mass production of *tanagrines,* obtained with the double moulds developed in the workshops of Capua, Cumae, Teano etc.; the latter is visible in a type of male head with hair done in prominent locks deriving from a portrait of Alexander and reproduced over a wide area from Capua to Pontecagnano. On the other hand the style of production which we may term "Italic" continued to exist, although without its former vigour, linked to the particular religious, ethnic and expressive traditions of the various centres. As Roman domination asserted itself so the "Roman" and Hellenistic forms prevailed, until they became hegemonic in the second century B.C. Architectonic terracotta work was markedly Hellenistic, probably through the influence of Taranto, and characterised by the diffusion of common types such as the head of Athena surrounded by vines which we find in the mid-4th century in Pompeii in the temple of the Triangular Forum in high relief, to be imitated in increasingly schematic versions in Capua and Fratte (Salerno).

The opening of the great international port-cum-emporium of *Puteoli,* which superseded *Neapolis* at the beginning of the second century, gave a solid backbone to this economic and productive system. It is significant that, in addition to its flourishing commercial activities, it rapidly acquired artisanal productions to complement those of Capua, as for example metalworking and perfume manufacture (with the relative glass containers). In this period *Puteoli* was the true economic hub of the region, the most important in Italy and on an equal footing with Rome. *Negotiatores* from all over the Hellenic world gathered here to deal in grain, spices, wine, glass, slaves and Oriental luxury goods destined for the ever more demanding Roman market. Thus we can understand how in 126 B.C. the Roman poet Lucilius could speak of Pozzuoli as "the lesser Delos", likening it to the Aegean island which at that time represented the most important trading centre of the entire Mediterranean.

There are clear echoes of the commercial success of Pozzuoli in the contemporary Pompeii, which thanks to its prolific agricultural hinterland, specialised in the production of wine, was able to trade, albeit not on the scale of Pozzuoli, with Rome and overseas. The imports that derived from this trade give an idea of the extent of the exchanges: Spanish honey, wine from the Greek islands, braziers from Delos, and then again mosaics and, although we lack the material evidence, certainly cultured slaves, literary papyrus scrolls, and Hellenistic fashions and tastes. The city authorities set about a radical redesign of the principal public buildings in accordance with Hellenistic architectural canons. The restored walls were integrated with new gates decorated with sculpted archways; the area of the Forum was embellished with new colonnades, the Basilica, the new temple of Apollo and the temple of Jove; the quarter of the theatre and the archaic temple of Athena was masterfully reorganised in a single design including the new *propylon* and the porticus of the Triangular Forum,

the monopteros of Epidius, the Samnite gymnasium, the temple of Isis and the temple of Aesculapius. The project must also have envisaged the quadriporticus behind the theatre stage *(porticus pone scaenam)* and the odeon *(theatrum tectum)* which were both erected later by magistrates in the first generation of the Sillan colony. This renovation scheme was on the grand scale and undoubtedly involved private as well as public buildings.

One only has to think that the finest houses in Pompeii, such as the House of the Faun, date from this period, and their wall decorations stand among the highest achievements of ancient art.

Potters, masons and mosaicists, but also painters, architects, sculptors, goldsmiths and bronze workers made up a sizeable cohort of cultured artisans, none of whom alas is known to us by name, who catered to the Campanian and Roman aristocratic classes in the general rush to renew and embellish cities, sanctuaries and villas. We can glimpse the *modus operandi* of these peripatetic artisans and decorators in the activity of a workshop which specialised in decorating places of entertainment with stone inlay. The theatres of Sarno and Pietrabbondante (in Molise, in the heart of ancient Samnia) and the *theatrum tectum* in Pompeii all conserve specimens of its production of ornamental sculptures. A tangible sign that all this artistic profusion took place in a political and economic context that was inequivocably Roman can be read in the mosaic greeting to visitors with the Latin motto *"have"* on the threshold of the House of the Faun in Pompeii, at the time still a Samnite centre.

Large scale sculpture did not generally play a part in the artistic output of this period. One exception is the splendid *Aphrodite* of *Sinuessa,* an original creation of the second century B.C. which adorned the villa of a Roman nobleman at the foot of Monte Massico. Small decorative statues in bronze, however, were relatively common in Pompeii and of superlative quality (examples are the *Faun* of the eponymous house, and the *Narcissus and Satyr with wineskin).* Of particular interest as an indication of the complete assimilation of Hellenistic taste is the architectonic terracotta work such as the *frieze with battle scenes between two parties of cavalrymen* from the Triangular Forum in Pompeii dating from the third century. The subject imitates a prototype belonging to the genre of battle scenes which flourished under Alexander and his immediate successors and which found great popularity in Magna Graecia and Romanised Italy, as we see from the many and varied reelaborations, from the frieze of Civitalba to another which alas has been lost from Cales, or indeed the *mosaic of Alexander* itself. The same can be said for the fine series of figured capitals which adorn the doorposts at the entrances to the houses of the aristocracy in Pompeii.

The process of renewal in this period, which is so richly illustrated in Pompeii by virtue of its exceptional conservation, left traces which are less impressive but no less significant in the other cities of Campania. In Cumae, for example, the Forum, an open space measuring 120 metres by 50 with *tabernae* round the sides, was remodelled in the work done on the main temple of Jove: the third century edifice, consisting in a podium and shrine with triple nave, surrounded by a colonnade in tufa with two rows of Corinthian columns and semi-columns on pillars, and a rich epistyle with a frieze decorated with weapons added at the end of the second century. Or again in Pozzuoli, where the first Serapeo to be constructed in Italy is only known to us from the famous *lex parieti faciendo,* but substantial remains are to be seen of the first phase of the *Capitolium* in Rione Terra, with traces of an impressive *pediment decoration* in terracotta which is still to be studied.

This was the golden age of places of entertainment, both theatres and amphitheatres. Examples of the former are known at Sarno, belonging to a sanctuary complex, Nocera, Cumae (documented in inscriptions), Teano, *Cales* and the *theatrum exaggeratum* in Capua, recorded in an inscription of the *magistri Campani* in 108 B.C. Campania had no equal anywhere in Italy for the diversity of its amphitheatres: the first arena in Capua, from the time of Gracchus or a little later, that of Pozzuoli, from the end of the second century in *opus incertum* of tufa, that of Cumae, currently being investigated, and another recently discovered example in Benevento. This proliferation of costly building projects was encouraged and accompanied by the development of new methods in building technology: the readily available slave labour was exploited in the adoption of *opus cementium;* a mortar known as "malta di pozzolana", which we find in use as early as 168 B.C. in the restoration of the walls of *Calatia;* the first experiments with domes made of squared off stone blocks, such as the one dating from the middle of the second century in the baths in the lower part of the sanctuary of Diana Tifatina, and the use of *opus reticolatum,* known from the first decades of the first century B.C.

Another fundamental element which accompanied the process of Romanisation was the development of the villa. Conceived as a place for the spirit rather than a physical space, it represented the solution elaborated by the Roman aristocracy, albeit in the private sphere of *otium,* to the conflict between the straitjacket of public protocol and the fascination with Hellenistic culture which was emblematic of the progressive spirit in the Roman world of the time. To the Romans Campania, with its ancient Hellenic traditions emanating from Cumae to Poseidonia and Velia, and more vividly still in the actuality of the culture of *Neapolis,* represented the nearest and most authentic embodiment of Greece. It has been plausibly argued that the various members of the Scipio family played a fundamental role in establishing this *forma mentis.* There is no doubt that among the first residents in the Phlegrean Fields we find Cornelia,

the daughter of Africanus, with a villa at Miseno, and earlier still the consul in 176 B.C, Gneus Cornelius Scipio Hispallensis, who came to cure his infirmities in the waters of Cumae. For over and above its intellectual fascination, Campania could also offer the benefits of a prodigious wealth of mineral waters, which were highly prized in Hellenistic medicine. This aspect was not restricted to the Phlegrean area. A few years later Aemilius Paulus went to treat his complaints in the balmy climate and waters of Velia, site of a famous school of medicine which traced its origins back to Parmenides (and the recent discovery of a Hellenistic spa linked to a grandiose edifice with terraces near the source of Hyele gives confirmation to this ancient tradition). Many years later the physician Marcus Antonius Musa cured Augustus at *Atella* with a new therapy of cold baths of his own invention.

The name villa is also given to the constructions which accompanied the transfer of colonies or in general the installations in agricultural areas and which were thus primarily productive, although according to the precepts of Cato they could still include a residential area. The villas of Falerno and Caleno gave their names to the most celebrated Roman wines, while other such rural sites are known to us in the locality Posto di Francolise (CE) and round the southern and western slopes of the Massico, in the *ager* of Falerno, in the territory of *Sinuessa* and *Cales* and at Lauro di Nola (NA), some of them still built on the old-fashioned polygonal groundplan. The countryside was also dotted with sanctuaries, some of them going back to the Archaic period, often with rural hamlets that had grown up around them. Such is the case of the Dionysiac temple in contrada Sant'Abbondio in Pompei, which possessed a fine pediment in relief showing Libero and Libera, now in the Antiquarium, or the recently discovered sanctuary in the locality Privati in Castellammare di Stabia.

There was a rapid acceleration in the process of Romanisation as a result of the Social War (91-89 B.C.) and the consequent defeat of the Italic peoples. Colonies of veterans who had fought under Silla settled in new centres (this seems to be the case of *Urbana* in the Falerno plain) and in preexisting cities such as *Suessula,* Pompeii (now renamed *Colonia Cornelia Veneria Pompeianorum),* Nola and *Abella.* The territorial reorganisation was carried out under the strict supervision of the senatorial aristocracy and was largely the work of Silla and his lieutenants. The fate of Stabiae, an ancient Oscan stronghold in the federation of *Nucera,* sacked and annihilated as an autonomous urban entity, and that of the sanctuaries of the Samnite hinterland which were razed to the ground, testify to the harshness of the punishment inflicted on the losers. In cultural terms the new cycle of Romanisation was radical in the extreme: laws and administrative institutions, altars and rites in honour of the deities, the system of weights and measures, all was changed, and the Oscan language went into decline and rapidly disappeared. Of the ancient Greek colonies only Naples and Velia were

The main centres of Roman Campania

On the next page:
Marble relief with scenes of gladiators, from Pompeii, outside Porta Stabiana, tomb of Clovatius or A. Clodius Flaccus

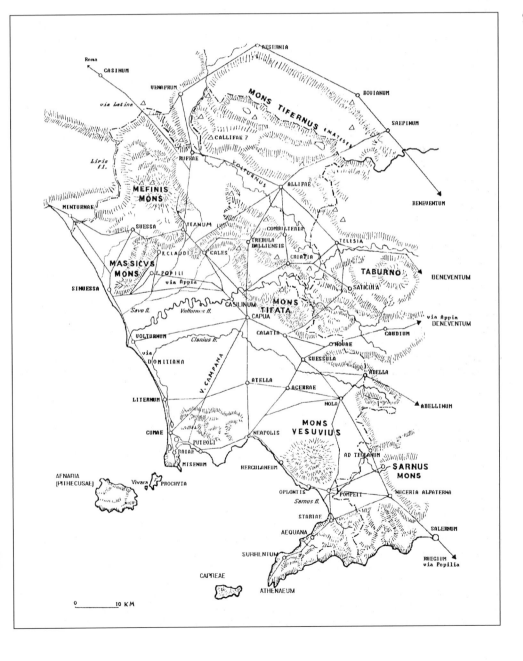

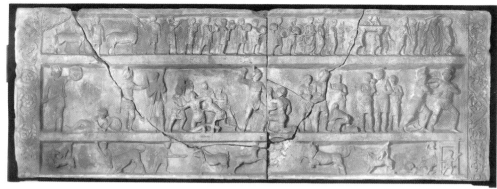

allowed to maintain, and indeed exalt in their continued use of the Greek language, the cultural traditions of Hellas which, now that they had no further political significance, represented no threat to Roman hegemony. Silla himself laid aside his toga when he stayed in Naples and donned the Greek chlamys. Roman youth (including Virgil) hastened to frequent the philosophy schools of the peripatetic Staseas, the academic Dion and the epicure Philodemus. The female portrait painter Iaia of Cyzicos was accredited with continuing the great tradition of classical painting, and doctors and naturalists, grammarians and orators, poets, writers and theatre producers completed the cast of the foremost cultural centre in contemporary Italy.

Nonetheless it is Pompeii which, up until 79 A.D. of course, best allows us to follow the evolution of a medium-sized Campanian city during Roman times. As well as signs of continuity with the pre-Silla phase, such as the completion of the reorganisation of the theatrical quarter which we mentioned above, new projects were set in motion. Some, such as the building of the amphitheatre at the eastern edge of the city or the new baths in the Forum, were related to the Campanian tradition of entertainment and spas; others, like the new terraced sanctuary dedicated to Venus as protector of the new colony, evoke traditions which were more typically those of Rome and Latium.

Such large-scale public works relied heavily on the support of illustrious figures connected to the Roman aristocracy, whose influence went beyond the individual city. A typical example is Caius Quintius Valgus, who appears in Pompeii as the magistrate who promoted the construction of the *theatrum tectum* and the amphitheatre, in Frigento (AV) in an inscription referring to a still unnamed *municipium* as the artifice of a wall of fortification, the town gates, forum, *porticus* and *curia*, and again in *Aeclanum* (Mirabella Eclano, AV) where he was active in similar projects. All these works show significant affinities, so that they evidently reflect a repertoire of monuments considered indispensable for the dignity of a town. In the same way the monuments which have come down to us often have counterparts: the baths in the Forum of Pompeii and *Cales;* the amphitheatre

of Pompeii and its virtual twin in Avella *(Abella),* as well as the less famous ones in *Atella,* Nola, *Telesia, Cales,* Teano, Sesso Aurunca, Paestum and the theatre of Alife. A typical architectonic feature of the period, related to the construction in terraces, was the cryptoporticus, of which the largest was in Capua, in the area of the Forum, and others at Rione Terra in Pozzuoli, Sessa Aurunca, Alife and la Starza di Mondragone (CE) *(pagus Sarclanus).* Much effort went into the upkeep of city walls, which as well as being a physical necessity seem to have been a mark of the prestige of the community. The examples in *Allifae,* Atripalda *(Colonia Veneria Abellinatium), Telesia* and *Aeclanum* were constructed using all the various techniques in vogue *(opus incertum, reticolatum, quasi reticolatum).*

In this period architectonic activity seems to have been particularly intense in the Phlegrean area. It was here that Roman aristocracy built luxurious villas laid out on successive terraces, *more Baiano,* to take advantage of both the proximity of the sea, at the lowest level, and the incomparable panorama over the Bay from higher up on the slopes of the Phlegrean craters. It is not difficult to imagine the lines from the opening of Lucretius's *De rerum natura* being composed, if not actually written down, here: *"dulce, mari magno turbantibus aequora ventis...",* an emotional tribute to the beauty of the seascape. The volcanic nature of the region with its active and extinct craters inspired local men of a practical bent to invent, or rather perfect, appliances catering to the growing *luxuria* of the Roman aristocrats. Two such inventions made the name of the *eques* Caius Sergius Orata: the tanks for oyster beds (mussels were already represented on coins from the Greek Cuma) and fish farming *(vivaria),* activities which were particularly suited to the lakes of Lucrino and Fusaro or purpose-built on the coast, and the *balinea pensilia* or baths equipped with *suspensurae,* which may have depended on the volcanic *fumaroli* activity. Taking full advantage of Nature's bounteous liberality, in this period the first spa establishments were developed. The complex named Sosandra, which was laid out over the highly scenographic terraces that were a feature of contemporary architecture, comprised, as can be seen today, a porticus at sea level, a nymphaeum-cum-theatre half way up and residential quarters at the top.

Not much, alas, remains of Capua, the other centre which underwent a spectacular development. It owed its prosperity to its intimate links with the emporium of *Puteoli* and its strategic position in the road network of Campania (highly advantageous for its ancient tradition of specialised arts and crafts, in particular the small statues in bronze known as "*Campana supellex*"). Among the significant building episodes of this period we can recall the reconstruction, at Sant'Angelo in Formis, seat of the ancient and highly venerated cult of Diana Tifatina, of the temple and columns with treasury funds. This was instigated by the *magistris,* as recorded in the dedicatory inscriptions in the mosaic pavement which is still *in situ* in what became a Christian church. A largely new element in the architectonic repertory of Campania was the funerary monument, a consequence of Romanisation. There had been occasional examples in the Hellenistic cities, above all in Naples but also elsewhere (Capua, Atella, Atripaldi), of the hypogeum tomb type, with extremely interesting achievements in decorative painting and plasterwork and in the accompanying reliefs. But in spite of these precedents, the real transformation in Campanian necropolises can be dated from the arrival of the Roman colonisers with their specific ideology of noble birth. From this time on roads leading away from the urban centres began to be lined with large and small burial monuments, adorned with sculptures and reliefs. In this context the production of sculpture has conserved singular examples of the swan song of the Italic stylistic language: between the end of the Republic and the first decades of the Empire numerous half busts were set up in the Hellenising roadside shrines in Capua, deeply incised in the manner of wooden sculptures and using the same, rather démodé language as the last "mothers of Capua" which also date from this period; or again the vivid realism of the reliefs with scenes from working life illustrating the calling of the deceased; or, from the necropolises of Pompeii, singular gravestones which fall midway between being non- representative and portraits. However, apart from these quirks, the predominant style in funerary art, while respecting local peculiarities, was undoubtedly the language of Hellenism reelaborated by the Romans. Specialised craftsmen set up shop in each centre. On the one hand we find a homogeneous diffusion, especially in the plain and round the coast, of the most common types inspired by Hellenism already in favour with the Roman *nobilitas*: with a circular base (in Capua the "Carceri Vecchie" from the end of the Republic, and in Pompeii the tomb of Eumachia, early Empire), cube-shaped with funerary lions, in the form of a *naiskos*, a housefront, a triclinium or a simple enclosure. On the other hand, especially in the interior, there is a prevalence of local subtypes, probably in connection with the migratory patterns of the colonisers: tombs with decorations of figured metopes and triglyphs, anthropomorphic *cippi* and funerary shrines with figures inserted, particularly common in the inland areas (Capua, then Benevento, *Abellinum* and also Pompeii), and representations of city gates (*Abellinum, Aeclanum,* Capua).

Naples too harks back to Greek tradition, but its production was clearly differentiated from that of the rest of Campania. In reusing some of the Hellenistic hypogea, during the first century A.D. it produced a series of *funerary reliefs* in marble and terracotta which, unique in Italy, derive directly from Greek models, and in particular the late-Hellenistic reliefs of *Rhenea* and, slightly later, *Paros, Naxos, Syros* etc.; set in architectonic frames, the characters are invariably portrayed in the gesture of the farewell handshake, which was typical of Greek funerary ideology, just as the language and formulae of the inscriptions are Greek, such as the characteristic *chreste chaire* («farewell, the best»).

In due time we shall trace the development of house building in the Vesuvian cities. For the moment we must just recall the influence of the cultural model of the great villas of *otium* which thronged the Neapolitan coastline. Once the figure of a *princeps* began to be surrounded by an imperial court, and he himself acquired the habit of residing for longer and longer periods in Baiae, in palaces either built to order or purchased from citizens, owning a villa in Baiae must have become the ultimate dream of the *crème de la crème* of Roman aristocracy. The continuity of these imperial seaside residences is seen in the sequence of the visitors: Augustus, Tiberius, Claudius, Nero, Domitian, Hadrian, Settimius Severus, Alexander Severus, while both Marcus Aurelius and Antoninus Pius owned estates there. The imperial palace itself has still not been identified with certainty. At the east end of the Bay of Baia, at Punta Epitaffio, the recent discovery of a nymphaeum-triclinium submerged by bradyseism, which was adorned with an extraordinary ensemble of statues dating from the middle of the first century A.D., has suggested that this was the *praetorium* of Claudius. In fact the ensemble includes, as well as statues of Ulysses and Baius from a scene of the blinding of Polyphemus (the same theme recurs in the grotto of Sperlonga in Tiberius's villa) placed in the alcove in front of the entrance, two statues of Dionysus and representations of members of the imperial family (the ensemble is on display in the Museo dei Campi Flegrei in the castle of Baia).

However, the imperial court and its entourage were not limited to Baiae in their pursuit of the delights of villa life. The Emperor had also inherited, from the extremely wealthy *eques* of Benevento Publius Vedius Pollio, the Neapolitan villa of *Pausilypon,* which gave its name to the headland of Posillipo. This was an enormous property, of which so far the only visible remains are a theatre with a swimming pool for aquatic entertainments (unique in its kind), an *odeion* and spa chambers. The Naples Museum has some very fine sculptures found there, including the group of *Nereids on a pystrix* and the *statue of a negro*. Another vast imperial villa was situated in Sorrento, and still frequented in the second century (one example of sculpture from Sorrento in the Museum is the *statue of a boxer* signed by Aphrodisia Koblanos), and then again there were further properties in Pompeii and Nola, where Augustus died. Yet the most celebrated of the imperial properties round the Bay was the complex of villas with which Tiberius endowed Capri. It is no exaggeration to say that the island, which became entirely imperial property under Augustus, was one great villa, with various ramifications at Villa Jovis, Palazzo a Mare, Damecuta and the Grotta Azzura, and represented a *summa* of all the possible refinements and architectonic features of the villa in that epoch. The superlative quality of the architecture and decoration transpires from the fragments that have come down to us: precious paved floors in coloured marble like the one which was relaid in the palace of Capodimonte; decorative sculptures and the marine group from the Grotta Azzura, which was transformed into an extraordinary nymphaeum belonging to the complex of le Gradelle above and possibly linked to the villa of Damecuta. There can be no doubt that this grandiose example of an entire natural environment enhanced with the architectonic marvels of a villa served as a model for Nero's later creation in Subiaco, the Domus Aurea, the villa of Domitian in Castelgandolfo and Villa Adriana near Tivoli.

Naturally the premise for all this *otium* was the new political status of the realm. The conclusion of the civil wars with the battle of Actium and the assertion of the new regime of Augustus signalled, for the whole of Italy, the beginning of a phase of consolidation, stabilisation and recovery of the urban organisms. In Campania the direct link with the capital had now acquired institutional recognition in the creation of the single *Regio I (Latium et Campania),* and the seeds sown in the previous two centuries now bore fruit. Throughout the region a vast programme of public works was put in hand, with the creation or reinforcement of both military and civilian infrastructures. The regional road network was developed, and the most visible signs of this today are the portentous tunnels opened up in the Phlegrean area: that of Monte di Cumae, from the Forum of Cumae to the port, that of Averno, between the Lake and Cumae, that of "the Sibyl" between Lucrino and Lake Avernus, that of Seiano leading to the villa *Pausilypon*, and the *crypta Neapolitana,* going under the hill of Posillipo to join Naples to the Phlegrean Fields.

The grandiose project of Nero to link the port of *Puteoli* to the Tiber with a canal *(fossa Neronis)* had to be abandoned, although there are still tangible signs of it along the coast, and the completion of the road network came about in the age of Domitian with the construction of the highway named after him (95 A.D.) from *Puteoli* to Sinuessa, running entirely along the coast through the inhospitable marshes at Cumae (Arco Felice); and, under Trajan, the opening up of the *Appia Traiana,* an offshoot of the Appia from Benevento to Brindisi. Another innovation of great importance for both the Vesuvian and Phlegrean areas was the construction, in the Augustan age, of the aqueduct of Serino. Designed to supply the naval base at Miseno and restored by Constantine, it was one of the most remarkable achievements of its kind for its carrying capacity, length (about 100 km) and the feats of engineering involved: long stretches of viaduct, deep galleries through the mountains of Forino and Laura and then the enormous tanks which stored the water in the Phlegrean region – the spectacular *piscina mirabilis* in Bacoli, the "cento camerelle" and the "piscine" in Pozzuoli (Cardito, Lusciano etc.) which can now be integrated with the recently discovered *castellum aquae*. Numerous offshoots supplied cities along the route, such as Nola, *Atella,* Acerra, Pompeii and also Naples, where a few remaining arches, known as the "Ponti Rossi", have always been one of the traditional landmarks.

It is once again in Pompeii that we can get a complete idea of the transformations that followed on the arrival of an aqueduct in a city. Old tanks for collecting rain water and wells were replaced by a capillary network of water distribution, new public fountains were erected and many laundries opened up. Private houses were embellished with fountains in the form of statues, urns, nymphaea done in mosaics, aquatic tricliniae, all elements taken over from the decorative repertoire and philosophy of the urban villa and, in social terms, from the *nobilitas,* whose life style was beginning to be imitated by new social classes such as the urban *bourgeoisie* and the most upwardly mobile of the freed men. Naturally the development of the water supply network, which in *Puteoli* was integrated by the Campanian aqueduct, was not restricted to the territory of Naples and Pozzuoli: we know of other aqueducts at *Abellinum* and *Beneventum,* at Capua, carrying the waters of the river Tifata, and at Cava dei Tirreni and Pontecagnano, near the site of *Picentia*.

In the Imperial era the Phlegrean area continued to be the core of Roman Campania, above all because here, at Pozzuoli and Miseno, were situated the two major ports, for commercial and military traffic respectively. From the age of Claudius Ostia began to vie with Pozzuoli, until it took over completely as the port of Rome, but up until the third century A.D. Pozzuoli remained an emporium of prime importance for the Mediterranean basin, and was treated with special regard by the imperial administration. In the Augustan age it was endowed with an impressive new pier (the so-called *molo caligoliano)* comprising arches built on pylons resting on the seabed *(opus pilarum)*. The coast round to Baiae *(ripa Puteolana)* was gradually covered with buildings, prevalently for commerce or for celebratory functions, constituting a sumptuous and intricate *continuum* which contemporaries considered an extraordinary sight. Some idea of it has come down to us in the schematic representations of the urban landscape which adorn a series of glass beakers (end of 3rd-4th century A.D.), veritable souvenirs complete with messages of greetings.

As for the naval base which had originally been located in Pozzuoli when the new colony was installed there in 194 B.C., the events of the war against Sextus Pompeus had shown the necessity for new and more efficient facilities. Agrippa, the commander of Octavian's fleet, designed a new and exclusive base, the *portus Julius,* in a pair of natural basins, former volcanic lakes, situated on the coast between Pozzuoli and Baiae. One was Lake Avernus, which was stripped of the woods covering the slopes of the crater, and hence of that aura of religious mystery which had hitherto enveloped the ancient entry to Hades. It was linked by a purpose-built canal to an entry port in Lake Lucrinus, which ran on into the sea. It is likely that the engineer behind this project was the same Lucius Cocceius *architectus* who was responsible for building the road through the high ground between Lake Avernus and Cumae and who also, probably on the occasion of the installation of a new colony under the auspices of Augustus, erected in Pozzuoli the marble temple commonly referred to as being in honour of Augustus but in actual fact the *Capitolium.* This building, a pseudoperipterum in Corinthian style which has been perfectly conserved inside the cathedral of San Procolo in the Rione Terra, represents a marvellous example of Augustan classicism in the slightly academic clarity of its lines and down to the details of the vegetation decorating the marble antefixes. However, the *portus Julius* was not destined to see many years of service, possibly because Lake Lucrinus was prone to silting up. Immediately after the battle of Actium it proved necessary to move the fleet to a new base at Misenum. Here again two basins (Mare Morto and the harbour of Misenum) were linked by a broad canal over which a road ran on a swing bridge. As the base of the Pretorian fleet, Misenum received a military colony which is recalled in the theatre and in parts of some buildings in the Forum including the shrine of the Augustals, whose rich decorative ensemble with marble statues and inscriptions is on view in the Museo dei Campi Flegrei in the castle of Baia.

All the cities in the Phlegrean area were significantly enlarged during the early Imperial era, partly as a result of the policy of Augustus aimed at restoring the most ancient cults and traditions from the Roman past. The Phlegrean Fields naturally had a significant role to play in this revival, including as they did the grotto of the Sibyl and the entrance to the Underworld, celebrated in the new national epic, solicited by Augustus himself, Virgil's Aeneid. We know that the monuments relating to those cults and myths were restored at this time, from the temple of Apollo in Cumae, which sent the Sibylline books to Rome, to the temple of Demetra, also in Cumae, where in earlier times the Romans obtained the priestesses

who ministered to the cult of Ceres in Rome. The same spirit of renovation affected similar monuments in other cities, as for example the temple of the Dioscuri in Naples (later the church of San Paolo Maggiore) and the restored temple of Apollo in Pompeii, in honour of which the new *ludi Apollinares* were inaugurated. An interesting testimony to this religious atmosphere is the marble base in Sorrento (in the Museo Correale there) showing relief figures of deities in procession, a perfect expression of the ideology and the classicist artistic tendencies of the moment. Another interesting specimen is the statue of *Diomedes* from Cumae (in the Naples Museum), a copy of a Greek 5th century original attributed to Cresila, in which the hero is shown in the celebrated episode of the abduction of Palladius from the Trojan epic. The effects of this new climate are also visible in buildings and shrines either connected with the imperial cult or of a more general religious nature which now testify to a profound renovation of public architecture in the cities of Campania, as we shall see in detail in the cases of Pompeii and Herculaneum.

One more element which enriched the architecture and other manifestations of religious art in Roman Campania was the presence of foreign cults which passed through Campania on their way to Rome, arriving either at the port of Pozzuoli or overland from Brindisi with the commercial traffic. We have already mentioned the *lex parieti faciendo* of 105 B.C., an inscription recording the existence in *Puteoli* of a temple of Serapis. Although we have found no trace here of the temple of Isis, its twin in Pompeii can give us quite a precise idea of such a cult building in Imperial times. Thus it is indeed regrettable that so few fragments, obelisks and sculptures have come down to us from the restoration of the temple of Isis in Benevento that Domitian carried out in 88 A.D., in a sanctuary that had been flourishing for over a century. We have no remains of the analogous temple in Naples apart from an inscription in Greek and the famous statue of the Nile, found in the quarter which in medieval times was called "of the Alexandrians". Documentary evidence shows that the cult was widespread also in the other centres of the region, including Acerra, Carinola and Capua. A rapid review of the subject would enable us to identify, especially in the Phlegrean area in the cosmopolitan milieu of the *classiarii* (naval servicemen) of Misenum and the merchants of *Puteoli* (recent discoveries of graffiti have revealed names of some of these immortalised in Nubian wadis on the caravan routes to the Red Sea), evidence of the most exotic cults, from the *Magna Mater,* the Phrygian Cybeles who in Baiae was known as *Magna Mater Baiana,* to Ma, another Phrygian goddess identified with Bellona, *Syria* (*Atargatis* of Hierapolis), the various Baals from the cities of Syria *(Jupiter Heliopolitanus, Damascenus, Dolichenus)* the Punic *Caelestis* to whom a temple (*thalamis*) in Pozzuoli is recorded in an inscription, down to the Arab Nabatean *Dusares,* recorded by an altar with ritual stones found in the sea and some inscriptions from Pozzuoli; this same deity has recently been identified with a colossal marble bust from the end of the second century in the Vatican Museums, formerly believed to show the god Hadad and also from the Phlegrean Fields. Even more remote worlds are conjured up by the ebony statuette found in Pompeii showing the Hindu goddess Lakshmi.

However, it is the cult of Mithras, the Persian god who vied for supremacy with Christianity over a long period, which has left us various monuments of considerable importance in the region. Above all the temple in Capua, from the end of the second century, a subterranean place of worship comprising vaulted galleries decorated with religious paintings and an image of the god killing the bull in the holy grotto, surrounded by other mythical figures. The same scene, evidently from other temples, has survived in reliefs from Naples and Capri.

The desire to celebrate the imperial dynasty gave rise to the vogue for honorary arches which spread throughout the cities of Campania. The integral preservation of the Vesuvian cities gives us examples of several arches in *lateritium* covered with marble slabs and surmounted by statues, in Pompeii, and one with four passages covered in stucco and decorated with bronze sculpture groups in Herculaneum. The finest example is the Arch of Trajan in Benevento, the most important monument of official sculpture in Campania and one of the greatest in Roman art. Another arch in the same city, called *arco del Sacramento*, survives only as a bare structure. Other commemorative and honorary monuments in the various cities of Campania are only known to us from the scantest fragments. This is the case of the honorary arch of Capua, on the stretch of the Appia leading to *Casilinum,* a 2nd century structure with three passages of which only a few architectonically simple fragments remain which, like the one in Benevento, could have been related to Trajan's renovation of the road. In this class of monuments we should also mention an Augustan age relief from the area of the Forum of Salerno; the *marble base from Puteoli* recording the cities of Asia struck by earthquake; one from the reign of Antoninus, also from *Puteoli,* showing personifications of the provinces (while alas no trace is left of the triumphal arches richly decorated in marble on marine subjects which are known to have stood at the ends of the pier in that city); another, circular marble base from the forum of *Abellinum;* the reliefs with a frieze of weapons, dating from the second century A.D., found in Sorrento (in the Museo Correale there); and the *marble bust clothed in a cuirass (lorica)* found at Fuorigrotta in Naples, part of an official monument from the reign of Antoninus which stood near the *via per cryptam* leading to Pozzuoli. And in this respect we can also recall the host of statues of emperors and princes which ornamented town squares and public monuments, and often private houses, as a sign of devotion and political loyalty throughout Campania. Numerous examples are to be found in all the museums in the region. Then too there was a great vogue for statues of private citizens: everyone, from the freshly nominated *sexvir Augustalis* to the most decorated consul, hankered after, and more often than not secured, one or more likenesses in the hope of perpetuating his own, possibly illusory, fame. An enormous quantity of statues, busts, armed images and equestrian statues in both marble and bronze thronged the forum, theatres, amphitheatres, spas, sanctuaries and tombs.

As in Rome at this time, the munificence of the *princeps,* or of the municipal authorities who enacted the directives of the new regime at the local level, was glorified in all the cities of Campania with new public buildings, and in particular those with the most popular appeal: spas, amphitheatres and theatres. At Pompeii no less than five public baths confirm the great popularity of these facilities even in a city which was by no means large. The last to be built, occupying four *insulae* which were destroyed during the earthquake of 62 A.D. and known as the *Terme Centrali,* indicate that in Campania too there was a definite proclivity for large suburban establishments. While the most ancient baths were still located right in the centre, just off the forum, the crowds and disorder that they tended to attract, and also the necessity for large open spaces to take ever more colossal establishments, frequently prompted the magistrates to locate the new baths outside the city itself, even at the cost of violating the sacred ground or *pomerium* immediately beyond the walls (*post murum*). This was the case in Pompeii, outside Porta Marina, Herculaneum, Capua and Naples. In Pozzuoli we can still see the grandiose ruins of the *baths of Neptune,* dating from Hadrian's reign, *of the Forum* (*Balnea Orthodonica*) and *of via Ragnisco,* and in Cumae the *baths of the Forum* from the reign of Domitian. However, it was above all in Baia that the construction of bathing establishments reached new heights of technical prowess, foreshadowing the achievements which were to distinguish such structures in Rome. Great halls were erected on a circular or polygonal groundplan and covered over with aerial domes (known as «trugli» in medieval times and «templi» to the humanists) which still evoke wonder today for their impressive dimensions and await proper investigation to establish their exact function within the establishments. The fashion for «taking the waters» continued unabated during Imperial times. The mild climate and abundance of spas constantly attracted adepts, and on occasion this tradition inspired re-evocations of classical models, which on Ischia, on the soil of the ancient *Pithekoussai,* managed to appear remarkably genuine. In the sanctuary of the Nymphs of the Nitrodi the local goddesses of health-restoring waters were honoured in relief sculptures which were of clearly Greek descent.

While in Rome the theatre was long viewed as an art

form from an alien culture, in Campania its roots went back to the remote past, both Greek and Italic, for the latter peoples also had their own theatrical traditions, such as the *fabula Atellana*. Thus it is hardly surprising that the precocious development we have already registered continued, and even gathered pace, during Imperial times. We do not know the most ancient theatre in Naples, although we can suppose that it occupied the site on which, during the first years of the Empire, the theatre in which Claudius and Nero later performed was constructed. As in Pompeii, beside the theatre there was an *odeion*, or *theatrum tectum* to give it its Latin name, of which little remains. It should be remembered that the musical competitions were always an essential part of the Neapolitan games, including the great four-yearly events which Augustus inaugurated, styled *Isolympics* (that is, of equal dignity to the Olympics). The theatre of Hercu-laneum is of great interest, both for what it reveals about architecture in the Augustan age and for its fine state of conservation. In the first excavation in the Vesuvian area, in the 18th century, it was found intact under the crust produced by the eruption with all the decorative sculpture of the proscenium and primarily the numerous statues of its munificent patrons, the *Nonii Balbii*. Little remains, in contrast, of the Augustan age theatre in Misenum, or indeed of those of Liternum and Capua, of which the latter was refurbished under Tiberius. Further north, investigations still have to be carried out on the examples in Sessa Aurunca, characterised by important work dating from the late 2nd-3rd century, and Treglia (*Trebula Balliensis*). The theatre of Benevento was inaugurated in 126 A.D. and is well preserved in the external arches and the stage area, while the large theatre of Teano was remodelled during the reign of Severius with luxurious marble ornamentation and sculptures adorning the proscenium.

Once again, it is above all in the construction of the amphitheatres, together with the baths, during the Imperial age in Campania that, to quote Piranesi, «the magnificence of the ancient Romans» continues to impress us as it did the humanists. As the gladiatorial contests superseded plays as the most popular urban form of social entertainment, the evolution of the amphitheatre into ever more elaborate and imposing forms gave it pride of place in the panorama of municipal monuments. It is an open question whether the second example in *Puteoli* dates from the reign of Nero or Flavio, or in other words whether it predates or postdates the extraordinary project of the Colosseum in Rome. What is certain is that the two gigantic constructions, erected in the space of a few years, both testify to the maturity of Roman engineering in dealing with enormous problems of calculation, construction, transport, hydraulics and organisation of works sites. Monumentality is also the hallmark of Capua's second amphitheatre, built at the turn of the second century, restored by Hadrian and dedicated by Antoninus Pius, and outdone in its dimensions only by

the Colosseum. Built partly out of stone blocks and partly in *lateritium,* comprising four Doric orders tapering as they go up, it was decorated with an impressive array of sculptures and reliefs, including the *Aphrodite, Aphrodite with Psyche* and *Adonis* in the Naples Museum, while the keystones in the arches, representing the heads of divinities, were taken as a model by the sculptors working for Frederick II of Swabia on the Gate he erected on the bridge over the Volturno. More in general the passion for the arena, radicated in the souls of Campanians from the most remote times, inspired all sorts of monuments, the products of popular craft traditions, and not just the architectonic giants. This is seen in the decorations in stucco, marble statues and painting in tombs in Pompeii, or sculptures reflecting popular taste such as the gladiator with Priapus in tufa found in the amphitheatre in Pompeii, or the simple representations in terracotta figurines or on the discs of the mass-produced lamps, right down to the most ordinary manifestations of daily life such as the graffiti and acclamations which crop up all over the place in the Vesuvian cities.

Another characteristic phenomenon of the early Imperial age, determined by the Augustan policy of bringing up the young in the traditions of their homeland and also by a revival of classicism which in the traditional culture of Campania found fertile ground, was the construction *ex novo* of large *palaestrae*. We find the most significant examples in the Vesuvian cities, with large open spaces equipped with a *natatio* and surrounded by an ample *porticum*. This revival took on an even more explicit form in the great ludic festivals which were instituted in the Greek cities, such as the Isolympics in Naples and the Eusebeia, in honour of Hadrian, in Pozzuoli. They required the erection of a stadium, which was a totally anomalous architectonic type in Italy, undoubtedly catering for a sizeable population of Greek and Oriental residents. We know of its existence in Naples from numerous written references, and in Pozzuoli from actual remains. In the same context can be placed the Neapolitan hippodrome and circus, for which again we have only documentary evidence.

The reorganisation of the civic functions in Roman cities can also be seen in the rapid diffusion of another architectonic type of Greek origin, the *macellum*. This was a building with an internal courtyard surrounded by a porticum designed as a food market, replacing the unsatisfactory practice of selling foodstuffs in the forum or other public squares. The example in Pompeii, situated in the north-east corner of the forum, shows better than elsewhere how it was integrated into the urban lay-out, but the finest specimen in Campania is the so-called temple of Serapis in Pozzuoli. Built along the *ripa* overlooking the harbour, it measured an impressive 58 metres by 75 and was distinguished by an extremely rich decoration in marble and exotic statues. The latter included the copy of the *Serapis* by Briassides, which accounted for its mistaken identification, various statues of emperors and famous men of the city and Empire, and neo-Attic sculptures like the famous group of *Orestes and Electra* from the reign of Tiberius. Another *macellum* which has been investigated and can now be visited is located in the heart of Naples beneath the monastery of San Lorenzo Maggiore.

We shall leave consideration of paintings and mosaics to the chapter on domestic architecture in the Vesuvian cities. In cities elsewhere the figurative arts are represented above all by stucco work. In the Phlegrean area we must mention the remains of the ceilings in two rooms in the baths of Sosandra in Baia, dating from 40-50 A.D., and two impressive survivals in Pozzuoli: the coffer vaulting in the amphitheatre of Flavius, recalling analogous constructions in the Colosseum, and the remarkable decoration seen in various *columbaria* which, being made of material that had to withstand the damp, were destined to survive well. Among the most significant examples, not least for their state of conservation, are the twin columbaria dating from the reign of Vespasian situated in the *fondo Caiazzo* on the Via Campana. Although the style is elementary to the point of verging on popular art, their complex architectonic disposition shows a complete adhesion to the repertoire of Roman funerary iconography with the abduction of Proserpine, Hercules at rest and the standard imagery of female figures making offerings, dancers with the *kalathiskos,* marine creatures, *Erotes and Psychai,* laced with garlands, festoons, candlesticks and so on. We find the same repertoire in two mausoleums near San Vito, also on Via Campana. One is in ruins, but shows the same architectonic disposition, while the other, which may be slightly earlier, presents in the apse of the lower floor the traditional Dionysiac couples in flight and in the semi-domes scenes of a Dionysiac maritime procession and Hercules in combat with the Hydra, with obvious funerary significance. This fashion for stucco continued through the middle period of the Imperial epoch, both in the baths (in Baia we can single out a ceiling in the baths of Sosandra, from the Domitian period, with satyr masks in the medallions, and another dating from 170-180, with a Nereid on a sea panther holding up a plate of fruit) and in the columbaria (in Pozzuoli, in a tomb in Via delle Vigne from about 130, with flying figures, Victories carrying candelabra, marine creatures, centaurs, a maritime procession with Erotes and an alcove with a shell held up by kneeling Tritons). Finally this fashion is seen as a more precious version of painted decoration in villas, as indicated for example by the fragments from the end of Hadrian's reign found at Pausilypon, including the figure of a satyr making the gesture of *aposkopein.*

As for decoration in mosaic, it too, thanks to the destiny of the Vesuvian cities, is in general sufficient for us to trace its development, which is in line with the overall evolution of this technique in Roman Italy. Here we shall just mention the extraordinary surge in popularity of mosaics in the spa establishments during the second century. Marine deities, Aphrodites, Nereids and Tritons were all recurrent in the typical black and white style, of which alas the Museum possesses no example, although it is very common in excavated sites throughout the region, such as the villa of Minori, the baths at Agnano, via Terracina in Fuorigrotta, one which went missing from a villa in Boscoreale, Torre San Limato in *Sinuessa,* and others showing a hare hunt and a radiant *Helios* from the lower level of the Venus complex in Baia. There are also some remarkable polychrome mosaics, such as the fragment with the chorus of children, late second century, from Sant'Angelo in Formis, displayed in the Museo Provinciale di Capua, and one showing a hunting scene from the fourth century, analogous to those of Piazza Armerina, found on the hillside round Lucrino and regrettably since lost.

Turning to the most fragile of the decorative genres, wall painting, its history in Campania after 79 A.D. has left no evidence apart from a few walls dating from the second century in Baia which show just how far the architectonic schemes of the IV style had been degraded. A funerary painting from the Neapolitan hinterland is more instructive. The *columbarium of Caivano,* from the end of Hadrian's reign, presents a scheme of yellow sections forming panels which are decorated with stylised chalices. Of particular note is the lunette, with a delicately drawn marine landscape on a white background, and the dome with geometric partitions adorned with floral garlands. For the sake of completeness we should also refer to the description of the picture gallery of a suburban Neapolitan villa filled with mythological pictures, many on the themes of the Pompeian repertoire, which, perhaps with a dash of rhetorical invention, we find in the writings of the brilliant sophist Philostratus of Lemnos, dating from the turn of the third century.

Another aspect of artistic production to undergo profound changes during the Imperial age was funerary art. In some parts of Campania, especially the Phlegrean Fields, which were closely linked to Rome, the new cultural models and architectonic typologies were adopted immediately. The chronic lack of space in these overpopulated areas and hence the prohibitive cost of a burial vault tended to limit more and more the use of an individual or family tomb in the Republican fashion. Thus from the middle of the first century onwards the *columbarium* became increasingly common, often designed to hold all the urns from one funerary district. It was largely built underground with walls divided up into tightly packed rows of niches (*loci),* often decorated with one or more aedicules and exquisite decoration in stucco. From the mid-2nd century onwards, when in addition to cremation the practice of burial also became common, the necessary trenches (*formae*) were dug in the floor at the base of the walls. The tombs of the lower classes were merely trenches protected by two tiles leaning against each other or by an amphora. The roads leading out of Pozzuoli were lined with numerous mausoleums in the Republican style and *columbaria*. The most notable complexes are in the necropolis of Via Celle, where there is a group of edifices dating from between the mid-1st century B.C. and mid-2nd century A.D., the necropolis of Fondo di Fraia, containing a famous mausoleum in *lateritium* built on two storeys, a cylinder on a square base, and a no less characteristic mausoleum in Quarto with a pyramid-shaped cusp. The practice of burial entailed the use of a *sarcophagus*. Of the many examples from Campanian necropolises in the Naples Museum, we can recall a fine second century example from *Atella,* showing the finding of Achilles at Scyrus; one from località Toiano at Pozzuoli, near the Via Domitiana, in the Asia Minor style of the *kline,* datable to the mid-3rd century; and another, fourth century example from Pozzuoli, made in a local workshop, showing the myth of Prometheus creating man and Eros bringing him a soul, symbolised by Psyche. Slightly older, from the end of the third century, is the famous specimen from Auletta, on the borders of Campania, which combines the iconography of Ariadne abandoned and sleeping with a scene of Erotes harvesting grapes.

The tendency which emerges so clearly in painting and the other figurative arts to take over refined models and propagate them on a wide scale thanks to the low cost of materials and mass production techniques extends to every sort of similar artisan production. However, the realisation of this phenomenon in the world of Imperial Rome has no parallel anywhere in pre-industrial times. We can point for example to the anonymous ceramics works in Pompeii, outside Porta Ercolano, or the factory for lamps and beakers *(fritilli)* near Porta di Nocera, which turned out mass objects with no identification which are practically impossible to distinguish from other makes.

It is difficult, in the absence of a systematic investigation, to make sense of the enormous quantities of artistic craftwork which the Vesuvian cities in particular have bequeathed us, filling the collections of the Naples Museum. It is still, for example, very arduous to distinguish, among the thousands of bronzes, those produced in Capua and celebrated in documentary sources as the prestigious *Campana supellex*. That there was a similar local production in Pompeii is borne out, among other indications, by a marble relief displaying the sign of a workshop which produced metal vases (Museo Nazionale, inv. 6575). There is the same difficulty in identifying the examples of *vicus vitrarius* made in Pozzuoli among the rich series of glass vases, or the workshops which produced the abundant silver vaseware or the numerous brooches in gold, silver and precious stones. In the ceramics sector it has so far been possible, on the basis of kiln rejects, badly fired examples and moulds, to attribute to Pozzuoli, Cumae, Naples or the Vesuvian cities some groups of *red varnish vases* and *vitreous pottery,*

cheap mass-produced objects for use by the lower classes, even abroad, but there is no doubt that the bulk of this investigative work is still to be done. In any case we are dealing with objects which, since they come from two medium-sized provincial cities, reveal the capillary presence of such ware, while the more exquisite objects, and particularly the bronze and silver ware from Pompeii, can give us some idea of the quality of the household objects in the noble residences of Naples, Capua and Pozzuoli, not to mention the villas in Baia and on Capri.

As we mentioned above, another remarkable example of decoration, from late Imperial times, is the production of glass souvenir flasks with scenes of the *ripa Puteolana*. Given the subject matter this class of material must be assigned to Phlegrean workshops, and they may also have produced the engraved glass which turns up in the Campanian hinterland and Samnia, such as the *glass of Sepino* (CB) and the glassware from Campochiaro (CB), regions which probably benefited from traffic along the *Via Campana*.

As for the other forms of artistic production, there is no doubt that the imperial palace in Baia and the villas of the nobility would have been catered to by workshops, probably based in the cities, which assembled painters, plasterworkers, sculptors and mosaicists. A particularly large haul of sculptures has come to light in Baia and Cuma, and the discovery, in a room in the baths of Baia, of numerous fragments of plaster moulds for important classical models is significant evidence of the activity of a sculptor specialising in the reproduction of the master-pieces of the classical world. Similarly an unfinished statue of *Pudicitia* found in the sea, together with other works either finished or only roughed out from the same area, indicates the existence of another workshop. Moreover, we know the signature of one local sculptor, *Karos Puteolanus,* found on one of the two copies of the *Hera Borghese* from the sea off Baia, while a mosaicist who signed himself *T. Senius Felix civis Puteolanus* is known to us from a mosaic found at Lillebonne at the mouth of the Seine. Similar finds have also occurred at Pompeii (for example the *torso of Jove* from the *Capitolium* and an unfinished statuette of Fortuna from *Oplontis),* showing that in a region like Campania in which demand was high, there must have been lots of workshops, naturally of differing quality, to meet the demand.

From as early as the middle of the second century there were signs, in Italy as a whole but even more so in Campania, of a serious economic crisis. The forms of specialised agriculture which had distinguished the late Republican and early Imperial period were abandoned, while *Puteoli* and neighbouring cities fell into a progressive decline, which dealt a severe blow to the urban economy consisting in craftwork and commerce that had interacted with and been supported by the considerable profits of industrialised agriculture. In terms of artisan and artistic output, the crisis of the municipal aristocratic classes, who were no longer able to play the role of munificent benefactors which had contributed so much to the development of the Campanian cities in Roman times, coincided with the increasing financial difficulties of the central authorities, who now intervened only in an emergency, such as the restoration of the Serino aqueduct or of city walls when a barbarian invasion threatened, and suspended all new building work. Already in the third century the construction of new public buildings had become a rare event, although there were occasional signs of activity under Severus, such as the small temple of Via Terracina in Pozzuoli or the renovation of the theatre of Teano. Now began the era of the great ransacking and reuse of the artistic materials from previous epochs involving sculptures, reliefs and epigraphs. Local craftsmen turned their hand to this sort of activity now that they could no longer count on public commissions.

The cities decayed and the population declined. Archaeological evidence shows that most of the residential quarters were uninhabited by the end of the second century and in any case after this period houses were only restored in exceptional cases. The cities which resisted best were the larger ones which were well placed to receive the residual economic activity. Thus Capua, which Constantine designated *caput Campaniae* and the seat of the *consularis Campaniae,* benefited from the traffic along the Via Appia, while Salerno was the joint seat, together with Reggio Calabria, of the *correctores Lucaniae et Bruttiorum.* Above all Naples seems to have withstood the crisis well, strengthening its ties with the agricultural hinterland, which once again, as in the Archaic period, became primarily the supplier of cereals for a subsistence economy. The presence of Syrian and Jewish colonies maintained some touches of cosmopolitan vivacity and the cultural traditions of the city that conserved its Greek language survived undaunted. It is significant that Plotinus, travelling through regions whose cities were largely deserted, still wanted to implant here his *Platonopolis,* the city of the philosophers, or that another intellectual from the late ancient world, Simmacus, reevoked in the villas of Baia his literary infatuation with the classical world. Yet again archaeology reveals that between the third and fourth centuries in Naples too the inhabited area of the city dwindled progressively, in spite of the rather over optimistic impression recorded by Cassiodorus in the second half of the fifth century: *"urbs ornata multitudine civium, abundans marinis terrenisque deliciis".* The process of urban decay did not spare any of the cities in the region, albeit with differences of degree and chronology, and the destructions which followed in the fifth and sixth centuries by Alaric (in 410: Eboli, Nola, Cimitile, *Abella),* Genseric (455: Capua, Nola, Abella), the Goths (490 and 542: Benevento; 554: Capua, *Compsa,* Paestum) and the Byzantines (662: *Aeclanum)* simply put an abrupt end, in one site after another, to a process which was already drawing to an inevitable conclusion.

However, it is also true to say that the end of the classical city did not automatically mean the end of a city or settlement in that area. In Campania as in the rest of Italy the new propulsive force was Christianity, and this gave rise to the only new artistic expressions to see the light in this epoch. They ranged from the palaeochristian churches in Naples (the basilica of Santa Restituta commissioned by Constantine with the adjacent baptistery of San Giovanni in Fonte, the oldest in the Western world, which still conserves splendid mosaics in its vaulted roof) to the basilicas of Cumae, erected in the fifth century on the ancient temples of the acropolis, the monumental complexes of catacombs and cemeteries in Naples and Cimitile, copiously decorated in painting and mosaics, and the rich remains in Capua. This, however, is another story, and the province of another Museum.

The decoration of public monuments in some of the Roman cities in Campania: Pompeii, Herculaneum, Puteoli, Capua

One topic of particular importance which is well illustrated in the voluminous collections of the Naples Museum is, as we have already mentioned in passing, the decoration of public buildings in the Roman cities. Campania was as rich in cities of outstanding importance as it was subject to the most dramatic phenomena of natural obliteration by means of eruptions or bradyseism. The fortunate conservation of such monuments as the theatre of Herculaneum, which the first excavators discovered with all its sculptures intact, and the Sacellum of the Augustals in Herculaneum, also extraordinarily well preserved with its full complement of paintings and now able to be compared with its counterpart in Misenum, makes it possible to study in depth, at least up until the first century A.D., the concept of the *loca publica*. It was through these monuments that the imperial regime expressed the image of itself that it wished to impress on citizens, and in the trading cities on foreigners too. As is well known, the attention paid to image and the propaganda deriving from it were one of the features of the heritage of Roman culture in the Western world.

There is no doubt that, apart from Rome itself, Pompeii is the city in which public spaces are best conserved, starting from its groundplan. Unfortunately the depredation which followed the eruption of 79 A.D., and to some extent also the state of decay which was a result of the earthquake 17 years earlier, deprived us of much of the decoration, and particularly the scupture, of the main public buildings. Some compensation for this lies in the fact that the architecture itself is better preserved than elsewhere, so that at least the bases of the missing statues remained in place, and also in the vast repertoire of painting which provides some exceptional evidence, such as the paintings in the House of Julia Felix with scenes of life in the Forum and the reliefs from the lararium of Cecilius Giocondus representing the Forum during the earthquake of 62 A.D. The buildings which largely escaped depredation give us a fair idea both of the level of artistic accomplishment current in the city and of the criteria which guided the authorities in their choice of statues for the civic monuments.

Once every form of municipal identity and trace of the former autonomy had been subsumed in the Roman system, the prevailing criterion seems to have been an ostentatious loyalty to the ruling dynasty, not only in the imitation of new buildings put up in Rome at imperial instigation and reiterated portraits of the *princeps* and members of his family but also in the adoption, in both private and public portraits of the citizens of Pompeii and Herculaneum, of the styles of dress, poses and hairstyles then in vogue at the imperial court. This phenomenon was widespread throughout Italy and the Roman world. The close relations that the nascent aristocracies, both urban and municipal (the *domi nobiles*), that emerged following the civil wars maintained with the new regime led to a rush to build anew or renovate the public monuments in cities large and small. In emulation of the archetypes in Rome, these schemes had to give visible expression to the support of all the citizens for the dynasty and at the same time to the general contentedness in an epoch which the court poets celebrated as a return of the golden age. One material, marble, which after centuries of use in Greece became the virtual symbol of classical art and culture and was vituperated in Rome by the upholders of indigenous values when the Roman *nobilitas* began to make profuse use of it in their residences, now comes to symbolise the new architectonic morality. Augustus himself, who was grudging in his *privata luxuria* as Suetonius's *Life* shows, set a widely acclaimed example of *publica magnificentia* by leaving to posterity a capital resplendent in marble which, in its architecture too, could at last take pride of place in the rollcall of the world's great cities.

This was also the prevailing spirit in Pompeii. The building belonging to Eumachia, which yielded the statue of this eminent Pompeian woman of Greek origin, imitates celebrated contemporary Roman counterparts even in the address of the dedicatory epigraph, with its mention of *Concordia* and the *Pietas Augusta*. The same goes for the groundplan of the building itself, which is reproduced identically in the Forum in both Cumae and Herculaneum, and for the cycle of statues of *summi viri* and the *elogia* which in the *chalcidicum* celebrated, following the illustrious model of the Forum of Augustus in Rome, the founder of the Julio-Claudian dynasty and its mythical ancestors Aeneas, Romulus and Caesar. To complete this local revisitation of the Augustan mythopoeia the portal was decorated with high quality marble reliefs composed of acanthus volutes populated with little animals and insects which undoubtedly called to mind famous ancient urban models, signally the reliefs on the *Ara Pacis,* and evoked gratifying notions of that return of the golden age which the new regime claimed to have inaugurated. Another analogous block from a portal, also belonging to a building in the Forum of Pompeii, shows just how widespread this set of images was. The same goes for the temple of the imperial cult known as the Temple of Vespasian, where the representation of the scene of the *inauguratio* of the temple on the front of the altar conforms closely to the urban models. And also for the layout of the *macellum,* with the marble columned *chalcidicum* embellished by a gallery of two rows of statues facing each other, once again local *summi viri* in all probability, who would have financed the renovation of the building in keeping with the new Augustan *mores.* The sacellum on the far wall of the porticoed courtyard at the centre of the building was dedicated to the cult of the emperor. At the back of a small temple an aedicula displayed on a base the statue of an emperor of which only a hand holding a globe has survived. The alcoves on the side walls held four honorary statues, two on each side, of which two have come down to us, one male and the other female: formerly held to represent *Marcellus* and *Octavia,* they are more probably local figures from the age of Nero, members of the munificent *gens* which financed the temple's renovation. The echoes of imperial iconography are evident and not coincidental: the woman is shown as a priestess, as were the imperial princesses, and the youth, perhaps already dead, is represented in the "heroic" type of the nude athlete, his cloak wrapped round his waist.

The ensemble of sculptures and epigraphs from the temple of *Fortuna Augusta* is of particular interest. This cult was instituted to celebrate the miraculous capacity of the *princeps* to ensure prosperity for the state and, at the same time, to give the emerging social groups, such as the freed men or even the slaves of the leading families who were excluded from the magistracy and the major priesthoods, the chance to affirm their ambition with a show of solidarity with the regime that generously conceded them this opportunity. One of the inscriptions found in the temple provides the names of the first *Ministri Fortunae Augustae:* Agatemerus, servant of Vettius, Soave servant of Cesia Prima, Potus servant of Numitor and Anterote, servant of Lacutulanus. The consular date of 3 A.D. which marked the institution of the priesthood is also quite probably that of the inauguration of the temple. The building shows, on a small scale, the typical features of the Augustan *aurea templa*: marble for the most visible surfaces, Corinthian style, with a pronounced elaboration of the pediment area, alcoves on the side walls of the shrine to constitute, as in the sacellum of the *macellum,* a gallery of local

dignitaries flanking the statue of *Fortuna,* probably portrayed canonically with a rudder in her hands. Two of these statues were found during excavations, one a female statue with a reworked face, in the typical attitude of *pietas,* and the other male, wearing a toga, possibly showing the munificent dedicator *Marcus Tullius.* In Pompeii we also find a few dissenting voices from this chorus of acclamation of the ruling culture. This is the sense of the parody of the *incipit* of the Aeneid written on a wall in the city: *Fullones ululamque cano, non arma virumque* (I sing the fullers and the falcon, not arms and the man).

The most important temple in Pompeii was that of Venus, particularly venerated in the Augustan religious system as the mother of Aeneas. Unfortunately its decoration was lost, and all that remains are the bases for two statues, one equestrian and the other pedestrian. There is also evidence of two portraits, tentatively ascribed to Marcellus and Caius Caesar, while some inscriptions found in a tip at the foot of the sanctuary attest a statue of Eumachia and another of Nonius Balbus, a member of the *gens* in Herculaneum which was famous for building the temple. It was also here that the famous *gold lamp* was found (see individual description). In comparison, the dedication made at the temple of Apollo by two *duoviri* of the Augustan age is much more modest. These men financed the construction of a sun dial set on an Ionic column in cipollino marble, which helps to bring alive for us the "solar" climate inaugurated by Augustus's own gigantic sundial in Campo Marzio (*horologium Augusti*).

One inscription gives an idea of the great religious festivals which at this time received a new lease of life, such as the *ludi Apollinares.* A local nobleman, Aulus Clodius, recalls that during his various terms of office as a *duovir* his contributions to these games in the Forum and Amphitheatre included parades (*pompam*), corridas with bulls, bullfighters and assistants (*tauros, taurocentas, succursores*), combats with wild boar and bears, various pairs of gladiators, fencers, boxers in groups and singly, shows with clowns of every description and every sort of pantomime, among which a Pilades who had evidently made a name for himself, as well as public donations running into thousands of sestertii. Another atmosphere, much more exotic and picturesque, would have greeted the visitor to the sanctuaries of the foreign deities. These had now acquired public dignity, and in fact, albeit less overtly, they were no less permeated with the aura of the regime. Good examples are the temple of Isis in Pompeii and the *Magna Mater* in Herculaneum, for both contained portraits of individuals set up in *loco publico* as well as the customary dedications of private citizens on religious statues and ritual objects. The temple of Isis in Pompeii is an example of the renovation of an entire temple at the expense of one individual, the youngster Numerius Popidius Celsinus. His father Ampliatus would undoubtedly have considered the great expense money well spent if it permitted his son to break through the rigid class barrier separating the freed men from the *ingenui*.

Among the public buildings which offered the greatest opportunities for acts of public munificence, because the decoration was particularly apparent, were the venues for public spectacles. The amphitheatre in Pompeii has come down to us in a relatively unadorned state compared to the richly ornate arenas of Capua and Pozzuoli, conserving only the bases for the statues of the Cuspii Pansae, but we have much more evidence for the theatre. It was one of the most advantageous sites for public expression of *munificentia* and the concomitant honours. The concession of the *bisellium,* the seat of honour in the theatre, was among the most common honours of the time, whereas to have a statue put up in the alcoves along the *scenae frons,* constantly in full view of the citizenship who were thus forced to keep in mind the merits of the man so honoured, must have been one of the supreme ambitions of any career-minded entrepreneur. Thus it comes as no surprise that the restoration of theatres (or indeed their total renovation, as was the case in Naples and Herculaneum) was one of the tasks which the affluent families of the municipal aristocracies were only too ready to accept. In Pompeii the job of remodernising the old Hellenistic theatre was taken on by the most important family of the Augustan age, the *Holconii*. A series of inscriptions were set up all over the building to exalt in the eyes of contemporaries and posterity the contribution, *sua pecunia*, of the brothers Marcus Rufus and Marcus Celerus to the construction of the *cryptam, tribunalia* and *theatrum,* and work to embellish the edifice and make room available for several hundred more spectators from the poorer classes. As an extra honour, in addition to the ritual statue and the various epigraphs, a permanent bronze *sella curulis* was set up for M. Holconius Rufus in the middle of the theatre, on the lowest step of the *media cavea,* in a position which significantly upstaged the other noblemen in the *ima cavea* and may be an allusion to a tendency on the part of the Pompeian worthy to pose as one of the populace.

Another characteristic of these official enterprises was the commissioning of a famous architect who would sign his projects (Vitruvius is one example). The big name in the Phlegrean Fields was Cocceius, and his counterpart in the less prestigious environment of Pompeii was *M. Artorius M.l. Primus,* whose signature we find on the projects of the *Holconii* in the theatre and elsewhere in the restoration of the temple of Venus from the same years. The monument which has given us an almost complete picture of these practices, thanks to its integral conservation at the time of its excavation, is the theatre of Herculaneum. This was the work of the architect *Numisius,* whose name is recorded in one of the entrance arches. The whole building was richly adorned in marble slabs and statues in honour of illustrious

citizens: the *summa cavea* carried the great bronzes of *L. Mammius Maximus,* Augustal in the period of Claudius and a relative of the founder or restorer of the building, and *L. Annius Maximus,* quinquennial *duovir;* in the cavea there were six large equestrian statues in gilded bronze (the fragments that were found were melted down in the 18th century to make medallions for the King), while other statues of Appius Claudius Pulcher and Marcus Nonius Balbus stood on the *tribunalia*.

The other large public building which emerged virtually intact during excavation was the Basilica of Herculaneum. Situated on the *decumanus maximus,* it was erected by Marcus Nonius Balbus, who in an inscription claimed to have financed the construction of this and also the city walls and gates (although perhaps their restoration would be nearer the mark). He was an illustrious son of Nocera who became governor of Crete and Cyrenaica. The building contained marble and bronze statues of him, his father of the same name and his mother Viciria Archade, as well as various members of the imperial family. It was also remarkable for the paintings with which it was decorated. The famous scenes of *Hercules and Telephus, Theseus the liberator, Achilles and Chiron, Marsyas and Olympus* were all removed from the apses and the minor alcoves.

Among the most emblematic monuments of the new aspect of Roman cities were the honorary arches, which were set up in the Forum and every other strategic point to exalt the figure of the emperor (and of his loyal subjects). Thus the position of absolute preeminence attained by the *Holconii* in Augustan Pompeii is borne out by the four-sided arch which occupied the most central crossroads in the city, at the junction of Via dell'Abbondanza and Via di Stabia, in front of the main entrance to the *terme Stabiane.* Surmounted almost certainly by a statue of the *princeps* and probably paid for by Rufus, he had a statue of himself in military dress set up alongside it.

An even more magnificent collocation for statues of the emperors were two symmetrical arches erected on each side of the temple of Jove. The one on the left of the façade still stands, made of lateritium. The other was razed to the ground *ab antiquo* so that it is only from the uneven appearance of the paving of the Forum in correspondence with its location that we can be sure of its existence. It is likely that this was the arch of Nero (subsequently eliminated, perhaps on account of the *damnatio memoriae* which was imposed on all monuments to him) while the other one celebrated another emperor. The obvious archetype for this combination of arches with a temple is the temple of the holy Julius on the east side of the Roman Forum, flanked by the arch of Augustus. A third honorary arch embellished the northeast entrance of the Forum, with two alcoves for statues overlooking the forum and two fountain basins on the other side, while a fourth, known as the arch of Caligula from a bronze equestrian statue mistakenly identified with this emperor, was set up at the beginning of Via di Mercurio as if to give visible emphasis to the new extension of the Forum, stretching from the insula to the northeast of the square down to the Forum baths.

The Vesuvian cities also help us to make important comparisons in another category of buildings, the public baths. Provincial cities such as Pompeii and Herculaneum, which were already well provided with baths, never caught up with the innovation of the large-scale imperial baths, which provided a golden opportunity for displaying works of art, as can be seen in the ensemble from the Baths of Caracalla (from a much later date), part of the Farnese collection in the Naples Museum. But they are also outclassed by the bathing establishments in the Phlegrean area, as in Baia, which yielded masterpieces like the *Sosandra and Hermes,* and also the unique group of plaster casts indicating a sculptural workshop which worked from the supreme models of classical art; and lesser establishments, such as Agnano, where the decorative sculpture was considerably more impressive than the modest herm of Mercury found in the Stabian Baths in Pompeii or the bronze braziers donated to the two main baths of Pompeii during the reign of Silla by *M. Nigidius Vaccula*. The same goes for another important architectonic feature of such establishments, the mosaics, which in Baia and Agnano achieved the status of important works of figurative art during the second century.

Thus although it is generally less rich than that of the Vesuvian cities, the architectonic evidence found in the Phlegrean Fields is just as important inasmuch as it gives a more immediate reflection of the major events and tendencies afoot in the *Urbs* (see for example the *Pozzuoli base*). Regrettably a large part of the ancient monuments in this region was destroyed. Much of the buildings and their marble embellishments was transformed in the lime kilns or built over, and only the engravings on glass exist to give us a faint idea of the splendour which greeted sea voyagers arriving at *Puteoli,*

with the *ripa Puteolana* gleaming with marble temples, arches laden with sculptures, villas and other buildings. If the *colossal heads from the temple of the Forum of Cumae* can give a good idea of the standard of official sculpture, the Sacellum of the Augustals in Misenum, which evaded the lime kilns because it was engulfed by a landslide and is now on display in the new Museo Archeologico dei Campi Flegrei in the castle of Baia, has recently filled in our knowledge concerning a building which is analogous to the Sacellum of Vespasian in Pompeii one century after the destruction of the latter. Erected in the Augustan age, the sanctuary was restored on several occasions and embellished with sculptures dedicated by the members of the priestly college of the Augustals, vying with each other to display the greatest munificence and prestige. The cult statues of Titus and Vespasian represented as Greek heroic nudes, installed inside the shrine during the reign of Flavius, were followed by a bronze equestrian statue of Domitian, later remodelled to depict Nerva, which stood in the courtyard. During the reign of Marcus Aurelius, in the second half of the second century, the façade of the temple was completely refurbished in the form of a porticus in cipollino marble. The pediment, in lunense marble, was decorated with the busts of the husband and wife who sponsored this renovation, placed within a wreath of oak supported by two Victories, in a pompous gesture of self-glorification which sums up the taste and culture, permeated with dynastic loyalty, that prevailed in this fundamentally military city.

However, the crisis was looming. In the Phlegrean Fields as in Rome, the sun had set on first the Golden and then the Silver Age of the Empire, and in the gathering gloom iron and bloodshed was the order of the day. Dedications of public monuments became a rarity, and restoration came to involve the marble adapted from preceding destinations. Further damage was carried out in iconoclastic forays by the rampant Christians, as has been borne out by the recent discovery of the decapitated sculptures from the temple of Isis in Cumae.

Model of Pompeii

This 1:100 model of Pompeii, made of wood, cork and paper, was manufactured in several stages from 1861 onwards to crown G. Fiorelli's project for the reorganisation of the excavations, and features accurate watercolour reproductions of the painted walls.

Although it is not updated to the present-day extension of the excavations, it still stands as an instructive centrepiece of the exhibition of the materials from Pompeii and the Vesuvian cities in the Museum, to which it provides a useful guide.

The model gives an aerial view of the city, with its streets, *tabernae*, houses, squares and public buildings.

So-called Jupiter Meilichius, from Pompeii
inv. 22574

This fictile sculpture, found in the 18th century in the small temple on the via di Stabia, in the theatre quarter, is actually a portrait of Asclepius, as Winckelmann had already observed. Its identification with Jupiter Meilichius was proposed by Nissen on the basis of his interpretation of the temple as the *kaila Iuvieis Melichieis* mentioned in the *Oscan inscription of Porta di Stabia*. Actually, the inscription certainly refers to an extra-urban centre, a context much better suited to the cult of a nether world deity such as Jupiter "sweet as honey". While the identification as Meilichius is hence to be rejected, there are no objections to an identification as Aesculapius, god of medicine and salvation, like the nearby Isis (see description on p. 262). 3rd-2nd century B.C.

Fictile statue of a goddess, from Pompeii
inv. 22575
This great statue of a female deity was found in the so-called temple of Zeus Meilichius, along with the preceding statue and a terracotta bust of Athens. Its stylistic features are rather generical (it belongs to a type that was very common in the late Hellenistic period); it was certainly not originally paired with the figure of Asclepius, which is almost a full head shorter. Held to be a Juno, but nothing contradicts its identification with Hygeia, a paredra of the god of medicine. 1st century B.C.

Marble bust of Jupiter, from Pompeii
inv. 6266
This bust was an acrolith (see following object) of the cult statue erected in the *Capitolium* of Pompeii, identified with a beautiful marble head inspired by the 4th century B.C. type called "of Otri-coli", which introduced in the iconography of the god a new benign face of transfigured tenderness, with sunken and slightly moist eyes under the dark shadow of thick locks of hair. The *Capitolium*, like almost all the public buildings, was in a state of abandon at the moment of the eruption. Inside it, more statue fragments were found, including colossal shoes and a bust reworked at the back, possibly from official statues originally standing in the Forum.

108

Marble busts and heads of Jupiter, Juno and Athena, from Cumae
inv. 6267, no number, 150082
The busts and colossal heads of Jupiter, Juno and Athena from Cumae originally stood in the cella of the *Capitolium* of the city, in the Forum, where they represented the Capitoline triad, the main cult of the city in the Roman period.

They are acroliths, i.e. only the visible parts of the figure, the head, hands and feet, were made of marble, while the rest of the body consisted of a wooden skeleton concealed by the dress. It is evident that they are inspired by the great Greek chrysoelephantine statues (the Zeus of Olympia, the Athena of the Parthenon), a type appropriated by the classicist trend of Roman art.

Apollo, from Pompeii
inv. 5629

This statue of Apollo drawing his bow was found, in several fragments, in a dump in the western area of the city. It was attributed to the sanctuary of Apollo, mainly on account of the discovery there of a similar bust of Artemis, also drawing a bow.

The comparison of the heads, with the identical rendering of the curls, leaves no doubt that the two sculptures were made in the same workshop and belonged to the same group, probably derived from a Greek model in which the two divine archers killed the Niobids with their arrows.

The finding of another female arm holding a bow may indicate that there were other statues of Artemis in the sanctuary. It has also been suggested, on the basis of a graffito on the base of the statue of Apollo containing the name *Mumi*, that the two statues were part of the famous spoils of Corinth, taken when the city was captured by L. Mummius (146 B.C.), and that it was given to Pompeii as a present to the Campanian *socii*, as in other cities where epigraphs with the dedication of the conqueror of Greece are well attested (*Trebula Mutuesca*, Curi, Norcia, Parma, *Fabrateria Nova, Italica* in Spain).

Marble statue of Diomedes,
from Cumae
inv. 144978
The creation of this figure of Diomedes
is generally attributed to the sculptor
Cresila, around 430 B.C. The hero, a
mythical traveller to the West after the
capture of Troy, originally must have
held in his hands a statuette of the
Palladion, the figure of Athens that had
been the divine guarantee of the invio-
lability of Troy, until the hero, together
with Ulysses, stole it, thus propitiating
the taking of the city. Many cities of Italy
claimed noble "Trojan" origins through
their possession of the Palladion, which
Diomedes had brought with him to the
peninsula. The Cumaean copy, found in
the crypt under the Acropolis, bears
under its base a Greek inscription men-
tioning a certain Caius Claudius Pollio
Frugianus, possibly the dedicator of the
statue.

Marble base of the cities of Asia, from Puteoli
inv. 6780

The base, which in ancient times bore a statue of Tiberius erected in the last months of 30 A.D., is a smaller-scale copy of a similar monument erected in Rome as a sign of gratitude by the fourteen cities of Asia (Sardi, Magnesia, Philadelphia, Tmolos, Kyme, Mostene, Aegae, Hierokaisareia, Temnos, Kibyra, Miryna, Ephesos, Apollonidea and Ircania), which had received donations from the Emperor after several earthquakes hit them between 17 and 29 A.D. The cities are represented by symbolical figures sculpted in relief all around the base, an interesting iconographic testimony of celebrated ancient sculptures mentioned in the literary sources, which became the emblem of the cities where they were erected (for Ephesos, the Amazon of the famous competition, cf. p. 296).

Gold lamp, from Pompeii, Temple of Venus
inv. 25000

This golden bilychnous lamp, found in 1863 in the temple area of the most important sanctuary of the city, featuring *repoussé* work with lotus flower motifs and a high reflector decorated with the same system, is an absolute *unicum*. As epigraphic and literary sources attest, golden objects were offered to the main sanctuaries from the Classical period.

Like the golden lamp that, as Pausanias informs us, glowed day and night in the Erechtheum, the sanctuary of Athena Polias on the acropolis of Athens, this specimen too was doubtlessly an exceptional votive gift to the sanctuary. The lamp was a typical object of Venus, as erotic poetry and the tale of Love and Psyche tell us.

Two graffiti found in the house of Julius Polybius a few years ago attest that this Pompeian lamp is almost certainly one of the gifts of the Augusti Nero and Poppaea to the city and the sanctuary, possibly going back to their famous Neapolitan sojourn of 64 A.D. The first graffito, written in vernacular Latin, narrates with emphasis: "as soon as Caesar came to the temple of the saintly Venus, when, O Augustus, your celestial feet carried you inside, there were thousands of pounds of gold"; the second recounts the gifts of the Augusta. A date in the time of Nero also fits well with the style of the lamp.

Statue of a Doryphoros, from Pompeii, Samnite Gymnasium
inv. 6011

Tradition reports that the bronze sculpture made around 440 B.C. by the great Polycletus of Argos, known as the "lance-bearer" (*doryphoros*), and probably representing Achilles, was also known in antiquity as *Kanon*, i.e. "canon", because it was the image of the metrical and musical law for the construction of bodies according to mathematical ratios between their different parts. Actually, in this replica of the statue, the best one that has reached us, what is especially evident is the principle according to which the figure is constructed. The attitude of the figure is based on a chiastic pattern (from the form of the letter X, the Greek *chi*) elaborated by the master: the right leg is held straight and the opposite left arm bent, while, conversely, the left leg is bent and the right arm extended. The appeal of the figure, however, lies in the less accentuated movements of the head and the torso, giving life to the statue, which remained the most accomplished attempt to represent the harmonious ideal of the Greek man, *kalòs kai agathòs* (beautiful of body and noble of intellect). The presence of this early Imperial copy in the Samnite Gymnasium in Pompeii is especially significant. It reminded the young aristocrats of the Campanian city that they were part of the Classical world and shared the ideals of Hellenic culture, of which the Romans felt themselves to be the heirs.

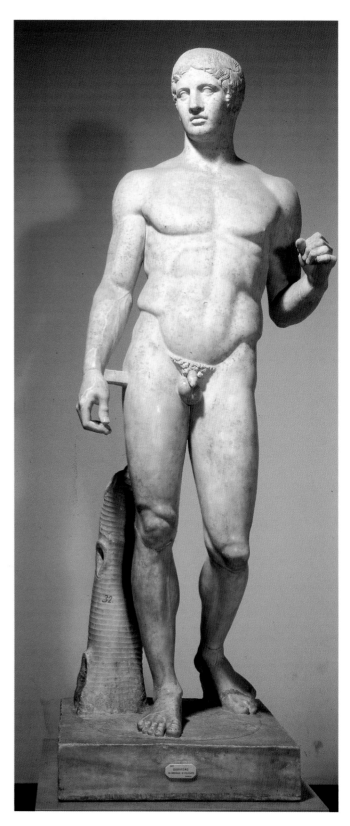

Statue of a Palaestrite, from Sorrento
inv. 119971

This statue, found in 1899 among the remains of a gymnasium, represents a boxer (note the *cesti* or thongs armed with metal studs, on his hands). The olive wreath on his head proclaims him as a winner, while the herm of Hercules beside his right leg symbolises the world of the gymnasium, the *athlia*. The statue, datable to the first half of the 1st century B.C., is signed, on the front of the base, by Koblanos of Aphrodisia in Caria (*Aphrodiseus Koblanos érgastolos*). Here, under the stimulus of Roman demand and thanks to the presence of excellent marble quarries, a celebrated school of sculpture flourished from the Augustan age to the end of the Western Roman Empire. It is attested by about thirty-five signatures of Aphrodisians, almost all of them on statues found in Italy.

Marble statue of Aphrodite "pudica", from Herculaneum

inv. 6283

Some of the features of this Roman copy are traceable to a famous work of art, Praxiteles'Cnidean Aphrodite, by way of a Hellenistic re-elaboration of the 2nd century B.C. (the so-called Capitoline Venus). Praxiteles was, in fact, the first to undress the body of the bathing goddess (already shown through transparent wet robes by the generation of sculptors after Phidias), and make it the subject of his masterpiece. The statue was bought by the inhabitants of Cnidus, after the customers of Cos who had commissioned it decided they would rather have a dressed Aphrodite by the same master, and was displayed in a round small temple where it could be admired from every angle. Hellenism stressed the theme of *pudicitia* by raising the hand to cover (actually to emphasise mischievously) the breast, or by varying the rhythm of the figure by adding a falling dress. The figure was then adopted, for ornamental purposes, by the Romans, who used it very often as a decoration for public buildings (e.g. thermal baths) or the gardens of houses and villas.

Bronze female statue, from Herculaneum, Theater inv. 5589

The priestly attitude of this figure, with its head covered by the cloak (*palla*), is found in other statues from the same theatre as well (see the following object), and in the statue of Eumachia. The model must have been a statue of Livia as *Salus* or *Pietas*. The statue is dated to the Tiberian period by the style of the portrait and the rendering of its drapery, very similar to that of the Eumachia mentioned above.

Bronze statue of Tiberius, from Herculaneum inv. 5615

This splendid bronze, found in the theatre in 1741, represents the emperor as *pontifex maximus*, with veiled head in the act of sacrificing, according to the type created at the time of Augustus, the best example of which is the Augustus of Via Labicana.

It reflects the ideology of the principate by relinquishing the heroic interpretations of the figure of the prince as a Hellenistic dynast, typical of the late Republican period, to stress the values of *pietas*, i.e. of adherence to the religious traditions of the Republic, which Augustus proclaimed repeatedly and had his poets exalt. The statue is one of the best in Herculaneum.

Head of a horse, from Herculaneum, Theatre
inv. 115391

It was especially on occasion of the discovery, in 1739, of these great equestrian bronze statues, that the archaeological method employed in the Herculaneum excavations revealed its limits. These horses were extracted in pieces, often confused, and some of them, regarded as "useless junk", ended up in the smith's crucible to make portraits of the King and Queen. The head, still showing remains of golden leaf, belongs to a statue of remarkable technical and artistic quality that bears witness to the excellent level of decoration even in such a small town as Herculaneum.

Painting of Achilles and Chiron, from Herculaneum, so-called Basilica
inv. 9109

The centaur Chiron was the tutor of the Thessalian hero Achilles. The theme of mythical pedagogy returns in the other picture, this one's *pendant*, representing Marsyas and his musical disciple Olympus. The boy-hero holds the lyre in his hand while the centaur, in a solicitous attitude, teaches him to tune it.

The figures are conceived as Classic statues against the architectural background of a podium adorned with metopes with bucrania and rosettes.

The original of this painting, of which other copies are known in Pompeii, was certainly a famous sculpture, probably of Greek origin, that Pliny the Elder records as having been on display in Rome during the *Saepta Iulia*.

The image met with great fortune in the 18th century through the *Antichità di Ercolano*, and was taken up on porcelains and ivory plaques.

119

Painting with Hercules and Telephus, from Herculaneum, so-called Basilica inv. 9108

The original of this famous painting, depicting Hercules - whose ponderous figure clearly recalls the Lysippean type of the Farnese Hercules (see p. 333) - discovering his young son Telephus being suckled by a doe, is possibly a celebrated painting by Apelles, "Hercules turning around", mentioned by Pliny and well known in all of Italy, as it was on display in the temple of Diana on the Aventine. The scene takes place in the presence of a solemn figure of Arcadia, comparable to a similar figure on the frieze of the Pergamon ara, of a young Satyr, symbolising the pastoral character of the country, and a winged figure impersonating Mount Parthenion, the southern boundary of Arcadia, where Telephus was born. Between the child and his father stands the eagle of Zeus, father of Hercules and hence grandfather of Telephus. The painting was probably a homage to Telephus, the father of the well-known poet and philologist Philetas, who established a centre of literary culture on Cos, the island on which Apelles took residence. The extraordinary still life with basket and fruit was probably already in the original.

Marble statue of Marcus Holconius
Rufus, from Pompeii
inv. 6233

The statue, from an urban workshop, was placed at the foot of the arch erected at the crossroads of Via Stabia and Via dell'Abbondanza, and portrays the most important citizen of Pompeii of all time (it should be pointed out, however, that no Pompeian was ever admitted, as far as we know, into the equestrian order...). The model is the iconographic type of Mars Ultor in the temple of the Forum of Augustus in Rome, and the military attire alludes to Holconius' office as *tribunus militum a populo*, conferred on him by the emperor. It was a purely fictitious military title, but it gave him the coveted privilege of sitting, on his visits to Rome, in reserved seats second only to those of the *equites*. The inscription under the statue (*CIL*, X, 830) reminded the Pompeians of Holconius' *cursus honorum*: besides being a military tribune, he had been *sacerdos Caesaris Augusti* (the first in Pompeii), five times duumvir *iure dicundo*, two times quinquennal duumvir, and had received the most sought-after municipal honour, the title of *patronus coloniae*.

Painted frieze depicting life in the
Forum, from Pompeii, praedia
of Julia Felix (II, 4, 3)
inv. 9068
The frieze presents us, in a straightforward
but effective style, with a lively contemporary image of the appearance of the
Forum in a Roman city of the 1st century
B.C. A group of people, three adults and
a boy, are reading a public announcement suspended from the bases of three
equestrian statues erected in front of the
wreath-adorned portico surrounding the
square. Other sections of this frieze
"photograph" various aspects of the life
of the square, such as the trading of
metallic tools, pans, cooked food, and
the punishment of a schoolboy.

Painting of the brawl in the amphitheatre of Pompeii, from Pompeii, House I, 3, 23
inv. 112222

The owner of the Pompeian house where the painting was found had asked a painter of modest means, specialised in lararia and shop-signs, to portray for him on a wall the famous episode of the fight between the Nucerians and the Pompeians that took place during the games of 59 B.C. The event, although altogether unremarkable, and probably due to parochial hostility between Pompeii and its more powerful neighbour, was evidently regarded as "history" in the peaceable town of the 1st century B.C. In fact, it brought down on the city the closing of the Pompeian arena for 10 years and the banishing of some illegal associations. The representation of the event is lively and quite true; from an aerial viewpoint, we see the amphitheatre with walls in the background and the gymnasium on the left.

123

Gladiator's helmet from Pompeii, so-called Gladiator Gymnasium
inv. 5673

The elaborate relief decoration on this famous helmet represents the night of the capture of Troy (*Ilioupersis*), with the groups of Neptolemos killing Priamus, Aiax abducting Cassandra, and, of course, Aeneas' flight with Ascanius and the old Anchises. The latter episode was the main reason for the popularity of the theme among the Romans, as it was the prologue to the foundation of Rome. The helmet is that of the *Thraex*, the Thracian. The gladiators of this nation reached the Roman arenas after the capture of many of them who had fought in Mitridas' army. The other weapons of the Thracian include a shield, greaves, a protection for the arm (*manica*) and a curved sword (*sica*). From the Pompeian graffiti, we know that the Thracians fought against one another, against the *Myrmillones* and especially against the *oplomachi*.

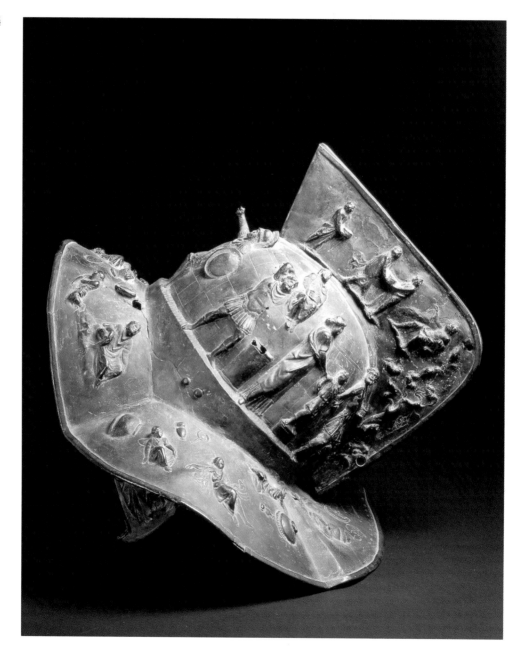

Marble statue of Aphrodite, from Santa Maria Capua Vetere
inv. 6017
This statue, part of the decoration dated to the time of Hadrian of the portico on the *summa cavea* of the Capua amphitheatre, gave its name to a famous type of Hellenistic Aphrodite, in the act of looking at her own reflection in the shield of Ares and resting her foot on his helmet (see the Pompeian painting). In the Roman age, this model was often adapted as a figure of Victory writing on the shield the name of the victory (Victory of Brescia), with the addition of wings and a stylus in her right hand.

Isis, from Naples
inv. 6372

The cult statue, datable to the II century B.C., documents, together with other evidence, such as the famous statue of the Nile in the square named after it or the dedication of M. Opsius Navius to Isis, the presence in Naples of a public cult of the goddess, probably introduced in the city at the time when this Alexandrine deity reached *Puteoli*, possibly even earlier. The presence of the Egyptian sanctuary was so characteristic of the quarter that it was called *Regio Nilensis*.

Isiac ceremony, from Herculaneum
inv. 8924

This painting owes its celebrity to its subject, a cult scene in an Isiac sanctuary. In the foreground a priest, with shaven head and the typical white linen dress reaching down to his feet, fans a fire burning on a characteristic "horned altar", in front of which stand two ibises, sacred to the goddess. Four more priests officiate, two on each side, while another on the right, a negro, is seated and plays a flute.

Behind them we see the courtyard of the sanctuary. Another priest directs with his wand the choir of the faithful, ranged on either side of the staircase of the temple, at the top of which, on a platform flanked by two sphinxes, against a background of palms and exotic vegetation, the high priest emerges from the door of the temple, announced by the sistra of a priest and a priestess, to perform the ritual display of the golden vase containing the sacred water.

Sarcophagus with the myth of Prometheus, from Pozzuoli
inv. 6705

This exquisite sarcophagus, dating from the 4th century A.D., was found in a mausoleum whose furnishings were still intact at the beginning of the 19th century. It is the product of a Roman workshop to which two more sarcophagi from Rome have been attributed, and represents the myth of Prometheus creating the first man. The hero sits at the centre of the scene, thoughtfully contemplating the clay body he has modelled and to which he is about to give Life personified by Psyche, urged forward by Erotes.

The supreme gods attend; they include Jupiter, Juno, Neptune, and Mercury, to whom Juno hands a bag of money to redeem the man's life from Pluto.

The sarcophagus, an entirely private monument, is a precious testimony of the cultural refinement of *Puteoli* even in the time of its decline in late antiquity.

An exemplary case: the temple of Isis in Pompeii

One example of the decor of a sanctuary which a well-documented excavation has made it possible to reconstruct in the Museum, giving us a good idea of the appearance of a sacred building in a Roman city, although naturally with the peculiar features of an Oriental cult, is the temple of Isis in Pompeii. It was explored in the years 1764-1766, in the first generation of Pompeian excavations. The finding of this Egyptian shrine, richly decorated with freshly executed paintings since it had been newly refurbished by the *isiacus* Numerius Popidius Celsinus and his father Ampliatus, provoked much excitement among the scholars of the time. It contained sacred objects and works of art alluding to the cult of the goddess who had travelled from Egypt to Italy and whose fame was perpetuated through the Middle Ages right up to modern times. Following the recent reorganisation, the complex is now displayed to give as realistic an idea as possible of the sanctuary as it appeared to the excavators. Some notion has also been given, with the exhibition of the original drawings and the bronze plates engraved for the publication of the find by the Accademia Ercolanese, of the sanctuary's reputation in modern times.

Marble head of Isis, entrance to the so-called ekklesiasterion
inv. 6290
This fine head, dating from the first half of the 1st century A.D. (40-50 A.D. circa), was part of an acrolith, a statue comprising a wooden frame covered in clothing with marble adjuncts for the visible parts of the body. In one hand the statue held a sistrum, the typical musical instrument of the cult of Isis.

The iconography of the goddess is derived from Aphrodite, and only the attribute which adorned the head, possibly a plume, made her identity explicit.

Sistrum, entrance to the so-called ekklesiasterion
inv. 409 AE

The sistrum was a rattle which was typical of the cult of Isis. It was shaken by priests and devotees during ceremonies to create that din that was so upsetting to the traditionalists in Rome. The numerous instruments in bronze and silver found in Pompeii, together with other significant objects such as painted lararia, statuettes, lamps and so on, go to show just how extensively the cult had permeated the society of this small Campanian city, due in part no doubt to the proximity of the cosmopolitan port of Puteoli.

Picture of Io at Canopos from the so-called ekklesiasterion

inv. 9558

Excavated on 18th November 1764 in the presence of King Ferdinand IV, the painting represents a subject that was quite a rarity (only one other treatment has come to light in Pompeii). The nymph Io, persecuted by Hera for her romance with Zeus, is seen arriving in Egypt where she is welcomed by the goddess Isis in her sanctuary of Canopos in the Delta. Here Io gave birth to Epaphus, founder of the royal lineages of Egypt and Argos in the brothers Egyptus and Danaus. This subject was obviously elaborated at the court of the Ptolemies in Alexandria in order to legitimise their dynasty by rooting it in ancient Heraclean and Argive origins which embraced the dual ethnic components of the new kingdom, the Egyptian and the Macedonian.

The prototype for this painting can likewise be ascribed to the milieu of Alexandria in the 3rd century B.C. A river god is seen casting up the fair-skinned Io on the rocks of Canopos, where Isis takes her by the hand. The goddess wears her hair in long ringlets produced by curling tongs and is characterised by the attributes of a cobra in her left hand and a crocodile beneath her feet.The altar adorned with horns and the priests accompanying the goddess denote a sanctuary.

Bronze herm of Caius Norbanus
Sorex, entrance portico
inv. 4991
The inscription on the pillar in cipollino
marble ("[herm] of Caius Norbanus
Sorex, actor of secondary roles, *magister*
of the *pagus Augustus Felix suburba-
nus*. Site assigned by official decree")
affirms the identity of the citizen being
honoured. He was probably the descen-
dant of another Norbanus Sorex, a
much more famous actor and friend of
Silla in the latter's retirement at Pozzuoli. The governor would have bestowed
liberal favours on his friend, and this
probably accounts for the presence of
his descendants in the Sillan colony of
Pompeii. Still clearly influenced by the
Hellenistic tradition, this handsome portrait can probably be dated to the years
30-20 B.C. Another herm of Sorex was
found in Pompeii in the building of
Eumachia, and a third came to light in
the sanctuary of Diana at Nemi (Lazio).
Here too there was a shrine dedicated to
Isis where the actor may well have taken
part in religious performances.

The cities buried by Vesuvius: private building
The decoration of the architectonic structure: painting, mosaics, stuccos

Houses in the style of villas

Among the many case studies which the eruption of Vesuvius in 79 A.D. consigned to posterity by burying the cities of Pompeii and Herculaneum and the sites of *Stabiae* and *Oplontis,* that concerning domestic architecture is one of the most interesting. The hundreds of houses and tens of villas investigated provide a virtually complete picture of the *modus vivendi* both in the city and in the country, in the hills and by the sea, of rich and poor alike. There is such an abundance of information about the architectonic models, decorative features, building materials and the use of space that these archaeological sites are unmatched for the study of Roman dwellings.

A by no means secondary aspect of this case study is the opportunity it offers of tracing the development of the house over more than two centuries, between the second century B.C. and the first century A.D., bearing in mind the different cultural and economic forces which affected architecture during this period. We are able to build up the complete picture only from the end of the second century onwards. Naturally there are examples of earlier houses, right from the city's Etruscan period (6th century B.C.) and the height of the Samnite presence (House of the Surgeon in Pompeii), but the information for this period is scant and perhaps less significant than in other sites. However, from the end of the second century onwards the evidence becomes more comprehensive. The fact is that many houses were built during this golden age of the Vesuvian cities, and many of them were deliberately conserved intact almost up until the end of the city's history as symbols of a glory which was perhaps never to return.

The traditional Italic family house was the *domus,* laid out round a courtyard, one of the names of which (*tuscanicum*) recalled ancient origins, which archaeology has confirmed, in the Etruscan culture. This model persisted through the period of the first Samnite domination with no significant changes, although when it came into contact with cultures from the Hellenistic world it acquired the new element of the peristyle. Now, between the third and second centuries B.C., it underwent a development, in the dwellings of the Samnite nobility

in Pompeii (Houses of Pansa, of the Labyrinth, of the Faun etc.) and Herculaneum (Samnite House), which was never to be equalled for sophistication and extent. In the groundplan the traditional rooms are flanked by new features coming from the Greek and Oriental traditions: peristyles, exedrae, guests' quarters (*hospitalia*) and nurseries. In the decor we find plastered walls painted to imitate structures in costly polychrome marble (the so-called I style), the first imported household ornaments in marble, figured terracottas and extraordinary mosaic floors (large areas of *vermiculata* such as the outstanding examples in the House of the Faun, but also *opus signinum* with tesserae, conglomerates, *lithostrota*), as well as objects which were typical of the Hellenistic world and scientific culture, such as the sundials which are found both in public buildings and in private houses.

Following the Roman conquest the model of the urban *domus* of the nobility built round an atrium appears to have rejected the horizontal expansion which characterised the previous phase in pursuit of that *amoenitas,* exemplified in the villas of Baia, which exploited panoramic views of the natural surroundings by means of porticos and belvederes (as in the houses built on the walls in the Regio VII and *insula Occidentalis* in Pompeii and those on the walls in Herculaneum) and also the *commodum,* hitherto unknown, of private thermal baths. Householders who did not have a panorama sought to open up perspectives within the house, buying up adjacent properties to instal new peristyles or extensive gardens (House of Ariadne, House of the Citharist in Pompeii). The model of the Hellenistic palace continued to exert its fascination, as can be seen from the proliferation in this phase of the reception areas built as colonnades opening onto peristyles, authentic examples of "architecture within architecture" endowed with intriguing oriental names: *oeci Aegyptii, Cyziceni, Corinthi.* As has been rightly pointed out, the lifestyle of a latterday citizen of Hellas was expressed not so much in the palaces of Rome, where nonetheless architectonic counterparts to the bronze columns entwined with budding tendrils are to be found (for example in the *horti Sallustiani),* but where the strict *mores* of the forebears was very inhibiting, as in the *voluptas aedificandi* that prompted the villas to grow in size and luxury. Once again it is a great loss that we have no more than documentary references for the villas in Baia of Marius and Lucullus, Silla, Pompey, Caesar, Hortensius, Cicero, Clodias, Lycinius Crassus, Piso and Martial, to name only the best known Republican dignitaries who could not forego the pleasure and prestige of possessing a *Cumanum* or a *Puteolanum.* Nothing remains of these villas today apart from the fulsome eulogies of contemporaries to the *amoenitas* of their belvederes, porticos and highly elaborate gardens, the precious marbles, pavilions, nymphaea, rooms for concerts and dramatic performances, the piers and miniature harbours from which elegant boats set out for genteel trips round the Bay, and again the fish tanks in which the most sought-after fish and shellfish were cultivated (a real craze of the age, the most gluttonous adepts earning the mocking epithets of *Tritones* or *piscinarii*) ... not to mention the exorbitant sums paid for such villas!

The eruption of Vesuvius has preserved some villas for us in Herculaneum, around Pompeii and in Stabiae where, after the destruction of the ancient Oscan city, the whole territory was given over to such constructions. The most famous example is undoubtedly the Villa of the Papyrus scrolls in Herculaneum, attributed to the *Pisones* or another *gens* of the Roman aristocracy. This building, which was excavated by means of tunnelling in the middle of the 18th century, stood on a hill to the west of the city and was provided with long arcades (*ambulationes*) and belvederes overlooking the Bay of Naples. Today it is best known for the rich collection of sculptures amassed by its owner and for the papyrus scrolls, concerning above all Epicurean philosophy, in its library. However, its architecture too must, as the reconstruction in the Getty Museum in Malibu goes to show, have been worthy of Baia. The same can be said for the villa excavated at Torre Annunziata (in ancient times this site, on the territory of Pompeii, was called *Oplontis)* and attributed, from the early Imperial age, to the *gens* of the *Poppaei.* Its first layout, from the middle of the 1st century B.C. or slightly earlier, shows an extreme simplicity with organically juxtaposed geometric shapes embellished with splendid paintings in the second style. It is notable that here in *Oplontis,* as in the Villa of the Mysteries in Pompeii and the Villa of Fannius Sinistor in Boscoreale, there was a zone set aside for agricultural produce, an interesting survival of the villa's original character as the hub of an agricultural holding.

With the affluence which derived from the *pax augustea* the dream of every inhabitant of the Empire, no longer restricted to the nobility but within reach even of freed men, was to possess a villa. We know this was the case of Horace from the frequent references to his *villula,* and it also emerges from the tens of paintings illustrating villas in the decor of Pompeii. Naturally, these buildings are only a pale shadow of the grandiose imperial villas on Capri or in Baia, or *villa Pausilypon,* as were indeed the

actual villas, often very sumptuous, erected by the wealthy Romans who, attracted by the fashion for the "villa way of life" and the presence of the Imperial court, as well as the natural beauties of the region, rushed to occupy virtually every site along the coast. Some of these buildings, fossilised by the same cataclysm as the Vesuvian cities, reveal the spirit of emulation which drove their owners to procure statues in bronze and marble and ornate pools. Shortly we shall examine the most famous example of all, the Villa of the Papyrus scrolls in Herculaneum.

From the age of Augustus onwards, the new standards of luxury and the influence of the villa model which, as we have seen, became so predominant round the Bay of Naples also brought about, without actually modifying significantly the traditional scheme of the *domus,* transformations and elaborations in the structure of urban houses: the very tall rooms of the more ancient houses were scaled down, by reducing the high tapering doorways and lowering the ceilings with imitation vaulting. The triclinia were elaborated in various sectors whose functions varied according to location and season (*triclinium vernum, aestivum, autumnale* and *hibernum*). Private baths became more and more common with the introduction of new technology involving a hypocaust built up on *suspensurae.* Either in substitution or integration of the peristyle, more attention was now paid to the garden, laid out on the lines of a park with trees, flowerbeds, avenues, semicircular seats, fountains and rivulets and looked after by professional slaves (*topiarii*). One famous example is the House of Loreius Tiburtinus in Pompeii with its extraordinary layout of two canals in the shape of a T and covered over by pergolas, crisscrossed by miniature bridges and set among little temples, *biclinii* and fountains, the whole creation adorned by decorative paintings and sculptures.

Of course such an architectural model could only develop in a city like Pompeii where there was still space available. Elsewhere, in Herculaneum for example, and presumably even more so in the dense conurbation of the Phlegrean cities, the lack of space made it necessary to adopt more concentrated building types and, in the poorer quarters, saw the rise of rented houses and apartments built on several storeys using the lightweight technique of wood and plasterwork *craticium* as seen in the eponymous house in Herculaneum, the archetype of the apartment blocks found in a typical *insula* of Ostia.

Painting

In the last years of the Republic the architectonic fantasies of the II style of painting in Pompeii got rather out of hand, with more and more complicated and artificial effects of perspective, leading Vitruvius (VII, 5, 3-4) to rail against things "which do not, nor cannot exist". The so-called "ornamental" or III style grew up in opposition to this excess, favouring a wall surface without any depth, decorated with blocks of elegant bright colours (red, white, black) divided up into three panels by slim candelabra or climbing vines. As the pictorial expression of Augustan classicism and the rendering in paint of the anti-spatial principles found in the *Ara Pacis,* this style became miniaturistic and precious, the spatial essence of the residual architectonic elements being nullified by the ornamentation. The slender columns were festooned with ribbons and embellishments, when they were not actually transformed into garlands of flowers: cornices and tympanums were crowned with minuscule statues, elegant and aerial constructions were finely wrought with precious ornamentation. Yet, difficult as it is to conceive, this style was embraced by a clientele that, after the excesses of the last years of the Republic, professed disdain for *luxuria* and the necessity of a return to the *dignitas* of the austere *mos maiorum.*

One element that has to be constantly borne in mind, however, is the fact that the main interest of a wall painted in the III style is the picture, illustrating an episode from narrative or myth as either a copy or a reelaboration of classic Greek originals, done in a sober and refined juxtaposition of sky- or marine-blue and white. The painter could practise his art not only at the centre of the middle panel but also in smaller scenes in the predella, above the plinth or in the upper frieze. The picture was seen as the principle feature of the whole. Unlike today, in antiquity no particular store was set by originality. A ruler such as Attalus III of Pergamum could be proud of his art gallery which included specially commissioned copies, and the owner of a house with good copies of Greek paintings could legitimately show off his collection as a mark of his culture.

The same revival of the classical style, going back almost to the severe style and bordering on the philological, can be seen in Rome in the paintings in the villa della Farnesina, and in Herculaneum in the Neoattic scenes on marble. In fact marble reliefs were featured in the houses of the rich, on rare occasions with Greek originals (such as the Attic 4th century relief showing *Aphrodite and her followers* from the house V, 3, 10 in Pompeii), but more commonly reelaborations of the Neoattic production: examples are the fine relief with scenes of the myth of Telephus from the house of the same name in Herculaneum, or in the same city that of *Orestes at Delphi,* or again *Orestes and Eurydice* from the seaside villa in contrada Sora in Torre del Greco. We can see the same classicising tendency in other artistic forms too, including the more run-of-the-mill production of vases. As well as conferring distinction and dignity on a copy, it served to reaffirm traditional values, a typical aspect of many classicisms, becoming a "vehicle for certainties". With their stories of heroes exalted and the impious punished, these paintings tended to form monothematic cycles which represented the moral order of the universe. In perfect accord with the anti-heroic atmosphere of the age – Horace's *mediocritas* comes to mind – the prevailing tone is one of restraint. Rather than epic

material, subjects tended to favour the idyllic or the sentimental and romantic: a mixture of the Bucolics of Virgil and the *Amores* of Ovid, in literary terms. One indication of the way in which these tendencies percolated down to the lower social classes is seen in the terracotta figurines, of no particular artistic merit, such as the group of *Perseus and Andromeda* standing on a rock with the slain monster at their feet or the group of *Pero and Mycos.*

Another typical feature of this style was a sort of "Egyptomania": emulation of the world of the Pharaohs as the cradle of a grand civilisation, a world of ancient wisdom and stunning magnificence, to which Rome made a generic claim to be heir, as shown for example by the importation of the towering obelisks. The past had already seen the importation from Alexandria of artistic and cultural models, not to mention the introduction of the cult of Isis; in painting the themes of the garden, parodistic friezes, wild animal hunts, idyllic-sacred landscapes and scenes of the Nile. Yet it still comes as something of a shock to see the reproduction, somewhere between the wide-eyed ingenuous and the antiquarian, of the Pharaonic customs, gods in animal form, cult objects, right down to the hieroglyphs whose true meaning was ignored and which were merely regarded as mysterious and sacred icons. It goes without saying that this fashion was by no means limited to the Vesuvian cities, as is shown by the few precious relics of paintings from the baths of Baiae.

This style has left us ensembles of superlative quality in both country villas and urban houses. Significant examples of the former came from the Villa of Boscotrecase belonging to Agrippa Posthumous, which is famous for its excellent idyllic-sacred paintings, although regrettably these are now divided up between Naples and New York, and some of the rooms in the Villa of the Mysteries and the Villa of Oplontis. Of the latter we can mention, in Pompeii, the so-called Villa Imperiale, the House of M. Lucretius Frontone, the House of the Theatrical Scenes, of the Caeii, of the priest Amandus, of the Orchard, of the Golden Cupids, of the Citharist, of Punished Love, of Caecilius Iocundus, of the Centaur, of the Grand Duke of Tuscany, of Jason, of Julius Polybus and many others.

Starting from the age of Claudius a new fashion asserted itself, known as the IV style, which by virtue of the fact of being current at the time of the eruption in 79 A.D. left behind the largest production, often in an excellent state of preservation because they were painted after the devastation of the earthquake in 62. Long belittled as the expression of a purely decorative taste, the sheer number of examples known to us – more than sixty ensembles of a certain prestige in the Vesuvian area – make this style a significant indication of the artistic tendencies of contemporary Roman culture. It tends to recuperate the architectonic designs, which now however are interpreted in a highly fantastic fashion without any of the constructive rigour of the II style, and frequently compressed and reduced to mere dividing partitions between the coloured panels, which still constitute the fundamental wall scheme. The fashion for mythological subjects is also retained, and, in imitation of the picture galleries of the great public and private collections, the art of wall painting, not in itself a noble occupation, becomes a very influential means for the diffusion of the imagery of Greek painting and culture in all the social classes, over and above its literary and contemplative evocation in the *otium* of the *nobilitas*. As the cyclical tendency diminished so the pictures became less allusive, while they reflected what we would call a "local" interpretation of the Greek heroes and heroines, as can be seen immediately in the Aphrodites with the elaborate curled hair-dos in vogue at the time. The quality of this production is on the whole not high, intended as it was for a largely literate clientele who sought to live in decorous surroundings but were not able or willing to commission works which as well as being decorative had a precise significance.

Most popular were themes from Ovid's Metamorphoses, the transformations of heroes and heroines who had a brush with divinity, a truly inexhaustible fund of images which with its characters who seem to have stepped out of a novel gave the citizens of Pompeii the illusion of getting to the heart of Greek culture: Narcissus, Daphne and Endymion recur over and over again on domestic walls, with few artistic pretensions but providing an interesting ancient case study in the diffusion of cultural models across wide sectors of the population.

One interesting indication of the influence of society on the themes represented is the evolution in still lifes. They first appeared as architectonic attributes in the depiction of sanctuaries in the II style, reflecting their original Hellenistic value as votive or hospitable gifts (*xenia*); from the transition to the III style they gradually became autonomous studies, sometimes of outstanding artistic merit, as in the fine series from the House of Julia Felix which reelaborate the original Hellenistic schemes. In the IV style what seemed to have crystallised into a tradition in its own right was permeated by new, realistic motifs which reflected the tastes of clients, such as typical forms of locally made vases or, even more striking, still lifes which included document cases (*capsae*), diptychs used for contracts and piles of coins which stand as a visual comment on the mottos set in mosaics extolling profit-making (*salve lucrum*) of which some examples are known to us in Pompeii.

A large number of decorative schemes were used in this style, all of them respecting the overall division of the wall into three panels, and one particularly important group comprised the walls which imitated the *scenae frontes*. These showed authentic scenes from plays with the characters on stage, as in the House of Apollo, with the myth of Apollo and Marsyas, or the House of Pinarius Ceryalis, or again the architecture of the Palaestra in the *Regio VIII*. A more heterogeneous group is the one which provides less impressive but no less articulate architectonic façades as frames for the pictures. The most significant ensemble in this group is that of the House of the Vettii which rehearses, possibly in two phases of execution, the whole decorative repertoire of the period: sumptuous, minutely wrought architectures overlaid with such elements as figures, images and pictures, other more lifelike architectures, almost after the II style, well balanced against the large pictures displayed on the coloured backgrounds. Large coloured areas almost imperceptibly set apart by fantastic architectonic elements are a pretext for friezes minutely populated with *Erotes* and *Psychai* busy in human tasks, gigantic still lifes, right down to miniatures with erotic scenes (*figurae Veneris*) in a small sideroom. Finally we should mention another heterogeneous group of walls with flat panels which range from the poor juxtaposed colour zones seen in the *Regio I* in Pompeii to the outstanding decorative achievements with carpeting effects visible in Herculaneum.

In the ensembles which go beyond mediocrity it is not difficult to identify the artistic spirit of the times, that progressive emancipation from classicism in the interests of a more plastic, pictorial, even «Baroque» vision which emerges in the earthy colours, the impressionistic and eclectic touch, the abrupt lighting effects and the heightened drama conveyed in the characters' gestures. This anti-classical interpretation must be borne in mind in assessing what many of the surviving pictures from this period can tell us about Greek painting. They are often of remarkable quality, such as *Achilles and Briseis* and the *Hierogamia of Zeus and Hera* from the House of the Tragic Poet; *Ulysses and Penelope* from the *macellum; Achilles in Syrus, Thetys in the smithy of Ephestus* and *Thetys with the arms of Achilles* in House IX, 5, 2; *Perseus and Andromeda* and *Medea* from the House of the Dioscuri; the large-scale pictures from the triclinium in the House of M. Lucretius, especially *Hercules and Omphale*; the delightful idyll of the *Nest of Cupids* from the House of the Diadumens; the similar *Olympus and nymph* from the House of Menander; the trilogy from the "Hall of Ission" in the House of the Vettii, *Daedalus and Pasiphae, Dionysus and Ariadne, the Punishment of Ission;* or again the large works from the Basilica of Herculaneum, *Theseus the Minotaur slayer, Achilles and Chiron, Hercules and the youth Telephus, Marsyas and Olympus, Zeus in the clouds* and *Medea*. Nor should we overlook the example of an unbroken frieze conserved in the triclinium of the so-called House of Loreius Tiburtinus with the cycles from the Heraclid and the Iliad.

Another topic which was greatly developed during this period was the depiction of gardens, both in the elaborate and loosely organised *paradeisoi,* thronged with somewhat emphatic animal figures, and in their scaled down versions set in blossoming plinths and minuscule garden scenes, miniature recreations of the great parks of the aristocracy. Both versions reveal the perhaps unconscious desire on the part of the lower classes to participate in the sophisticated expressions of the *otium* of the *nobiles,* and in particular that *ars topiarii* which was currently at its height. Among the most significant *exempla* we can mention the large villa in *Oplontis,* where the garden paintings, although similar in quality to those in Pompeii, are brilliantly integrated with the architecture so that they form a series of small internal gardens effectively alternating with rooms which give onto the *natatio* in a highly sophisticated blend of nature and nature recreated in art. The paintings commonly termed "popular", in the sense that they were done for primarily utilitarian purposes and stand outside the "styles" while nonetheless echoing them, have little artistic merit but are of considerable documentary interest. They include funerary paintings such as the ones on the tomb of Vestorius Priscus with scenes of a gladiatorial combat, a mountainous landscape and a garden, a table laid with silverware and a picture of the magistrate himself in the act of administering justice. This image recalls the wish of Trimalchio to have his tomb decorated with a picture of himself sitting in the law courts. They also include the pictures from the lararia with lively likenesses of the deities, sometimes ritualised like the Lares and Genius of the House of the Vettii or the Dionysus group from the House of the Centenary and on other occasions extremely expressive and realistic like the *Procession of the Carpenters.*

Some scenes narrate life in the Forum in a straightforward style which evokes the comments passed on to posterity in the graffiti on the walls of the city. Under the porticos of the Forum people gathered to gossip, read public notices or sketch while the baker, cloth merchant, cobbler, tradesman in household goods or metal hardware and all manner of food vendors plied their wares. Other pictures were intended as signboards for workshops, illustrating the work of felters, hide curers, washerwomen and dyers seen wringing out their cloth and pegging it up to be smoked or dried. The scenes of tavern life are particularly lively, with the customers engaged in an animated game of dice. Then we also find a visual record, in a sketchy style but achieving a grandiose effect in its sweeping bird's eye view, of the *Brawl in the Amphitheatre between citizens of Nuceria and Pompeii,* showing the antagonists gesturing excitedly and rushing about both inside and outside the arena, with unmistakeable evocations of such urban features as the palaestra, the city walls and the awnings of the amphitheatre. We find this same language again in another technique but in the same class of work, the lararium from the House of Caecilius Iocundus. Here the two marble reliefs which recount the earthquake of 62 A.D. show no concern for the laws of composition or perspective but are full of very vivid and realistic touches such as the crazed animals and the collapsing buildings.

Mosaics

The development of mosaic decoration during the early Imperial age went hand in hand with that of pictorial decoration. First of all, reflecting the miniaturising tendency, the tesserae of the geometric designs were made smaller. New motifs appeared, such as networks of linked hexagons, octagons, dodecagons and so on, or circular motifs surrounding or placed inside other figures, which clearly echoed the designs of ceilings. Some houses had vast areas covered with mosaics: in Pompeii it must suffice to mention the House of Paquius Proculus, where the floor of the atrium reproduces the effect of box vaulting interspersed with various polychrome genre and mythological figures. At the time of the IV style more and more houses adopted large areas of mosaics but the decorations tended to be more widely dispersed; rather than the underlying coffer effect they were characterised by an abundance of ornamentation, as in the House of the Mosaic Atrium in Herculaneum.

Figured compositions, which were rare in the III style, continued to be reserved above all for certain parts of the house; in vestibules we find, during the period of the III style, the famous images of a guard dog which bring to mind, as do contemporary paintings on the same theme, the passage from the *Satyricon* in which Askiltos was brought up short by such an image in the house of Trimalchio. Subsequently, as well as dogs on the leash, we find a wounded bear, in the house of that name, a wounded boar in polychrome mosaic, a boar attacked and savaged by hounds (a reworking of the bronze group which stood in the garden of the House of the Citharist) and a polychrome lion.

Mosaic decoration in baths continued to feature the typical themes of wrestlers (Pompeii, Palaestra VIII, 2, 21) and marine life, such as the octopus in the tepidarium of the House of the Centenary, but some mythological subjects were also introduced, as in the figure of Triton which, employed twice in the Baths of the Forum in Herculaneum, represents, also from the stylistic point of view with its highlighting in white of the black silhouette, an anticipation of later mosaic achievements in bathing establishments in the second century. An exceptional specimen is the little *emblema,* reused in flooring dating from the age of Flavius but certainly older, from the end of the first century B.C., with the *Portrait of a young bejewelled lady,* found in the floor of a cubiculum in the House VI, 15, 14 and recalling no less celebrated painted portraits from Pompeii such as *Paquius Proculus and his wife* or the *Portrait of a young girl.*

There was also no diminution in the popularity of *crustae,* now composed of little tiles of coloured marble from the provincial Imperial quarries. In the time of Claudius (Pliny, *N.H.,* XXXV, 1) the fashion spread for *opus sectile* both as portions of coloured marble with a geometric pattern inserted (or on occasions, in more modest houses, merely scattered about haphazardly) into tiled flooring or else more simply into new (or renovated) floors made of terracotta fragments, and in the floors of entire rooms with design and colour schemes carefully worked out, some even incorporating coloured glass (as in the triclinium of the House of the Ephebe), or again, in a few rare cases of figured scenes found in Pompeii, used above all to decorate walls, as with the two slabs with a Dionysiac scene in inlaid marble (a variant of *opus sectile*) from the House of the Figured Capitals with *Maenad and Satyr* in various coloured marbles; or the more modest *Aphrodite undoing her sandal* from the triclinium of the House I, 2, 10, or again the frieze with tendrils in numidian and porphyry from the House VIII, 2, 16.

However, the height of fashion in this respect was the wall mosaic, used to embellish columns, domes and other architectonic features (as in the eponymous Villa of the Mosaic Columns or in the domes in Baia) and above all in nymphaea and fountains which, as we said above, became available to city dwellers once almost everywhere in Campania was supplied with running water. Taking up the models current in contemporary painting, the gardens of Pompeii, Herculaneum and undoubtedly all the other cities in the region were adorned with aediculae which derived from Macedonian and Alexandrian models. They were covered with mosaics made up of seashells, marble flakes, porous limestone and spongy lava to give a grotto effect, and above all fragments of glass salvaged from broken bottles or produced on purpose, often in glass paste, with the *caeruleum* hue for which Cicero's friend Vestorius from Pozzuoli was famous. Thus these collages made use of material that was impermeable and water-resistant and achieved the precious effect of reflections in water of the most vivid colours, azure and seagreen for the bottom and yellows, reds, whites and greens for the ornamental motifs. We have an evocation of this fashion in the lines of Statius describing with wonder the baths of Claudius Etruscus, a figure at Nero's court: "the domes and roofbeams shine with multicoloured glass" (*effulgent camerae, vario fastigia vitro*...). Naturally the subject matter is marine, from fishes to more elaborate images of seaside villas, Aphrodite riding in a shell, a sea-borne procession and Poseidon Isthmios. The mosaic decoration is complemented by the painting, both in the interior of the fountain, with images of marine and riverside life, and with the intent of creating appropriate settings on adjacent walls, with compositions of gardens, animals hunting in the wild (the House of the Bear in Pompeii) and also marine landscapes with views of cities (Pompeii, House of the Small Fountain).

Stuccos

Only a few examples of stuccos have survived from the period of the III style, from the decoration of the *tepidarium* of the House of the Labyrinth in Pompeii, dating from the reign of Tiberius. They represent objects which symbolise the activities of a palaestra (amphorae, palm leaves, crowns, a circle etc.) and Victories in the lunettes, while the ceiling comprised a panels interspersed with figures (heads of Medusa, gryphons, Victories on *thimiateria*). The period of the IV style, on the other hand, affords abundant specimens. Stucco was now used freely both on ceilings and walls, alone or together with painting, and either white or in a range of colours. The design schemes of the fantastic architectures characteristic of the IV style were taken over, and gained from the plasticity of the material and the greater illusion of depth. The decoration of the ceilings tended to be centripetal with a central medallion and concentric partitions. Figured motifs were set in empty panels or medallions singly, so that the emphasis was on the particular modelling of the appearance or gesture of, for example, an Erote or an armed soldier. There were also large set pieces with figures, as for example in the palaestra of the Stabian Baths or in the baths of the Villa Petraro in Stabiae, and large-scale isolated figures, like the athletes in the peristyle of the Villa of St Mark in Stabiae or the boxers in the Petraro. At the other end of the scale we find minute figurines set against a coloured background, clearly imitating the sardonyx cameos. One example is the winged figure with a swan and a dolphin on a blue frieze in room E of the House of the Vettii.

Among the ensembles found in Pompeii we can mention the Villa Imperiale, whose decoration is outstandingly delicate but also very lively and colourful; the Stabian Baths, where the vaulted ceiling of the vestibule of the male *apoditerium* was worked in medallions and octagons, the main palaestra wall was richly decorated, and the male *calidarium* shows interesting remains of a scene with a ship and a harbour; the Baths of the Forum, the Suburban Baths and various private baths such as the recently recuperated example in the House of Alexander's Wedding in the *insula Occidentalis;* then there is the Temple of Isis, with its interesting Egyptian-style motifs, the delicate frieze based on the Trojan epic, showing the retrieval of the body of Hector in the House of the Trojan Shrine, and numerous tombs such as that of Vestorius Priscus. In Herculaneum we can recall the decoration of the four-sided arch on the *decumano massimo* and the Suburban Baths. A suburban villa near Portici contained a remarkable set of medallions from the ceiling with revelling centaurs and bacchants.

The eruption of 79 A.D. set a seal for all time on this treasure trove of paintings, mosaics and stuccos. If today we no longer go along with the ingenuous enthusiasm of the eighteenth century discoverers, who proclaimed the pictures of Pompeii "as beautiful as if by the hands of the Graces", surpassing the masterpieces of the divine Raphael, the Carracci or Guido Reni, the accumulated wisdom of two centuries of critical appraisal can today help us appreciate better the true value of this unique testimony to the history of art and artistic taste in ancient Rome.

The sorceress, mosaic from Pompeii, so-called Villa of Cicero
inv. 9987

This exceptional mosaic bears the signature, like another small scene from the same villa, of Dioskourides of Samos. It exemplifies the Hellenistic tradition at its best, and a recent hypothesis dates it to the third rather than the latter part of the second century B.C. The scene portrayed is either from Aristophanes's comedy *Synaristoi* or from a play of the New Comedy. Three women carrying masks are seated round a circular table, two of them youthful and the other an old hag.

The presence of vases on the table suggests that the sorceress might be preparing love potions, assisted by a serving girl seen on the right. The mosaic reproduces a painting characterised by pastel hues with colours that blend into one another and by a remarkable sense of volume, well embodied at the bottom by the steps and overhead by the perspective created by the wings in graded colours.

Sea scene with fish, mosaic from
Pompeii, House VIII, 2, 16
inv. 120177
The tradition of scenes of fish swimming at the bottom of the sea derives
from representations on Attic and Italiot
red figure dishes, but was greatly
enriched by the scientific precision with
which, following the precepts of the
Aristotelean school, Hellenistic scholars
proceeded to classify and also depict the

various animal species. The best evidence for this can be seen in the Pompeian
fish mosaics in the I style from the end
of the 2nd century B.C. (another famous
example was found in the House of the
Faun, and many others exist in the
collections of numerous museums).
They are undoubtedly refined products
of skilled workshops, done in the difficult
and painstaking technique of *vermiculatum,* and manage to do justice, by

means of thousands of minute tesserae,
to the delicate nuances of colour found
in the marine life of the Mediterranean.
Both fish and shellfish are easily identifiable: around the central scene of the
combat between an octopus and a lobster
we can see a moray eel, a squid, a
prawn, an eel, a bass, a skate, a red
mullet and a murex shell.

142

Cat and ducks, mosaic from Pompeii, House of the Faun (VI, 12, 2) inv. 9993

The existence of various versions in mosaic, albeit of inferior quality, scattered throughout the Roman world (Rome, Ampurias, Orange) of a painting in the Doria Pamphili columbarium and a statuette in the Cairo Museum found in the Delta, indicates that the scene of the cat trapping a bird undoubtedly derives from a famous original of the Hellenistic age, coming in all likelihood from Alexandria.

The same Nile environment inspired the motif of the ducks which here is combined with a still life of fish and birds.

Mosaic of Alexander, from Pompeii, House of the Faun (VI, 12, 2)
inv. 10020

This mosaic (measuring 5.82 x 3.13m.) is the most celebrated to have come down to us from antiquity. It was found on 24th October 1831 in the House of the Faun, where it adorned an exedra with a colonnade overlooking the central peristyle of the house. Impressive for its sheer size, the mosaic unquestionably derives, as can be inferred from its relatively limited colour range, from an ancient painting by a master of the first Hellenistic period, possibly Philoxenes of Eretria, of whom Pliny the Elder records (*N. H.* 35, 110) a battle between Alexander and Darius. The scene depicted here has Alexander the Great on the left, at the head of his cavalrymen, and Darius III on the right, fleeing in his chariot, the last of the Persian "king of kings", whom the Macedonian defeated and ousted from his throne. The breadth of conception of this composition is unprecedented, with the masses of men and horses caught up in a frenzied travail, highlighted by the juxtaposition of the long lances against the light sky. As the only element of landscape, the gnarled

tree is highly suggestive, and all the more striking when we think that it still figured in the accounts of the battle that Marco Polo heard fifteen centuries later in the steppes of Asia.

The painting must have been very famous in ancient times. An Etruscan urn from Perugia has an extract from the same scene worked in relief, and another allusion is to be seen in a Roman ceramic cup from the workshop of Gaius Popilius.

The technique used for the mosaic, which is every bit as much of a masterpiece as the original painting, is the highly sophisticated one of *opus vermiculatum*. It comprises something like a million tesserae, with between 15 and 30 in one square centimetre. As Goethe wrote in 1832: "Neither the present nor the future will be able to comment fittingly on such a remarkable work of art, and we shall eternally be obliged, after all our studies and explanations, to contemplate it in wonder pure and simple". Circa 100 B.C.

Satyr and nymph, mosaic from Pompeii, House of the Faun (VI, 12, 2) inv. 27707

An exact replica found at Thmuis near Alexandria suggests that this mosaic too can be ascribed to the milieu of Alexandria. As in the small paintings of the Satyr and Hermaphrodite or Polyphemus and Galatea (see descriptions), the erotic theme is used as a pretext for a composition that sets the animal rapacity of the Satyr against the soft femininity of the Nymph. Extraordinarily effective are the coloured gradations of the muscular masses heightened by the play of white light.

Large-scale painting with prince and philosopher, from Boscoreale, Villa of P. Fannius Sinistrex
inv. 906
The main characters in this frieze are certainly a Hellenistic philosopher and a young Macedonian prince (wearing the typical felt beret or *kausia* and armed with the famous long lance, *sarisa,* and shield with the star motif), but their identity has given rise to several hypotheses.

The prince has been variously identified as Antigonos Gonata, Antigonos Doson, Pyrrhus and Demetrios Polyorcetes, and the teacher as Menedemos or Aratos, with corresponding attributions for the other figures in the frieze.
There is no doubt that it reproduced a frieze extant in the palace of a Macedonian ruler, and the theme was assimilated by Roman art once the conquest of Macedonia and the other Hellenistic

states made the Romans the heirs of the empire created by Alexander.
Yet it is difficult to imagine what prompted the owner of this villa in the II style (circa 60-40 B.C.), whom we imagine to be a new citizen arriving from Rome at the time of Silla's colonization rather than a long-standing Pompeian resident, to commission such a frieze.

Entrance to sanctuary from Boscoreale, Villa of P. Fannius Sinistrex

no number

With its architectonic representation, this wall is one of the most representative examples of the II Pompeian style and illustrates well its characterisation as "illusionismo prospettico". The scene represents the *propylon* of a building with an internal colonnaded portico glimpsed through apertures half revealed by curtains hanging down over the partitions which flank the entrance door.

The central element of the composition, framed between two Ionic columns, is an imposing panelled door, the lintel painted with a hunting scene which closely resembles the decorations on Macedonian tombs (for example tomb II from Vergina) and the gable decorated with volutes above which hangs a lamp adorned with an Eros, which may allude to Aphrodite as the presiding goddess of the sanctuary. Another motif of considerable interest are the decorated shelves with Dionysian statues running round the top of the par-

titions, and, on top of the latter, two tragic masks, while in the top lefthand corner a frieze depicts a contest of centaurs.

The wall is a fine *summa* of the ornamental possibilities of the II style both in its overall scenography and in the details. As well as the masks, we can mention the rich elaboration of the candelabra with Victories and Erotes, which are both actual objects and decorations that seem to anticipate the most characteristic traits of the III style.

Architecture with tholos and still lifes, from Pompeii, House VI, insula occidentalis 41
inv. 8594

In the usual tripartite architectonic layout, this II style wall, which was removed from its site in the 18th century, can be dated to the middle of the first century B.C. or possibly slightly earlier. It repre- sents the entrance to a sanctuary, flank- ed by two wings provided with fountains spouting water into a basin. The *propylon* comprises a colonnaded gateway which opens onto the interior of the sanctuary with a *tholos* at its centre.

The gateway is flanked by partitions from which hang bunches of fish and birds, undoubtedly *ex voto* offered by fishermen and hunters. Such a custom is familiar from many of the Hellenistic epigrams in the Palatine Anthology.

On the partitions are placed two theatrical masks from the New Comedy. In the Museum another fragment from the same room can be seen (inv. 9847), with a hare hanging on the wall.

Architecture with green monochrome design, from a villa on the site of the Royal Stables in Portici
inv. 8593

This important fragment, discovered in the first phase of the excavations in Herculaneum, illustrates the passage from the II style, of which it conserves the architectonic monumentality and sense of perspective, to the III style, identifiable above all in the ornamentation which now tends to the Arabesque, the new taste for columns emerging from corollas and the range of colours used. The monochrome panel with a landscape and figures of travellers executed in green, was already to be found in the II style, as for example in the villa of Oplontis. Penultimate decade of the first century B.C.

Fragment of architecture with satyrs
inv. 9878
The fragment, from Herculaneum, is a typical example of decoration in the mature III style. By now the depth of the wall has been entirely annihilated.

The architectural motifs are traced against the black and bright red background as a mere pretext for ornamentation in brilliant cold colours, drawn with calligraphic precision and set out according to a calculated geometric scheme.

The acroteria in the form of satyrs are virtuoso creations which were to be retained, without the same fantasticating lightness of touch, in the IV style, as for example in the House of the Vettii.

Wall with a picture, from the Villa of Agrippa Postumus, Boscotrecase
inv. 147501

This large fragment preserves the whole central portion of a typical III style wall with columns and pilasters covered in elaborate polychrome ornamentations in a miniaturist taste. The same calligraphic delight in delicate embroidery is seen in the vegetal garlands, the cranes placed as acroteria of the aedicula, and the miniatures with masks in the upper section. The wall is dominated by the large central picture which represents a rural sanctuary emerging from the white background like an island, built on an outcrop of solid rock and grouped round the customary column with a ritual vase placed on the abacus and sacred tree in the background. At the base there is the statue of a goddess, possibly Cybele, with sceptre and drum. To the left is a goatherd surrounded by his charges; on the right three small figures, two women and a child, approach the shrine bearing either branches or torches. Behind them can be seen another *topos* of the idyllic-sacred landscape, the statue of Priapus. In the background, beyond a cylindrical monument which belongs to the sanctuary, there is a small walled garden, a tempietto with pronaos where a traveller is resting and, on the right, an aedicula and a cypress. The painting can be dated to the last decade of the first century B.C. or the first years of the Christian era.

Pan and the nymphs, from Pompeii, House of Fatal Love (IX, 5, 18)
inv. 111473

The three pictures from the same cubiculum (the others are *Europa riding the bull,* described next, and *Hercules and Nessus,* also in the Museum) share the same calm, majestic atmosphere and the presence of a landscape in which the human and animal figures take their place with great naturalness. Here it is the pine, sacred to Pan, which dominates the scene of the musical contest between the rustic god and one of the nymphs in a solemn and rarefied atmosphere.

The picture dates from the first two decades of the first century B.C.

**Europa riding the bull, from Pompeii,
House of Fatal Love (IX, 5, 18)**
inv. 111475

The myth of Europa abducted by Zeus in the form of a bull is here given a new interpretation with respect to the traditional one set at sea. In a sacred setting disposed round a column to which clings a twisted tree and opening out into a mountain landscape full of trees and strange rocks with steps cut into them, the group of the bull bearing the girl has a majestic air, attaining a kind of triumphal stateliness.

The girl has a far-off look with a hint of pride in her bearing, while three companions are seeing her off, one of whom is caressing the bull.

The Greek original from which this work derives dates from the end of the fourth century B.C.

Jason and Pelias, from Pompeii, House of Fatal Love (IX, 5, 18) inv. 111436

This picture gave the alternative name of "House of Jason" to this residence, which contains a remarkable series of pictures. The scene has a pyramidal structure: at the top of a staircase in his palace of Iolkos, we see the majestic and rather theatrical figure of King Pelias accompanied by his daughters; on the right next to a table, Jason stands enveloped in a cloak and with one foot bare, as the myth recounts; on the left an assistant, garlanded like the other characters, leads the bull to be sacrificed to Poseidon. The effect of the geometrical structure is heightened by the landscape with the colonnaded temple to the god, surrounded by trees and other more sketchy constructions. The vase below the table next to Jason recurs identical in the picture showing the prophecy of Cassandra (inv. 8999).

The punishment of Dirce, from Pompeii, House of the Grand Duke of Tuscany (VII, 4, 56)
inv. 9042

This large picture, dominated by a rural landscape in which a dolmen symbolising the mythical era introduces a disturbing atmosphere of mystery, shares the theme (and to some extent iconography) of the Farnese Bull. The hapless Dirce is already bound to the bull which Zethus, standing on the left with his mother Antiope, is about to set free, while Amphion is conversing with his tutor behind the bull.

The understated, almost serene representation of the tragedy exemplifies the classicising mood of the III style (this painting can be dated to the years either side of 30 A.D.), whereas the same topic was to receive a much more violent and Baroque treatment in the IV style painting in the House of the Vettii.

Mars and Venus, from Pompeii,
House of Punished Love (VII, 2, 23)
inv. 9249

The clear colours, light background and strong contrast between the swarthy complexion of the male protagonist and the lilywhite skin of the woman are typical attributes of the III style, which retains much of the Archaic. The Hellenistic topic of Ares (although with his plumed helmet he has more the look of an Italic Mars) fondling the bosom of Aphrodite enthroned in majesty, is here set against a bucolic background whereas elsewhere (the tablinum of the House of Marcus Lucretius Frontone) it is placed in a domestic environment. The cupid who is witnessing the scene not only plays up the erotic content but also alludes to the subject of the picture which stands as a *pendant* to this one, illustrated next (inv. 9257).

The Punishment of Eros, from
Pompeii, House of Punished Love
(VII, 2, 23)
inv. 9257
This small picture showing the punishment of Eros has the typically literary flavour of an idyll.

Aphrodite, seated on a rock, is looking down in the direction indicated by Anteros at her shoulder to where Eros is standing in chains and restrained by another woman, crying for the loss of his bow and arrows.

The picture derives from a Hellenistic original and is a *pendant* to the previous one, taking up the erotic content but giving it a delicate Rococo interpretation. It is thought to be by the same artist as the preceding *Mars and Venus* and also the *Punishment of Dirce* from the House of the Grand Duke (see description).

Satyr and Maenad (or Ariadne),
from Pompeii, House of L. Caecilius
Iocundus (V, 1, 26)
inv. 110590
In the III style we often find panels with characters from the Dionysian entourage inserted like windows in the side panels or upper margins of the walls. In the House of Caecilius Iocundus the small pictures with satyrs and maenads, depicted with a classicising clarity which tones down the erotic content and original violence of the scenes, were inserted at the centre of carpets with curving edges adorning the side panels of the tablinum. For the fantastic exuberance of its ornamentation, anticipating the grotesques of the IV style, the decoration of the house of the famous Pompeian banker stands as one of the richest examples of the III style in its maturity (towards the middle of the first century A.D.).

Erotic scene, from Pompeii, House of L. Caecilius Iocundus (V, 1, 26)
inv. 110569

The successful moulding of the man's biceps and back muscles, the fore-shortening of the composition, the highlighting and vivid chromatic contrast of the bodies and the carefully rendered drapery of the sheet all indicate that this is not the work of one of the usual caricaturists who adorned the brothels of Pompeii.

It must come from the same workshop that produced the III style decor on the other walls of the house. There was a time-honoured tradition of erotic painting: the famous Parrasius is recorded as having contributed to the genre and in the 4th century Atheneus mentions Pausias of Sikios as the author of pornographic works. In the Hellenistic age the genre expanded and in Roman times manuals existed illustrating the various "schemes of Venus".

160

Medea and the Peliads, from Pompeii, House of the Group of Glass Vases (VI, 13, 2)

inv. 111477

Medea, here seen on the right as a priestess of Artemis, tricked the Peliads into believing that they could rejuvenate their elderly father Pelias by killing him and cooking the pieces of his body in a magic cauldron in which she had resuscitated a lamb from the pieces of an old ram (scene shown on the left). An incredulous Alcestis keeps his counsel to one side.

The mythological theme is here less important than the architectonic setting, disposed like a theatrical set and still showing the influence of the perspectives or city prospects of the II style (see the wall from the Villa of Fannius Synistor in the Metropolitan Museum of New York).

Typical elements of the III style are the elongated structures and cold colouring. Another copy of the same picture was found in the House of the Vestals in Pompeii.

Small pictures of architectonic landscapes, from Pompeii
inv. 9406

The theme of architectonic landscapes, and above all of the villa of *otium* with its gardens and porticos, was particularly popular in the small pictures of the III and IV style. Here two such scenes are joined together, possibly coming from the side panels of one III style wall like those in the tablinum of the House of M. Lucretius Frontone. Pliny the Elder attributed the paternity of the genre to Studius, an Augustan age painter, although in fact he merely perfected a theme that was already popular.

The desire to own a villa – who can fail to recall Horace's longing for the *villula* of Licentia? – was typical of the Roman bourgeoisie, for it represented the foremost status symbol of the aristocracy. Thus this kind of painting, here representing two villas with a *porticus triplex* like the Imperial villa of Oplontis, served like the garden paintings as a kind of wish fulfilment, and at the same time showed guests that their host was perfectly *au fait* with the latest cultural vogue. The passage of Pliny alluded to bears this out: "[Studius painted] villas and porticos, gardens and copses .. all that anyone could desire..." *(qualia quis optaret)*.

Thetys and Ephestus from Pompeii, House IX, 1, 7
inv. 9529
This is the famous scene of the delivery to Thetys of a new suit of armour for Achilles manufactured by Ephestus, the famous "divine cripple" *(periklytos amphigueis)*. The scene is set in the palace of the god evoked by columns and drapes (in the Iliad, XVIII, 370 it is described as *aphthiton asteroenta*, "eternal and beautiful as a star").

Ephestus wears the habit of a blacksmith with a short tunic *(exomis)* and skullcap. With the help of his assistants the Cyclops, he is showing the "golden sandalled" Nereid, seated on the throne and accompanied by a handmaiden, the weapons that Achilles will use in the decisive clash with Hector.

All attention is focused on the famous shield, where the pictorial masterstroke of the reflection of Thetys served to free the artist from trying to do justice to the famous scenes that Homer described in the five sections of the shield. III style.

The Three Graces, from Pompeii,
House of T. Dentatus Panthera
(IX, 2, 16)
inv. 9236
Aglaie, Euphrosyne and Thalia, the
three Graces *(Charites),* daughters of
Zeus and companions of Apollo, symbolised beauty, grace and wisdom for the
ancients. Here the sense of beauty is
enhanced by the abundance of flowers
in their wreaths, in their hands and
adorning the rocky landscape, which is
a most uncommon feature in Pompeian
painting.

Destined to reappear in countless versions in painting and sculpture, the
group of the three nude maidens holding each other, one seen from behind
and the other two turning to one side in
mirror image, was skilfully composed by
an unknown Hellenistic sculptor and
reworked with unfailing success up until
Renaissance and Rococo times. III style.

Satyr and Hermaphrodite,
from Pompeii
inv. 110878

The group of the satyr attempting to rape Hermaphrodite derives from a famous Hellenistic sculpture that here is reproduced in painting but was also reproduced in sculpture (a fine example, reflected in the water of the *natatio,* adorned the villa of Oplontis) and in mosaic.

The picture's effect is entirely created by the contrast between the dark, sinewy body of the Satyr and the delicate fleshiness of Hermaphrodite.

However, the two-dimensional medium of painting detracts from the nuances in the facial expressions, so striking in the plastic versions, expressing the bestial intensity of the one and the half-teasing, half- alarmed reaction of the other. III style.

Polyphemus and Galatea, from Pompeii, House of the Coloured Capitals (VII, 4, 48)
inv. 27687

In the traditional mythological scenes the love of Polyphemus for the beautiful Nereid Galatea is frustrated as she is borne off by dolphins far out to sea. Here however the painter has adopted a version which is much kinder on the Cyclops than that of Theocrites. The Nereid is seen yielding languorously to his embrace, while around him are the attributes of the ram, the syrinx and the shepherd's knotty staff. Here too the effect of the picture depends on the chromatic contrast of the bodies. IV style.

The actor king, from Herculaneum,
insula Orientalis, II, Palaestra
inv. 9019
This indoor scene shows an actor wearing
the costume of a king, with gold sandals,
sword and sceptre, sitting on a *kline*. He
has laid his mask on a socle on which a
kneeling young girl is writing the name of
Dionysus in dedication, while a passer-by
stops to witness the scene. The whole has
an atmosphere of rarefied solemnity. III
style.

"The concert", from Pompeii
inv. 9023

This charming scene from the women's quarters of a house is a late example of the III style dating from 30-40 A.D. It was so greatly admired at the court of Ferdinand I that it was reproduced in one of the rooms decorated in Pompeian style in the royal palace of Capodimonte. In the middle of a colonnaded room a girl sitting on a *kline* is intent on tuning a small harp lying on the bed while in her left hand she holds a five-stringed lyre. Around her other girls are waiting with expressions of interest and wonder for her to begin playing, perhaps so that they can sing. Typical of the mood of the III style is the importance given to a moment of hiatus which precedes action.

Flora, from Castellammare di Stabia (Stabiae), Villa of Varanus or Ariadne
inv. 8834

The female figure seen tripping barefoot away from us, her veil and the hem of her dress fluttering in the breeze, has the heartaching allure of a fleeting apparition in a dream. As she moves she turns aside to pick with a gesture full of elegance white flowers from a bush which she will then lay in her basket.

We do not know whether she is human or divine, a nymph, Flora or Proserpine. But then the painter himself, who took his inspiration from 4th century models and produced this masterpiece of grace and fantasy as a vignette on a III style wall, made no effort to characterise with extraneous attributes the identity of this young maiden, whom it seems only natural to view as the embodiment of Spring itself.

Centaurs and centauresses, from Pompeii, the so-called Villa of Cicero inv. 9133

The Hellenistic theme of the family of the Centaurs, recurring in *Chiron and Achilles* from the so-called basilica of Herculaneum and the famous group of *Centaurs carrying off Nymphs* by the sculptor Arkesilaos which Pliny recorded in the collection of Asinius Pollio, is here interpreted in elegant vignettes which stand out like cameos against the dark wash of the wall.

The exquisiteness of the brushstroke, the tension of the movements and the elegance of line more than compensate for the rather literary dispassionateness. III style.

Rope-walking Sileni, from Pompeii, the so-called Villa of Cicero
inv. 9119
The refined vignettes from the Villa of Cicero were greatly admired by Winckelmann, who praised them as being "as fluid as thought itself and beautiful as if by the hands of the Graces", and again "the work of a cultured and genuine artist ... so that they seem to have been executed in a single brushstroke". The lithe and highly elegant figures with vividly striated skins which made such an impression on 18th century artlovers are an excellent exemplification of the spirit of fantasy and curiosity for the surreal that animated the III style of Pompeian art.

Garden, from Pompeii
inv. 8760

The finds to emerge from the so-called "new excavations" at Pompeii (House of the Orchard, insula Occidentalis, villa of Oplontis, etc.) added much to our knowledge of the genre of garden painting at Pompeii, but all the same this fine fragment in the III style deserves attention. It exemplifies a genre which originated in the funerary evocations of the Elysian Fields and acquired great popularity with the representation of profane gardens. In its depiction of the park, characteristic of the rich man's villa, it pandered to the desire of every self-respecting Roman to enter into the *beau monde* of the "villa society".

This fragment includes some of the genre's typical attributes, such as the trellis, the brightly coloured birds symbolising divinities (here a dove and a peacock), and the pilaster with *pinax* showing a theatrical mask, an allusion to that atmosphere of Dionysian revelry which the Roman garden invariably conjured up.

172

**Theatrical scenography, from
Herculaneum, insula Orientalis, II,
Palaestra**
inv. 9735

This large panel was removed in 1743
from the apsed room of the palaestra,
where some fragments of it are still to be
seen on the walls. The raised stage curtain,
hanging in sumptuous folds, here gives
the clearest indication of how artists drew
their inspiration from late Hellenistic
theatre. In the foreground we see an arch-
way with a central colonnaded aedicula
covered in highly elaborate ornamentation. The columns are festooned with
metallic spirals, the acroteria are metallic
statuettes of Triton and Pegasus and a
theatrical mask.

Above and behind this structure looms
another building with its tympanum
broken off, and still further off, a
colonnade on two tiers with the Delphic
tripod planted on a singular shelf. It is not
difficult to recognise in this typically IV
style representation from the reign of Nero
certain echoes of the II style.

Wall decoration in painting and
polychrome stucco from Pompeii,
House of Melager (VI, 9, 2)
inv. 9625
Decoration in stucco or a combination
of stucco and painting was common in
bath houses, whether public or private.
This large fragment, removed from the
tablinum of the House of Melager, thus
reveals a crucial moment of experi-
mentation with the two techniques, yielding felicitous results from the decorative
point of view.
The structure of the walls is the typical
one of the IV style with architectural
motifs delimiting sections into which are
inserted pictures or mythological figures.
The central picture, with stucco figures,
shows a drunken Silenus supported by
satyrs, and in the painted frieze below,
cupids.
The panels in the aediculae on either
side contain classicising figures of donors,
while in the outermost panels figures are
seen departing through half- open
doors. The rich ornamentation above the
architecture is also highly effective.

174

**Mars and Venus, from Pompeii,
House of Mars and Venus (VII, 9, 47)
inv. 9248**

The picture which gave its name to the House is one of the most famous re-presentations in Pompeii (at least thirty copies are known to us) of the theme of the love of Mars and Venus. Its favour with patrons of the arts and artists alike was undoubtedly due both to its idyllic-erotic content and to the fame of the Hellenistic painter who created the original.

The scene owes its effect to the pyramidal composition which sets the swarthy, muscular body of the god against the pearly, diaphanous curves of the goddess, and the exquisite elegance of the gestures, with Mars unveiling his beloved and touching her delicately on the arm while Venus abandons herself graciously against him raising one arm above her head. The cupids playing with the god of war's weapons, laid aside and worthless against the power of beauty, are an essential com-ponent of the picture, although occasionally they were left out by imitators or even treated as an autonomous topic. Here they are the occasion for a display of bravura, with a cupid who takes fright at the god's helmet.

Theseus the Liberator, from Pompeii, House of Gavius Rufus (VII, 2, 16) inv. 9043

This picture is a rather less successful version of a fine fresco from the so-called Basilica of Herculaneum (inv. 9049), and both derive from a famous original from the last years of the 4th century B.C. Emerging from the labyrinth where he has just slain the Minotaur, seen slumped on the threshold, Theseus is thanked by two Athenian children for having saved them from the monster.

The disposition of the masses of the building in the background may well go back to the original, for it successfully highlights the statuary figure of the Athenian hero.

The same probably goes for the triangular composition of the central figures, whereas the group of Cretans on the right, crowding in to stare and point in curiosity at the fearsome corpse of the beast, is probably a Roman addition.

Datable to the Flavian era, IV style.

Medea, from Pompeii, House of the Dioscuri (VI, 9, 6)
inv. 8977

This picture shows Medea on the right, standing in front of the house of Jason in Corinth, as she prepares to draw her sword to despatch the two children she bore to the hero. They are playing somewhat despondently, as if sensing their imminent death, and a tutor, who also seems to be waiting for something, is seen at the door. The lines of the composition draw the viewer's gaze to the eyes and fixed stare of Medea which are emphasised, in a touch worthy of Scopas, by the intensifying of the shadows. This *Medea* is less arresting but more complete in its overall composition and rich colouring than the other well-known replica from Herculaneum (inv. 8976). Both probably derive from a famous painting by Thymomacus of Byzantium from the beginning of the third century B.C.

Perseus and Andromeda, from Pompeii, House of the Dioscuri (VI, 9, 6)
inv. 8998

In the land of the Ethiopians Perseus has killed the monster to whom Andromeda was doomed in expiation of the *hubris* of her mother Cassiopea, who had dared to claim to be more beautiful than the Nereids (see the vase on p. 80). The girl, freed from the chains which bound her –

we still see one shackle round her left wrist – steps down majestically from the cliff, supported by the hero, also portrayed in a statuary pose with his sickle and the head of Medusa.

The pyramidal layout of the composition and the conception of the figures undoubtedly reflect the Greek original, which is probably to be ascribed to Nikias, the famous Athenian painter of the late clas-

sical period. Six other versions are known to us in Pompeii.

However, the treatment of the light, the softness of the fabrics, and the accentuation of the skilful use of colour which sets the light and dark shades in the foreground against those in the background, are all traits of the Roman reelaboration.

Datable to the Flavian era, IV style.

Traveller and sorceress, from Pompeii, House of the Dioscuri (VI, 9, 6) inv. 9106

The fragment comes from a longer frieze in the landscape genre which embellished the side panels of one of the walls of the tablinum in the house. In front of a reed hut a woman distinguished by the typical conical straw hat (*tholia*) of the Hellenistic tanagrines is seated on a cylindrical pedestal and offers a drink to a wayfarer, while his dog waits patiently.

This miniature, executed in the rapid daubs of the so- called "impressionistic" technique, exudes a faintly exotic fascination.

Hercules and Omphale, from Pompeii, House of Marcus Lucretius (IX, 3, 5)
inv. 8992

This picture is a fairly accurate copy of a famous Hellenistic painting from the third century B.C. Hercules, in female dress and footwear and bearing a thyrsus in his right hand, is at the centre of the composition, like a maenad stupefied by music, wine – we see an empty goblet at his feet – and the life of luxury which he is leading at the court of Omphale. The queen is seen beside him, proudly sporting the lionskin headdress and club which she has wrested from their rightful owner.

On the right Priapus bears up the unsteady hero, surrounded by Maenads and Erotes who allude to the amorous nature of Omphale's power. It is interesting to recall that the small lateral pictures on the wall from which this picture was removed evoked the same Dionysian atmosphere, showing two scenes of Erotes banqueting, one with a statue of Dionysus and the other of Hercules himself.

Datable to the Flavian era, IV style.

Hierogamia, from Pompeii, House of the Tragic Poet (VII, 8, 3) inv. 9559

This scene represents what for the ancients was the most sacred wedding of all, between Zeus, sitting in state on the right, and Hera, a majestic figure in a peplos that is as substantial and imposing as a Doric column.

The Erotes, in the bottom right corner, allude to the romantic aspect of the event, while the goddess is accompanied by a winged spirit who may personify Mount Ida, where the wedding took place.

The betrothed are separated by a votive column which functions as the crux of the composition, but they are united by the skilful play of hands holding up the two corners of the nuptial handkerchief. This picture was the *pendant* of the following illustration.

Achilles and Briseis, from Pompeii, House of the Tragic Poet (VI, 8, 5) inv. 9105

This picture in the IV style is one of the most celebrated paintings from Pompeii. Briseis, seen veiled on the right, is taking leave of Achilles (sitting in front of his tent) to be surrendered, against both of their wishes, to Agamemnon. Between the two, with his back to the viewer, is Patroclus, while behind the hero, in an attitude of consternation at the thought of the "divine wrath" which is bound to follow, stands Phoenix, the elderly king of the Dolopians, companion of Peleus and counsellor to Achilles. Around them are ranged the Myrmidon troops, armed but impotent, and the messenger whom we recognise by his wand. In the sad look of the two lovers and the dramatic and definitive gesture of Achilles with arm outstretched, the only movement in this completely static scene, we recognise the conception of the tragic which characterised the late Classic period (second half of the 4th century B.C.). This was the period of the original, possibly one of a series of works by Theon of Samos, conserved in Rome in the Portico of Philip. We should note the effective device of placing the shining disc of a shield behind the head of Achilles.

182

The sacrifice of Iphigenia, from Pompeii, House of the Tragic Poet (VI, 8, 5)
inv. 9112

Another very famous picture which also takes its subject matter from Homer. On the left is Agamemnon, his head covered to hide his grief, who has agreed to sacrifice his young daughter Iphigenia to Artemis, the goddess whose image with torches (identifying her with Hecate) and stags stands on the cylindrical plinth next to the king. On the right Ulysses and Diomedes carry off the girl while the soothsayer Calchas, who ordained that the sacrifice had to be made, holds his hand up to his mouth in the conventional gesture of consternation. In the sky above, the viewer can see the happy ending to the story.

Iphigenia, reprieved by the goddess *in extremis* and substituted by a stag, is welcomed by Artemis and will be taken to her sanctuary in Tauris.

Formerly considered a faithful copy of a famous painting by Timans described by Pliny, this picture lacks the Hellenistic unity of composition and is now held to be an original Roman elaboration based on several classical models.

Preparation of a satyr play, mosaic from Pompeii, House of the Tragic Poet (VI, 8, 5)

inv. 9986

The theme of this celebrated mosaic is the preparation of the actors for a satyr play, the performance that traditionally concluded the Greek theatrical trilogy in classic times. The action is portrayed within a portico with Ionic columns decorated with *oscilla,* garlands and streamers and a frieze comprising vases and herms. Seated to the right and wearing the same mantle *(himation)* as the statues of Attic playwrights from the 4th century B.C. is the leader of the chorus, possibly also the author of the comedy. He is watching two actors partly dressed in goatskin costumes who are practising dance steps to the music of an aulos played by a musician who is wearing a mask and a sumptuous costume with a garland on his head. On the right an assistant is helping another actor into the costume of Silenus. Masks from both tra- gedy and satyr plays are scattered about. In reproducing in mosaic the original painting, which dated from the late 4th or early 3rd century B.C. and may have been a votive offering for victory in a theatrical contest, the Roman mosaicist, working in the Flavian era, got the illusion of space created by the side pilasters in the foreground and the columns further back irremediably wrong. We have here a proto-II style similar to that found in Macedonian painted tombs.

**Dido abandoned, from Pompeii,
House of Meleager (VI, 9, 2)**
inv. 8898

The story of Dido is common to four other paintings from Pompeii, and was one of many subjects drawn from the mythical history of Rome enshrined in the Aeneid. The queen, in tears, is seated on a throne in her palace in Carthage, in the company of her sister Anna and a handmaid who holds a parasol over her. On the right is the personification of Africa, recognisable from the elephant's trunk and tusks. In the background Aeneas's ship is sailing away in prelude to the tragic epilogue. The motif of the handmaid shading her mistress with a parasol recalls analogous images on pottery. It was evidently a *topos,* and recurs again in the description of Pausanias of a painted marble stele standing outside the city of Tritea in Achaia: "a throne of ivory, and on it a young woman of surpassing beauty. Near her a servant, protecting her with an umbrella...". Datable to the Flavian era, IV style.

Paris as a shepherd, from Pompeii
inv. 9508
This painting belongs to the genre of mythological landscapes portrayed in an idyllic atmosphere.
The young shepherd Paris is sitting on a rock next to a sacred gateway, enhanced by the picturesque element of a bushy tree branching out either side of the arch.

Nearby a statue of Artemis-Hecate bearing torches stands on a tall plinth. Round the shepherd his animals graze and drink at a stream, while in the background rise up the slopes of Mount Ida. The god of the mountain, stretched out on a rock, presides over the scene, whose tranquillity is soon to be disrupted by the arrival of the goddesses for the fatal beauty contest. IV style.

Plato's academy, mosaic from
Pompeii, House of T. Siminius
Stephanus
inv. 124545
Many mosaics of this period (II style,
early first century B.C.) have a fine frame
with an ornate festoon of leaves and
fruit and comic masks.
Another good example from Pompeii is
the doves mosaic (inv. 114281), but
there are also specimens from elsewhere
(Teramo). The chosen theme for this
mosaic, possibly to underline the literary
pretensions of the villa owner who commissioned it, is a group of philosophers
characterised by the typical garments
associated with Greek orators and philosophers of the classical period. The second
and third figures from the left are thought
to represent Lysias and Plato respectively,
and in the background there is a view of
the acropolis of Athens.
The elements surrounding the philosophers, the sacred gateway with vases, the
tree and the votive column, are all typical
of a mythological landscape.

The so-called Sappho, from Pompeii
inv. 9084

This famous miniature, discovered in June 1760, has remained one of the most famous female portraits from Pompeii thanks to the air of gracious refinement that surrounds this girl caught in a moment of meditation before putting pen to paper.

In actual fact it cannot be viewed either as a reconstructed portrait of the renowned poetess nor as a portrait from life, for it shows no particular physiognomic traits. It is rather a model portrait showing the type of the cultured woman, recurring with the same attributes of wax tablet and stylus in other Pompeian pictures. The image of culture and affluence evoked by the hairstyle and the jewels, the gold hair net, earrings and ring, denotes the high social standing of the woman portrayed.

188

Paquius Proculus and his wife,
from Pompeii, House VII, 2, 6
inv. 9058

We know from documentary sources that painted portraits were particularly important in Roman times. Alas the vulnerability of their locations has meant that hardly any of them have come down to us, so that the few examples preserved as wall frescos in Pompeii, together with the Egyptian portraits in the Fayyum, are of outstanding importance.

This small picture, dating from the last years of Nero's reign, is thought to be the portrait of Paquius Proculus (Paquius or Pacuvius was a typical *nomen* from Campania) and his wife; another hypothesis identifies it with the jurist Terentius Neo.

The portrait of the man, with a short curly beard and curly hair, is intended to emphasise his dignity as a magistrate with the attributes of the toga and papyrus scroll.

His wife is portrayed in a literary pose with the stylus and wax tablet. Her hair is done in the latest fashion and she wears earrings with pearl pendants, status symbols which are apparently gratifying to this provincial bourgeoisie in imitation of the customs of Roman aristocracy.

Female portrait in mosaic, from Pompeii, House VI, 15, 14
inv. 124666

The portrait, which is undoubtedly taken from life, represents a young woman with her hair tied back in a bun. She wears pearl earrings mounted in gold and a pearl necklace with pendants of gold and precious stones, indicating her high social standing.

Found at the centre of a floor made of *opus sectile* from the last years of the city's existence, this mosaic is unique of its kind. There is no doubt that it is older than the rest of the floor, possibly dating from the end of the first century B.C.

"Memento mori", from Pompeii, House cum workshop I, 5, 2 inv. 109982

This *emblema* was significantly displayed in a triclinium and is one of the most striking for the clarity of its allegorical representation. The topic is Hellenistic in origin and presents death as the great leveller who cancels out all differences of wealth and class. It is a theme that has come down to our days, as for example in the famous poem *'A livella* by the comic actor A. de Curtis (Totò). In fact the composition is surmounted by a level *(libella)* with a plumb line, the instrument used by masons to get their constructions straight and level. The weight is death (the skull) below which are a butterfly (the soul) and a wheel (fortune).

On each side, suspended from the arms of the level and kept in perfect balance by death, are the symbols of wealth and power on the left (the sceptre and purple) and poverty on the right (the beggar's scrip and stick). The theme, like the skeletons on the silverware in the treasure of Boscoreale, was intended to remind diners of the fleeting nature of earthly fortunes.

Still life, from the praedia of Julia Felix (II, 4, 3)

inv. 8611 (right half)

This is one of the most famous examples of an ancient still life. Its fidelity to real life is borne out by the shapes of the terracotta vases which correspond perfectly to specimens found in Pompeii. The fruit, which fills the glass bowl producing a fine effect of transparency, represents one of the most popular subjects for still lifes, continuing a tradition of Greek and Hellenistic art. Varro, for example, mentioned the artist Possis, whose fruit fashioned in wax or terracotta could be mistaken for the real thing.

The tradition was also alive in literature, as is seen in this fine epigram by Philip of Gadara: "A pomegranate of yellow hue, a fig with wrinkled skin, a fresh green shoot broken off from a russet vine, a sweet-scented apple covered in faint down, a walnut enclosed in its green mallow, a fresh watermelon picked from the leafstrewn ground, and an olive almost ripe with golden skin, all this, O Priapus, friend of wayfarers, Lamo the gardner has dedicated to you, begging you to impart vigour to his trees and to himself" (in the version of S. Quasimodo). This final dedication recalls the ancient value of similar compositions of fruit and food as offerings to the gods and to guests (whence the name *xenia).*

Still life with fish, from Pompeii
inv. 8635
This still life clearly derives from the Hellenistic tradition of pictures of fish and marine creatures, familiar to us above all from mosaics (see description). From the golden years of the Imperial age, this fine representation of mullet, cuttle-fish, scorpion-fish and shellfish must naturally be associated with the contemporary passion for meals based on fish reared in fisheries in front of the seaside villas. Such an activity made the fame and fortune of Sergius Orata. The lengths to which such passions drove people drew down the scorn of Juvenal (Satire IV): "For six thousand sestertii Crispin the Egyptian has purchased a mullet, weighing as many pounds... Will you pay so much for fish scales? For less you might have bought the fisherman; farmsteads change hands ... for such sums".

Sacred landscape, from Pompeii
inv. 9418

This painting in the IV style showing a shepherd and ram approaching a rustic sanctuary is another example of a typically idyllic sacred landscape. We have an earlier instance of a rural sanctuary dedicated to Hecate in the hunting scene depicted in the tomb of Philip at Vergina, while an Attic vase shows a hunting scene near a sacred portal.

Under the influence of Alexandrian literature the idyllic landscape acquired all its features during the Hellenistic period and passed into Roman art both in painting and, as Virgil's Bucolics demonstrate, in literature.

About 25 B.C. in his *De Architectura* Vitruvius gave a very interesting definition of the sort of landscape that was painted in places where people went to take a walk. It contains many elements in common with the Pompeian pictures: "ports, promontories, beaches, rivers, fountains, canals, sanctuaries, sacred groves, mountains, flocks, shepherds".

Maritime landscape, from Stabiae
inv. 9514

The proposed identification of this scene with the port of Pozzuoli is not convincing, in spite of the arch on the quayside which recalls the one shown on the famous glass flasks from late Roman times. It is very likely that similar honorary or decorative monuments stood in many other famous ports as well as *Puteoli*.

Furthermore this kind of landscape is never a faithful representation of reality but rather a fantasy, as is borne out here by the inclusion of the same fishermen idling on the rocks that we find in other idyllic landscapes.

The passage from Vitruvius quoted in the previous description shows that ports, promontories and beaches were simply adjuncts of the genre of picturesque landscape painting.

The Judgement of Solomon,
from Pompeii, House of the Doctor
(VIII, 5, 24)
inv. 113197

The Old Testament tells (I Kings 3, 16) of two women who argued over a baby boy, each claiming to be the rightful mother. The case was brought before Solomon the Wise, King of Israel. He decreed that the baby should be cut in half so that each of the women could have a part. At that point the true mother implored the king to spare the child, as she was ready to renounce her claim. This famous story, already credited in earlier times to the Pharaoh Bocchoris, is represented in this miniature from the parapet of a small porticoed garden. The two companion pictures showed Nile scenes with pygmies, and here the characters in the story of Solomon are also comically depicted as pygmies. This confirms the impression that it originated in the Alexandrian milieu as a reelaboration of a story current in the flourishing Jewish community of the city.

Theseus and the centaur, miniature on marble from Herculaneum
inv. 9560

A famous painting from the Roman villa of La Farnesina has shown how in the Augustan age much store was set by copies on marble of monochrome pictures from the classical period.

They were highly refined paintings done in a single colour in which the graphic content was predominant, as in the Attic *lekythoi* on a white background (see description) or in the modern technique of *mezzatinta*. This celebrated example from Herculaneum was probably based on an original from the end of the 5th or early 4th century B.C., showing the struggle between Theseus and one of the centaurs who has already seized a Lapithean woman.

The same motif is seen on one of the metopes of the Parthenon.

Girls playing with astragals, miniature on marble from Herculaneum
inv. 9562

This miniature, signed by Apollonios of Athens, is in all likelihood an ecletic Neoattic reelaboration of an original which may have come from the workshop of Zeusis, the renowned Athenian artist famous for his monochromes on a white background (*monochromata ex alba*). The "florid" style of the scene seems perfectly in keeping with that period (end of the fifth century B.C.), bearing comparison with the painted ceramic ware of the Meidias Painter.

The Greek inscriptions allow us to identify with certainty the scene: Phoebe is trying to pacify Latona and Niobe while two Niobids, the young girls Hilearia and Agles, are playing with astragals, unaware of the tragic destiny in store for them.

Bacchus and Vesuvius, from Pompeii, House of the Centenary (IX, 8, 6)
inv. 112286

There has been much debate as to whether the cone-shaped mountain covered in trim vineyards is Vesuvius or the hill of Nisas, sacred to Dionysus. Both interpretations are possible, considering that a lararium could be decorated with either mythical or realistic scenes, and if one reflects for a moment, they are not even mutually exclusive, for Martial compared Vesuvius to the hills of Nisas in his famous verses lamenting the eruption of the former in 79 A.D.

The Dionysian connotation of the lararium is clearly affirmed by the presence of the god with his customary attributes *(kantharos,* panther and thyrsus), transformed into a bunch of grapes in a singular image which transmutes his body in the same way as an Ephesian Artemis is girt with innumerable breasts. The other elements in the picture, such as the garlands, birds and the beneficent divinity in the form of a serpent bearing an egg to the altar, belong to the most banal stereotypes of lararium decoration.

The other wall of the shrine remained *in situ* in Pompeii and shows the traditional figures of the Lares against a background of stylised trees.

200

The cities buried by Vesuvius:
the *instrumentum domesticum* and the artistic
production of furnishings and personal belongings:
sculpture, furniture, pottery, gold and silverware, ornaments

Looking back over two centuries of research into the cities and sites of Vesuvius, it is regrettable that the initial interest, characteristic of the 18th century with its encyclopaedic approach to knowledge, in all the aspects of life in ancient times which the excavations turned up soon gave way to the narrower approach of the art historian. Almost all the attention came to be focused on the artistic, architectonic and historical elements, interpreting the cities as if they were concrete illustrations of the works of Vitruvius and Pliny. It took scholars a long time to see beyond the emotional impact of the sudden fossilisation of daily life and realise how much scientific data could be gleaned from the less "noble" classes of material and used to reconstruct the social life, commercial activity and the way in which the individual houses were integrated in the world around them. Thus it is only recently that these materials have begun to be properly recorded and studied from an archaeological point of view as a context of *instrumentum domesticum*. Yet even after decades of excavation in other sites, the mass of information we possess about the Roman world from the Vesuvian sites – one only has to think of the thousands of voices from the past which are immortalised in the graffiti scratched on walls all over the place – remains without comparison.

A modern visitor would be amazed at the sparse furnishing of houses in Pompeii. It is true that the way in which this city was buried meant that wood was destroyed, leaving us to guess at the appearance of the furniture from the metal fittings of the more costly examples (although on occasions when the wood was coated in mud it has proved possible to take plaster casts from it). In Herculaneum, however, the mud slide which engulfed the city preserved all the wooden fittings (no examples are on view in the Museum because these are recent finds which belong to the collection formed at the site itself). One fundamental element was the bed, which took different forms according to whether it was used for sleeping, for dining in the triclinium, for resting and reading or was an infant's cradle. We have some intact examples from Herculaneum and a series of fine decorations in inlaid bronze from Pompeii. Then there were tables, stools, chairs, wardrobes and chests *(arcae)*. The latter were strengthened with iron bands and studs

and decorated with bronze ornamentation and often stood in the atria of houses as a sign of the family's affluence. The houses themselves were cold and dark in winter, making it essential to be well provided with implements for heating (braziers and warmers made of terracotta or bronze) and lighting (oil lamps in terracotta or bronze, sometimes with bronze holders, lanterns made of bronze or metal, bronze candelabra which were often highly artistic; then again much use would have been made of simpler objects which have left no archaeological trace, such as wax candles and torches of resinous wood).

Naturally religion was of considerable importance in the household, with the domestic cult of the Lares and Penates, the Genius of the householder and the gods which protected the family's various activities. The shrine or lararium was often made of brick and placed against a wall, although in Herculaneum interesting examples have been found in wood with a cupboard in the lower part. The images they contained may have been made of wood, as in the House of the Menander in Pompeii, or more often of bronze, and in rare instances of silver. As well as the traditional figureheads of the Roman pantheon, Jove, Juno and Minerva, the citizens often worshipped Dionysus, the god of wine, a product which was fundamental for the local economy, Mercury, the god of trade and profit, and Isis, the Egyptian goddess who protected seafarers and was assimilated to the goddess Fortuna. Cult objects included terracotta holders for burning incense, small movable altars for libations, and bronze musical instruments such as the sistrum, rattles and bells, which were frequently used as amulets to ward off ill fortune.

The sculptures of important personages played an important role in private houses. Displayed in the atrium where the *dominus* received guests and clients, and where in the houses of the Roman aristocracy one would find the *imagines maiorum* modelled in wax or a nobler material to recall the ancient lineage and the public offices held by members of the *gens,* the more modest sculptures in Pompeii and Herculaneum (bronze or marble busts and statues in the Houses of Caecilius Iocundus, Vesonius Primus, Epidius Rufus, and of the Bronze Herm in Herculaneum which were honoured on the *dies natalis*) were more likely to be the expression of the loyalty of the householder, often a freed man, to his former master or his protectors, usually local citizens but who could also be Romans (as in the House of the Citharist).

The sculpture which adorned gardens was only apparently more frivolous. Here too it is easy to see the desire of Pompeii householders to emulate the aristocratic Romans who owned villas with sumptuous sculpture collections, and this makes for an interesting indication of the different cultural attitude in different social *milieux*. In the gardens of city houses one almost invariably finds only the most decorative and superficial aspects of Hellenism, whereas in the decoration of the villas these are accompanied by more significant cultural allusions. In the city most of the motifs belong to the banalised repertory of the Dionysiac world, the idyll, nature as imagined in the *paradeisoi,* constantly linked with the element of water, which was made readily available by the numerous new fountains. Thus there are many, generally mediocre statues of little animals, satyrs, masks, *pinakes* with sleeping Maenads and Ariadne, images of Dionysus, short columns and pillars entwined with ivory in low relief, and *oscilla* or mobiles showing the same motifs. Many examples could be cited, from the House of the Vettii to that of the Golden Cupids and of the Citharist in Pompeii. The higher cultural level of the villas is always unmistakeable. We shall look later on at the House of the Papyrus Scrolls in Herculaneum; here we can recall the Villas of Ariadne and St Mark in Stabiae and, among the most recent finds, the sculptures from the gardens of the Villa of *Oplontis,* especially the eastern one boasting a grandiose *natatio* lined with a portico on one side while the other side gave onto a wooded park in which Hellenising statues stood (the *ambulatio* alongside the swimming pool was adorned with two herms of Heracles, two Nikai, an Amazon and an ephebe) in an excellent attempt to recreate the atmosphere of a Greek gymnasium.

Indulgence in *luxuria,* or at least as near to it as one's means allowed, had its climax in the banquet or *coena,* a social ritual which exalted in a single event all the opportunities for self-glorification of the householder in front of his guests. On that occasion the candelabra lit up the vivid colours in the paintings and the figures depicted, the images in the mosaic *emblemata* were the pretext for a show of literary culture or philosophical considerations on the brevity of life and the joys to be gathered while one may. A microcosm of handkerchiefs, greetings, dishes to be taken away and little civilities has come down to us in the various graffiti, of which those from the House of the Moralist in Pompeii are particularly well known. Naturally much store was set by the dinner service (*ministerium*). Most citizens of Pompeii could only afford earthenware, albeit of the highest quality, which in this period meant the so-called *terra sigillata* from the traditional workshops of Arezzo,

Pozzuoli and now also from Gaul and Spain, while some types of food were served up in particularly fine vases (known as "thin sided") which imitated the plasticity of metal vases. The models for these were of course silver vessels, the real status symbol and object of desire for every Roman. Vessels for eating (*argentum escarium*) and drinking (*argentum potorium*), both often reproducing classical forms, sets of cutlery and simple objects intended for display which conformed rigorously to rules of symmetry have all been found quite frequently in the houses of Pompeii, Herculaneum and the suburban villas and constitute some of the showpieces of the Naples Museum's treasures. Among the most significant examples we can recall the "treasure" from the Villa of Boscoreale (now in the Louvre) and, in Naples, that of the House of the Menander in Pompeii. However, silverware remained a luxury that only the truly rich could permit themselves. Most of the well-to-do householders in Pompeii and Herculaneum had to make do with services made of bronze. Bronzeware, no less than silverware and perhaps even more so, could boast an extraordinary artistic tradition, and antique bronzes were just as much collector's pieces as the specimens in the noble metals. According to Horace, the insane passions to which man was prey were pederasty, adulterous loves and the ecstasy brought on by bronzes and the splendour of silverware. The abundance of bronze vases from the Vesuvian sites kept at the Naples Museum and in the deposits of Pompeii and Herculaneum confirm the prevalence of this passion. They constitute tableware and banqueting services with a comprehensive repertoire of forms descending directly from the ancient Greek tradition, with rich decorations masking the join of the handles to the vases with animal and vegetal motifs and mythological figures, mostly from the Dionysian rites. Some of the houses in Pompeii have yielded quite outstanding specimens: either for their antiquity, which had already acquired status as archaeological finds and were prized as *necrocorinthia* by discerning collectors, such as the *hydria* dating from the 5th century B.C. awarded as a prize at the games of the *Heraion* of Argus and found as part of the service of the triclinium in the House of Julius Polybius, or the *situlae* with elaborately decorated handles in the style of the 4th century B.C. In the case of more recent vases, we find some whose decoration is exceptionally beautiful, like the bronze embossed crater showing a heroic scene, also from the House of Julius Polybius in Pompeii. This dwelling, which has recently been investigated, has also yielded, in the rich service of its triclinium, another of the bronze statues of youths (in this case an Archaic-style Apollo) which affluent worthies liked to keep as "dumb waiters" in the banqueting hall to support tables or the arms of the candelabra (*lichnouchoi*). They were undoubtedly very costly, and to judge from their scarcity in our excavations of Pompeii to date, something of a rarity. In addition to vases, the ritual of banqueting called for other objects, such as ingenious containers for heating water, the so-called "samovars", tripods and others whose function is still obscure.

Glass, on the other hand, was a new material, at least in many of its applications. Much of the glassware found in the Vesuvian cities must have come from the celebrated foundries of Pozzuoli. Most of it was used as tableware, toiletries (*aryballoi,* flasks) and above all in women's cosmetics. The finds from the Houses of the Menander and Julius Polybius have shown how women owned veritable "beauty cases" containing rectangular and cylindrical bottles and flasks of perfume. In Pompeii the *unguentarii* comprised a corporation known to us from their electoral activities, and they seem to have plied their trade in the *Macellum*. In Pozzuoli a reference to *clivus vitrarius sive thurarius* shows us that the production of perfumes (Capua was famous for *seplasium,* Naples for spikenard and rose scents, while Pozzuoli would undoubtedly have imported a lot from the East) went hand in hand with the relative containers. It would be nice to be able to attribute to the glassmakers of Pozzuoli, or to their senior partners in Alexandria, not just the objects of mass production (which included window panes) but also the precious few examples of glass cameos which managed to survive in Pompeii. These are exquisite masterpieces like the "blue glass" or the two plaquettes with mythological scenes from the *insula Occidentalis* in Pompeii, or the rare examples of glass portraits. Here we can observe that another vase in the same class, the Auldjo jug in the British Museum, decorated with ivy leaves and vine shoots and found in the House of the Faun, was also in all probability made in Pozzuoli, since it really is very similar to the two preceding specimens and can safely be attributed to the same workshop.

Of course women's toiletries did not stop at perfumes, and

while it is a great pity that we now have no trace of the cloths, silks coming all the way from China, linens, fans and parasols known to us from written records and pictures, some precious relics have nonetheless come down to us in the form of combs, brooches in bone and ivory, tweezers, and mirrors made of silver and bronze. And again in ornaments, which in Pompeii and Herculaneum include bracelets, whether simple or in the shape of a snake's head, earrings – favourite types were crescent-shaped or bars with dangling pearls – originating from India and Arabia, necklaces of pearls, emeralds and quartzes, signet rings either engraved or inlaid with precious stones (cornelians, amethysts, onyx, aquamarina, rock crystals, garnets, agates, etc.).

The world of work, too, is significantly illuminated by finds in the Vesuvian cities. The electoral rolls enumerate politically active associations drawn from the most varied walks of life, including the makers of farm carts (*lignari plostrarii*), dyers (*infectores*), greengrocers (*pomarii*), innkeepers (*caupones*) and so on. Representations in genre paintings, and also occasionally in mythological scenes, give us a clear idea of how they went about their daily work, whether in a laundry, as stonemasons, doctors or whatever. Discovery of the tools they used adds to this knowledge, as is particularly well illustrated by the *groma,* of which the Museum possesses the only known example. Found in the workshop of a *faber aerarius* in Pompeii, it is one of the most highly significant objects in Latin culture, for it was the principal instrument used in land surveying. It gave the name to the official who performed the surveying (*gromaticus),* and this was the basis of the *limitatio* or apportioning of land in a new colony which has played such an important part in shaping our concept of large parts of the Roman Empire right up to the present day.

Dancing Faun, from Pompei, House of the Faun (VI, 12, 2)
inv. 5002

The only two known replicas of this statuette of a faun who, notwithstanding his muscular body, dances lightly on tiptoe, come from the Nile Delta area. An Egyptian provenance appears to be in character with the general Alexandrine inspiration of the house in its I style phase. The statuette decorated the atrium, presumably near or inside the *impluvium*, giving a somewhat Dionysiac allure to the hall dominating the entrance to this noble dwelling. Another element of this type was the altar with a dedication in Oscan to the goddess Flora. This statuette is a high-quality, accurately made work, certainly imported from an artistic centre of the Hellenistic world, possibly Alexandria itself. End of the 2nd century B.C.

204

Dancing Faun, from Herculaneum,
Villa dei Papiri
inv. 5292
I have placed this colourful dancing faun here to emphasise its affinities with the specimen from the House of the Faun.
Both participate in the wild joy of the world of Dionysus, which confronted visitors as soon as they entered the atrium.

The statuette was found on February 25, 1754, in the atrium of the villa, along with a dozen more statuettes of Fauns, Sileni and Putti, all crowding around the impluvium as if around a mountain lake, in the possibly vain attempt, in the context of this, the most cultivated and urban of architectures, to evoke in the beholder a feeling of "natural" freedom.
1st century B.C.

Satyr with wineskin, from Pompeii, House of the Centenary (IX, 8, 3-6) inv. 111495
This statuette of a young satyr, possibly an element of a Dionysiac group, may also date from the late Hellenistic period (end of the 2nd-beginning of the 1st century B.C.).

The satyr, whose head bears a pine crown, is squeezing the skin to make the wine spurt out and pour into the cup he held in his hand. As in the analogous group of Ulysses and Polyphemus from Baia, the character who was to drink the wine is missing. In Pompeii, the single figure was used as it was to decorate a fountain.

Bronze portrait said to depict L. Caecilius Iocundus, from Pompeii, House of Caecilius Iocundus (V, 1, 26) inv. 110663

The sculpture was found in the atrium of the house of this banker, whose name and business are well known from the archive of wax tablets found in the same house. It is datable to the Augustan age, and hence may portray an ancestor of the famous *argentarius*. The date is based on the persistence of realistic elements of the Republican tradition, with a lifelike reproduction of the cunning and provincial expression of the subject, and without the least nuancing of the physical characteristics, not even the less pleasant ones, such as the wart and the ears that stick out. The herm under the portrait bears the inscription: "to the Genius of our Lucius, the libertus Felix erected" (Genio L[uci] nostri Felix l[ibertus]).

Portrait of a woman named Terentia,
from Herculaneum
inv. 6247
This fine female portrait, found in the
first phase of the excavations of Herculaneum, dates from the Claudian period,
judging from the typology of the elaborate terraced coiffure, with single
locks gracing the brow.

Apollo playing the cithara,
from Pompeii, House of the Citharist
(I, 4, 5)
inv. 5630
This Pompeian bronze of Apollo citha-
rodos, from which the house takes its
name, reproduces a type dating more or
less from the middle of the 5th century
B.C., known from other replicas (e.g. the
so-called Apollo of Mantova), which
some attribute to Hegias, Phidias' teacher.
The god held the cithara in his left
hand, and is still holding the plectrum
in his right. The Pompeian copy, datable
to the middle of the 1st century B.C., is a
rare example, for Pompeii, of appropriate
use of an illustrious work – as was the usual
practice in villas – instead of converting it
into a lamp-holder (*lichnouchos*).

209

Fictile statuette of a philosopher, from Pompeii, House I, 2, 16
inv. 109622
This fine earthenware statuette of a philosopher decorated the garden of the house. The pronounced features of the statuette identify it as a portrait of the Athenian philosopher Antisthenes, a pupil of Socrates and the founder of the Cynic school, whose portrait, with its characteristic unkempt hair and beard, is known from an inscribed herm from Tivoli.

The statuette was certainly one of a series of philosophers' portraits probably manufactured in a Campanian workshop.

A figure of the same series identical in size and style, bearing the name of Pittacos of Mytilene along its edge, was found in Pompeii, in the garden of the praedia of Julia Felix. Another fragment of the same type has recently been identified among the terracottas found in the town area of Cumae.

The presence in the garden of images of philosophers is no surprise, considering that the same theme is observable in the much richer decoration of the Villa dei Papiri (see p. 299).

The intention was to recreate the atmosphere of a philosophical circle, a sanctuary of the Muses.

Bronze group of two dogs and a boar, from Pompeii, House of the Citharist (I, 4, 5)
invv. 4899-4900-4901

The house, lying at the crossroads of the main streets of the town, was especially rich in painted and sculpted decoration. The central peristyle, adorned by a semi-circular basin, was peopled, like a painted paradeisos, by bronze figures of animals arranged arround the basin, including an attacking snake (MNN 4898), a running deer (MNN 4902) and an attacking lion (MNN 48497).

The group of the boar attacked by dogs is the most remarkable sculpture of the whole ensemble. It was set on a protuberance of the rim of the fountain, which was fed by a spout installed in the mouth of the boar. The group, dating from the Augustan age, derives from a Hellenistic-age original, and the accurate workmanship of its details makes it a work of remarkable artistic quality in its own right.

Bronze statue of a ram, from Nocera
inv. 4903

The Dionysiac theme – the ram is the companion of Pan and the Cyclops – indicates that this bronze statue was doubtlessly a garden sculpture, like the fallow deer of the Villa dei Papiri and the boar attacked by dogs from the house of the Citharist in Pompeii. The sculpture, found under the floor of a Roman building, is an excellent work of the early Imperial period. It is a hollow casting, well retouched with a burin after cooling down. It certainly belonged to the decoration of the peristyle of a rich domus of Nuceria Alfaterna, the most important centre of the Sarno Valley, not far from Pompeii.

212

Oscillum, from Pompeii, House of the Citharist (I, 4, 5) inv. 6551
One of the most typical ornaments of the Roman garden was the series of *oscilla*, i.e. circular or pelta-shaped marble shields bearing mythological figures in relief. The idea derived from shields hung as trophies, but their decoration eventually lost its military character in favour of Dionysiac themes, better suited to the hortus. The Vesuvian cities have yielded a considerable number of such decorations. This specimen, the work of a Neo-Attic workshop, is the best crafted of those found in Pompeii up to now. On one face, a young satyr uncovers a cist from which a serpent comes out, on the other, a satyr plays the flute in front of a figure of Priapus. End of the 1st century B.C. Its excellent workmanship attests to the high quality of the decoration of this sumptuous Pompeian house.

Fictile statuette of an elephant bearing a tower, from Pompeii, house VI, 15, 5
inv. 124845

This graceful statuette depicting a war elephant, originally a vase, seems to allude to the wars against Carthage or to those waged in the East. It bears on its back a square tower with merlons, tied to its belly by three chains and protected by two shields. The driver, a Negro holding a sickle-shaped prod, straddles the neck of the animal and holds out a morsel of food to its raised proboscis.

The statuette was a garden ornament. It was found at the end of the last century in a fountain niche at the bottom of a garden of the house, alongside the equally famous statuette of a drunken old woman (inv. 124844), itself a vase, two more glazed terracotta figurines representing, respectively, Mycos with Pero and a recumbent Silenus, and a marble statuette of a nymph.

Marble relief of Telephus, from Herculaneum, House of the Relief of Telephus
inv. 76/128

The Pentelic marble used for this work is in itself sufficient evidence of its origin from a Neo-Attic workshop of the end of the 1st century B.C. It was inserted as a picture – it must have been painted in gay colours – in the wall of a room fronting a triclinium, and was intended to display the refined Hellenising culture of the owner of this fine house, built on the walls of Herculaneum, to the guests of his *coenae*. The relationship with the thermae on the sea, lying further below, reminds one of the house of the Nonii Balbi.

The mythical theme represented is appropriate for a Herculanean house. Telephus, whom Achilles, following the instructions of an oracle, is curing with the rust of his spear (on the right), is in fact the son of Hercules, the eponymous god of the Campanian city. On the left, the preceding episode of the story is represented: Achilles consulting the oracle from whom he learns that he will only be able to reach Troy if guided by Telephus.

Marble relief with Orpheus and Euridice, from Torre del Greco, villa in contrada Sora

inv. 6727

This relief, found in a maritime villa in Torre del Greco, in the territory of Herculaneum, formerly in the collection of the Duke of Noja, depicts the parting of Orpheus and Euridice in the presence of Hermes, the guide of the souls of the deceased.

It is a replica of a remarkable Greek original of the end of the 5th century B.C., the work of a master educated at the Phidian school of sculpture (possibly Alcamenes).

The relief is part of a group of similar three-figure reliefs, originally making up the decoration of a choragic or funerary Athenian monument (possibly the altar of the Twelve Gods in the agora).

Besides admiring the loftiness of conception of the monument, it is worth stressing the significance of its presence in a Roman villa, attesting to the refined culture and taste of the owner.

Archaistic statue of Artemis, Pompeii, VIII, 3,14?
inv. 6008

This sculpture, made of Pentelic marble, probably derives (as the frequent occurrence in other statues of the same type of the striding goddess armed with a bow bears out) from a famous Archaic Greek sculpture, possibly that of Diana of Segesta mentioned by Cicero. The Pompeian replica, a re-elaboration executed by a Neo-Attic workshop, has maintained the outward appearance of the original, with its geometrically arranged zigzag folds, its "Archaic smile" and rosette crown. The free movement of the body, the polished surfaces and a certain softness of the drapery, however, date this work, which has been attributed to the school of Pasiteles, to the 1st century B.C.

Equestrian statuette of Alexander, from Herculaneum

inv. 4996

When Quintus Caecilius Metellus made of the kingdom of Macedonia a Roman province, a renowned work by Lysippus, viz. a group of statues representing the *turma* of riders who fell in the battle of the Granicus river (334 B.C.), fighting under the command of Alexander the Great, was sent off to Rome to adorn the new portico erected by the winner (they later became part of the decoration of the Portico of Octavia). This fine statuette is very probably a smaller-scale offshoot of this famous model, and depicts Alexander himself in the act of slashing down with his sword from his rearing steed against an enemy on foot.

The presence in Herculaneum of another similar horse and the popularity of the type, of which many re-elaborations exist, support the proposed identification.

Bronze statuette of a riding Amazon, from Herculaneum
inv. 4999

The identification of the type from which this statuette derives with the statue of the famous *"Euknemos"*, a riding Amazon "with beautiful legs", the work of the Greek sculptor Strongylion, active between the end of the 5th and the first half of the 4th century B.C., is very uncertain. The figurine, whose iconography is quite similar to that of the mounted Alexander by Lysippus, appears to be a later work, recalling in a classicist style the Amazonomachiai of the Classic age. It possibly was part of a commemorative monument of the same style as the Pergamene Small Donary.

Safe, from Pompeii
inv. 73021

In houses boasting claims to antiquity and nobility, the place of the safe (*arca*, originally used to contain the bride's dowry and the other riches of the house) was in the atrium, on a base, where it was displayed to the guests of the house as a symbol of the family's wealth (in the House of the *Vettii* there were two).

The wooden structure of the chest was coated with bronze and iron laminae, and large studs concealed the heads of the nails.

This particular chest is decorated with bronze appliqués, including a boar, Diana and Erotes. In other specimens, the lock was sometimes guarded by figures of fierce animals such as lions and mastiffs.

Tripod with satyrs, from Pompeii, House of Julia Felix (II, 4, 2)
inv. 27874

This tripod became famous in the 18th century thanks to its reproduction in the third volume of the Count of Caylus' *Recueil d'antiquités égyptiennes, étrusques et romaines* (1759).

Along with the renowned Tripod with Sphinxes, made famous by *Vasi, candelabri, cippi, sarcofagi, tripodi etc.* by G. E. Piranesi (1778), it was used as a model by designers of Neoclassic furniture and had an enormous influence on the creation of renowned objects in the style of the Empire.

The bowl, adorned by arched leaves, is supported by three figures of young ityphallic satyrs holding their hand out in an apotropaic gesture. Like the Tripod of the Sphinxes, it was attributed, for no good reason, to Tarentine workshops, but the fortunate and recent discovery in Capua of moulds for lost-wax bronze casting (the wings of one of which are very similar to those of the Sphinxes) has revealed that the Capuan workshops of the Imperial age produced not only vases, but furniture of this type as well.

Bronze brazier, from Herculaneum
inv. 73104

Roman houses were cold in the winter, and the brazier, normally made of earthenware (the less common specimens in bronze were probably used in the triclinia of opulent houses) was a necessity. In this portable specimen (provided with two handles), the edges of the rectangular chest where the charcoal was burned are decorated with a merlon motif. On its sides are appliqués representing theatrical masks and animal figures. The legs are lion-paw shaped. Some small-scale specimens, used as portable altars, are also known.

Mule-head appliqués, from Herculaneum
invv. 72734, 72736
The ancient triclinium beds were often decorated, on their visible parts, viz. legs, frame, headboard and footboard, with relief-decorated elements, modelled inserts and copper and silver inlays. In this case, the *fulcra*, the curved parts of the head- or footboard, were decorated with two mule-heads, a typical animal of the cortege of Dionysus, and hence well suited to a banquet context.

This Dionysiac character is enhanced by an ivy wreath that the animal wears on its head and by the panther-skin on its back.

"Samovar" from Pompeii
inv. 73880
One of the luxuries of a sumptuous *coena* was an unlimited supply of water, wine and warm drinks. The Vesuvian cities have yielded a number of ingenious devices used to warm liquids. This specimen, whose form is a combination of the ancient tripod and the crater, was equipped with a double chamber in which the liquid was warmed, and its flow was controlled by means of cleverly designed valves.

224

Situla, from Pompeii (?)
inv. 73146

The few bronze situlae found in the Vesuvian cities are all of exceptional artistic quality.

Their refined decoration, here a row of shields that fits well with the two figurines of gladiators applied to the join of the handle to the vase, and their depiction in mythological paintings of Hellenistic origin (e.g. the one representing Jason and Pelia) suggests they were used as ornaments in the triclinia of late Hellenistic houses decorated in the 1st and 2nd style, which remained in use until the last phase of the city's life.

2nd-1st century B.C.

Crater, from Herculaneum
inv. 73105
The calyx-shaped crater has a great tradition in Classic Greek ceramics, being the main vase of the symposium. In the Roman age, this shape was much less common, and mainly used for decorative purposes, e.g. as a marble garden ornament with Dionysiac overtones. In Pompeii, only a limited number of bronze specimens were found, when compared, for example, with the very numerous *oinochoai*.

An exceptional specimen with figures in relief was recently discovered in the triclinium of the Pompeian house of Julius Polybius. In this Herculanean example, the Medusa-head shaped join of the handles to the vase is especially interesting.

Bronze oinochoe, from Herculaneum
inv. 69033

The decoration of this and many other *oinochoai*, featuring lions with paws ending in wheels, consciously revives decorative models typical of the Archaic Greek age, such as those found in the so-called *heroon* of Paestum (Paestum Museum).

The boom in the popularity of Archaic bronzes (the *necrocorinthia*) began when Caesar's settlers discovered, in Corinth and later on in Capua, the splendid Peloponnesian and Capuan bronze vases.

This set off a frenetic quest for original specimens (such as the hydria found in the house of Julius Polybius, a prize received on occasion of the feast of Hera Argiva) and, when these were not to be found, imitations or free re-elaborations, the latter produced by the specialised workshops of Capua.

Oinochoe, from a Vesuvian site
inv. 69082
This is one of the most typical and elegant forms of *oinochoai* in use in 79 A.D.

The decoration of their handles was especially refined, featuring animal protomai (here a horse) at the rim and masks (here a gorgoneion) at the belly. A pair in Julius Polybius' set bears the initials *M. AT.*

The new discoveries in Capua seem to confirm that the cast and hammered parts were produced separately by workshops specialised in these two different techniques and then assembled.

Silver scyphus with a landscape, from Pompeii, House of the Menander (I, 10, 4)
inv. 145504
This silver *scyphus* is decorated with a landscape (featuring a boatman, a shepherd subduing a ram and a sacrifice in a rural sanctuary), a scene derived from the Hellenistic literary genre of the rural idyll, which became fashionable in the Augustan age.

The Greek signature "Apelles" scratched on the bottom of the vase is a testimony of the enduring superiority of the long Hellenistic tradition in the crafting of luxury artistic products.

The piece bears traces of ancient restorations.

Silver scyphus with the labours
of Hercules, from Pompeii, House
of the Menander (I, 10, 4)
inv. 145506
The house of the Menander yielded, in
1930, one of the largest silverware treasures
in Pompeii, no less than 118 pieces for a
total weight of 84 kilograms of silver.
Although weight was an important element of value, as the frequent ponderal

inscriptions bear out, there is no doubt
that, in the eyes of connoisseurs, decoration must have been much more
important.
The mythological theme of the labours of
Hercules was the subject of this vase and
of its twin (drinking vases, the *argenta
potoria*, usually come in sets of two, the
ones containing food, the *escaria*, in sets
of four), signed by the same Apelles of the

scyphus illustrated on the preceding page.
Signatures of silver *caelatores* are extremely rare, possibly because one did not
wish to deprive the buyers of the illusion
of possessing ancient silverware, that
argentum vetus which was the pride of
the great families, not to mention pieces
truly belonging to the Classical age made
by the great metalworkers Mys, Mentor
and Kalamis.

Silver cantharus with olive twigs, from Pompeii, House of the Menander (I, 10, 4)

The olive-twig decoration of this vessel, also one of a set of two, is an example of the vegetal decoration (also featuring wreaths of oak, laurel and pine, and leaves of platan, vine etc.) that became fashionable during the late Republican period – it is commonly featured, for example, in II style paintings – and remained in vogue for a few decades. It reflects religious and literary motifs and, at the same time, alludes to a sentiment of complete natural *felicitas*, awakened in the new golden age of the Augustan *pax*.

Silver cantharus with Tritons and
Nereids, from Pompeii, House I, 6, 11
inv. 144802
The theme is the struggle of two Tritons,
one young, the other elderly, assisted
with trepidation by two Nereids, against
a lion and a dragon. In spite of the
small scale of the figures, the remote
influence of the Pergamene Baroque
can be perceived in the rendering of the
tense muscles of the contenders.

Silver calathus with apotheosis of
Homer, from Pompeii
inv. 24301
The buyer of this refined bucket with a
depiction of the apotheosis of Homer
obviously had literary interests. The poet
ascends to the sky mounted on the eagle
of Zeus and escorted by swans, symbols
of poetry. The two allegoric figures flanking the scene are extremely interesting.

One is a female figure in military dress
personifying the Iliad while the other,
dressed as a sailor, represents the Odyssey.
The use of silver vases was one of the
favourite targets of contemporary mora-
listic literature: "Great is he who uses
clay vases as if they were of silver, but no
less great is he who uses silver vases as if
they were of clay" (Seneca, *Epist. ad
Lucil.*, I, 56).

Obsidian cup, from Stabiae
no number
These two precious cups from Stabiae have the same traditional form as precious metal *scyphi*. They are decorated with inlaid Egyptian-style scenes and figures of white and pink coral, lapislazzuli, malachite and gold. The decoration alludes to the land of origin of Roman obsidian, discovered in Ethiopia by a man named *Obsidius* who gave it its name. Glass imitations of this material, called "obsidian glass", were also made.

Rock-crystal cup, from Santa Maria Capua Vetere
inv. 124701
The silver-*scyphus* form and the vegetable-motif decoration of this rock-crystal cup indicate an approximate date in the Augustan period. It is one of the largest known objects of this material.

This specimen is of colourless and transparent quartz, often used in antiquity both for jewellery and to make small objects used as trinkets or amulets.
The Egyptian (or Indian) origin of the material endowed it with a magical aura that is always associated with things Egyptian.

234

Ribbed cup of blue glass, from Pompeii
inv. 13810

These cups were made by melting the glass in a mould and then finishing it on a wheel. This is one of the most popular shapes, found both in monochrome and polychrome glass in the period between the end of the Republic and the 1st century B.C. Pliny, a contemporary of the Vesuvian cities in their last phase, says that, in his times, most people tended to favour glass vases over precious metal ones. The same author mentions that Puteolan workshops, certainly among Pompeii's providers, had access to an extremely fine white sand extracted between Cumae and Liternum, from which it was possible to obtain pure glass.

**"Millefiori" glass cup, from a
Vesuvian site (?)**
inv. 13558
Polychrome vases in the styles known as
"sprinkled", "millefiori", "golden ribbon"
and "pseudo-murrhine" inherited from
the Oriental and Hellenistic world and
enthusiastically renewed by Roman craftsmen, were very popular in the Roman
world in the early stages of glass vase
production. The "pseudo-murrhine" vases
enjoyed great favour, due to their lively
colours, imitating the polychrome transparencies of the "murrhine" precious stone
vases. Vases of this type, however, are
exceptional. In Pompeii and the other
Vesuvian cities fairly pure monochrome
glass is the rule.

236

"Millefiori" glass cup, from a
Vesuvian site (?)
no number
We do not know to which production centre to attribute this work. Along with the traditional Egyptian centres, the new Puteolan laboratories must have been very active. The main asset of this set of two is the lively combination of vivid colours. They call to mind a passage in which, speaking with the tone of a refined connoisseur, Martial (XIV, 113) states: "if you drink your wine warm, the material of the murrhine vase is suited to the ardent Falernum, and the wine acquires a better taste".

Marbled south-Gaul cup, from
Pompeii
inv. 109640
Although the wealthy employed metal
vases, made of bronze or silver, the
crockery of common people was made
of the so-called *terra sigillata*, i.e.
pottery coated in a coral-red varnish,
whose production had extended from
Arezzo to all of Italy and the provinces.
In southern Gaul, workshops soon
created their own series and forms, and
invaded the Italian market with refined
products such as this cup, covered with
a varnish with marble-coloured streaks.
Martial reminds the snob, who looks
down on a table on which such vases
are set, of the ancient glory of earthenware vessels: "do not despise Aretine
vases too much; I warn you, the Etruscan
fictile vases were Porsenna's luxury"
(Martial, XIV, 98).

238

Pair of canthari of glazed pottery, from Pompeii, IV, 6, 28
inv. 133315 and 133316
It is still unclear in which factory these vases, glazed with a siliceous paste or leaden varnish, were fashioned. They are attested in the Vesuvian cities. One centre of production was certainly Egypt, where a factory is known in Memphis, and many of the decorative motifs employed are also Egyptian. In other instances, as in the case of this pair of calyxes, the shapes are, more generally, Hellenistic, and obviously derive from silver prototypes.

One is reminded of Varro's words (*Lingua Latina*, VIII, 31): "any glass will do for a thirsty man, but it is not enough for a refined man, if it is not beautiful as well…"

Oven, from a Vesuvian site
no number
Most of the population warmed their food and drink on simple earthenware ovens, equipped with a closed compartment for the fire and an open one on which the vessels to be warmed were set.
In the Hellenistic period the braziers from Delos, with Satyr-head handles, became very popular in Pompeii, as in many centres touched by sea trade. In the Imperial period, the demand for braziers and simple ovens such as this specimen was mainly satisfied by local potters.

"Thin walled" human-faced jar,
from a Vesuvian site
no number
These bowls, commonly featured in the
crockery of the *tabernae*, were used as
drinking vessels for warm drinks. They
were probably produced by local workshops, and must have certainly been less
expensive than the *terra sigillata*. On
these products, the stylised caricature of
human features is rather frequent.

Bronze syrinx, from Pompeii
inv. 111055
Musical instruments, such as this syrinx found in 1876, could be used in the course of the banquet. They were also essential in the sacred rites and theatrical representations.

The syrinx was, for example, a typical element of the satyresque drama and of the mime. This nine-pipe specimen is especially interesting for the decoration of the body, with three appliqués representing aedicules making up the façade of a theatre stage.

Lamp-bearing Silenus from Herculaneum
inv. 72199

Banquet time was at night, and feasts were carried on in the dim light of lamps. As Horatio sings (*Carmina*, II, 21): "if Liberus comes, and gay Venus, and the Graces who stop to untie themselves, the live lamps shall remain awake with you until the sun disperses the stars".

Silenus, the companion of Dionysus in the thiasos, is an appropriate character in a banquet context.

Bronze statuette of a placentarius, from Pompeii, House of the Ephebus (I, 7, 10-12)
inv. 143760
This statuette, evidently a grotesque caricature of a popular theme of late Hellenistic origin, belongs to a group of four identical figurines found in a box in a room near the atrium of the house. They were probably used as fancy meal-course holders – delicacies were placed on the silver tray – on the table of their rich owner.

A passage in Cato suggests their identification with *placentae* (flat bread) sellers.

244

Bronze statue of an old donkey, from a Vesuvian city
inv. 4955
This statuette, a hollow casting retouched with a chisel, probably decorated a piece of furniture or carried a pack-saddle used as a food-holder. Its artistic quality, at all events, is remarkable. The statuette certainly derives from a Hellenistic prototype providing an amusing psychological interpretation of the patient character of the animal.

Silver disc with Apollo, from Herculaneum
inv. 25492

This disc, featuring a high-relief bust of Apollo of excellent workmanship, is paired with a similar one representing Diana. Both are mounted on a movable bronze lamina support, certainly decorating furniture or some kind of prestigious object, displayed by the owner on important occasions. The theme of the young bow-wielding gods became very much in vogue after the consecration of the temple of Apollo on the Palatine at the time of Augustus, to which these reliefs probably belong, a date confirmed by the strong Classic influences of their style.

Fictile statuette of Pero and Mycos, from Pompeii, VI, 15
inv. 128486
This statuette, with its plumbiferous glaze, is an example of the tradition of grotesque parodies of myth commonly attributed to the Alexandrine environment. It depicts the characters of the famous myth, also featured in painting, of Pero suckling her old imprisoned father. The statuette was found with a duck-shaped jug, also glazed, and other analogous objects reflecting the exotic tastes of the owner.

Bronze statuette of Venus,
from Herculaneum
inv. 5133

It was found on February 22, 1757.
Venus, here in the iconography of the
Hellenistic Aphrodite untying the laces of
her sandal, about to bathe (the anklets
and armlets are of gold, the inlays of the
base of silver), was one of the main
deities of the Vesuvian area. Th Romans
gave her name to the colony of Pompeii,
calling it *Colonia Cornelia Veneria
Pompeianorum* in honour of the dictator
Sulla, who claimed to be the goddess'
protégé. Venus, however, was important
in the Vesuvian region even before the
Romans, as the cult of *Venus Physica* in
Pompeii and a Herculanean inscription
with her Samnite name of *Herentas* bear
out. The goddess formed, with Dionysus
and Hercules, the local triad in Pompeii,
mentioned in a well-known epigram by
Martial. A painting in the Pompeian
house of Mars and Venus (VII, 9, 47)
represents a procession in honour of the
latter, with the participants pushing
forward *fercula* and the sacrificial bull.

Statuettes of Lares, from Pompeii, House of the Golden Cupids (VI, 15, 7) invv. 133327-28

The lararium of this elegant house contained a set of statuettes of deities typical of the most pure of Latin traditions. Jupiter, Juno and Minerva formed the Capitoline triad, while Mercury was the traditional Latin god of trade. As to the Lares, represented in their usual aspect of dancing youths with buckets and drinking horns, they are the traditional gods of the house, and gave the domestic sanctuary its name. The cult of traditional gods inside the house was accompanied by ancestral magical rites, such as this ceremony to keep ghosts away described by Ovid (in *Fasti*, V, 431-444): "the father, recalling the ancient rite and fearful of the gods, stands up on bare feet and snaps his fingers to chase the shadows from his face, he spins around and, after having put black broad-beans in his mouth he throws them over his shoulder saying: 'I throw these broad-beans and, with them, I release myself and my own'. Nine times he says these words without turning around; the shadow is said to gather the broad-beans, unseen, and to follow him. Again he wets his hands [...] and asks the shadow to leave the house. After having said: 'Spirits of my fathers, go out', he turns around and judges he has carried out the sacrifices in a pure fashion".

Bronze statuette of Fortuna enthroned, from Pompeii, House IX, 7, a ("of Fortuna")
inv. 111697

Fortuna was the goddess of the good and bad fate of men, cities and peoples. At her caprice, they prospered or perished. To symbolise her power to direct destiny she is often represented as a helmsman, holding the helm in her hand.

The marine world, dominated by uncertain destiny, is evoked here by Tritons playing a *buccina* adorning her throne. The goddess holds in one hand a silver patera and in the other another typical attribute, the cornucopia. A bronze lamp in the shape of a human foot, found in the same niche, must have hung in front of the statuette. Like the cult of Mercury, that of Fortuna in the lararia is meant to bring good luck on the house, as the traditional offering on the lararia of fruit, pine cones and eggs, symbols of prosperity and fertility.

Bronze statuette of Athena, from Herculaneum

inv. 5228

This statuette, inspired by the Classic 5th century B.C. types, with its crested helmet, the aegis with the head of Medusa, the *phiale* and the lance, well expresses the classicist trend that started with the Augustan age. It certainly comes from a lararium, where the goddess, the protector of the arts and of wisdom, had the role of Minerva of the Capitoline triad.

251

Group of silver lararium statuettes,
from Scafati
invv. 125709-711
This group of silver statuettes belonging to
the same lararium was found in a rural
villa in the Pompeian countryside. They
include a figure of Isis with ears of wheat,
the rudder and the lunar crescent on her
head, Venus, naked, beside a dove, and an
agathodaemon snake, the god of good
luck so often painted on Pompeian lararia.

Bronze votive hand of Sabatius, from Herculaneum

inv. 5506

These hands, with fingers bent in the traditional gesture of blessing still known to the Latin Christian ritual, are typical of the cult of the Phrygian or Thracian god Sabatius, a god of vegetation already known in Greece in the 5th century B.C., and transplanted in the Roman age, as so many other Oriental cults, to the Latin West, where he was assimilated to Zeus or Dionysus. The hand is loaded with symbols.

Sabatius himself, dressed in Phrygian attire, sits on the palm with his hands held up in blessing, the sacred serpent beside him, Dionysus' pine cone on his left, a deer's head at his feet and, above him, on the fingertips, Zeus' lightning-bolt, formerly held by an eagle. On his wrist are the figures of a mother and child inside a cavern, certainly an allusion to a story concerning this god's childhood.

Fictile statuette of Bes, from Pompeii
inv. 22583

Bes is a typical character of the fantastic
world of Egyptian religion and magic, a
good dancing dwarf with a misshapen
body, his tongue hanging out as that of a
Gorgon, and wearing an ostrich-feather
headdress. He was thought to bring good
luck and protect the sleep of women and
children, and was reproduced since
ancient times on amulets suspended from
necklaces, such as this Egyptian-faience
(i.e. coated with a silicon-based glaze)
statuette. In the Roman world, the motif
was also used for merely decorative purposes. Statuettes such as this one were
used, like the figures of crocodiles, sphinxes
etc. as ornaments in "Egyptian-style" gardens, a token of the craze for the land of
the Nile (generally called "Egyptomania") that seized the Romans after their
conquest of Egypt.

Cymbals, from Pompeii
inv. 76943
These cymbals, formed of two bronze concave discs connected by a chain, are a typical instrument of Oriental cults, especially Isis and Cybele, but Dionysus as well, as in a famous Pompeian picture with Bacchic symbols (panther, horn etc.; inv. 8795). Their noise and that of the hand-drums aroused the indignation of Roman traditionalists.

Marble relief with a scene representing a boilermaker's workshop, from Pompeii

inv. 6575

This panel, a shop sign or funerary relief (the latter instance, however, is less common in Pompeii than in Ostia), illustrates three typical phases in the activity of the boilermaker: on the left, the weighing of the metal on great scales; at the centre, the beating of the hot metal on an anvil; on the right, the cold-working of a plate under a figure of a recumbent dog.

The upper part of the scene shows the display, on whose steps various vessels are depicted, including the typical seashell shapes for the making of cakes; at the centre lies the furnace.

This work displays the simple style typical of popular monuments of this kind, but is also remarkably expressive, e.g. in the detail of the figure of a child holding his father's hand on the left.

**Steelyard with a weight shaped as
a child's head, from Pompeii**
inv. 74039

The steelyard is of the type still used today, based on the principle of the lever. It has a plate on which the object to be weighed is laid, counterbalanced by a movable weight, here shaped as a child's head, sliding along a graded shaft.

This steelyard had two scales, one from 1 to 14, the other from 10 to 50, corresponding to two possible positions of the fulcrum. On the short arm of the shaft, a dotted inscription recalls the consular date of 47 A.D., and attests that both the steelyard and the weights were of the type specified in the decree issued in that year in Rome by the aediles *Marcus Articuleianus* and *Gnaeus Turranius.*

Painting showing fullers at work,
from Pompeii, fullonica VI, 2, 31
no number

The painting represents, in the simple style of popular painting, two scenes that must have been common in Pompeii. At the centre, a worker is teaseling a woolen cloth, i.e. combing the hairs of the wool so they can be shaved evenly. For this purpose he is using a fuller's teasel, a brush (*aenea*) made of quills or bristles. On the right, another worker is carrying on his head a wooden cage to bleach the cloth with sulphur fumigations.

The owl perched on the cage alludes to the goddess Athena, the protector of the fullers' art.

In the other panel, young slaves, their feet in the washbasins, wash the laundry immersed in an ill-smelling liquid based on urine by trampling on it.

Cupids at work, from Herculaneum, House of the Deer (IV, 21)
inv. 9179

The theme of Cupids playfully imitating man's activities is typical of the Hellenistic repertory. Like the renowned frieze in the House of the Vettii, this Herculaneum painting has become famous as a representation of working activities. The scenes include perfume-making, field measuring, cobbling and carpentry. Their most interesting features are the gestures used in work, the machines and the closets.

Silver lid of a medical box,
from Herculaneum
inv. 25699
Comparisons with complete specimens
and the decoration of the lid, made of
copper with inlaid silver figures, indicate that the lid belonged to a medical
box in which instruments and drugs were
kept. The figures represent the guardian
deities of the medical profession, viz.
Aesculapius with the snake curling around
his stick and Hygeia with an olive twig. In
Herculaneum, as in Pompeii, doctors are
attested rather frequently, e.g. in a graffito
referring to Vespasianus' doctor, Apollinar,
who *optime cacavit*.

Surgical instrument (so-called "Herculanean forceps"), from Pompeii inv. 78029
These large tongs with S-shaped curved extremities testify, along with several other similar objects found in the Vesuvian cities, to the rather advanced level of technical specialization attained by ancient surgery.

The instrument is identified as an *odontagra*, i.e. dentist's tongs, to extract teeth and roots, but may also have been used as an *ostagra*, to extract bone splinters and other extraneous bodies from wounds.

Painting showing the wounded Aeneas, from Pompeii, House of Siricus (VII, 1, 25)
inv. 9009
This fresco, the work of a mediocre painter, is interesting because it shows, through the medium of myth, a doctor – Iapyx in the myth – at work, operating with a surgical instrument with which he extracts from Aeneas' thigh the cusp of the arrow that hit him (Virgil, *Aeneid*, XII, vv. 398 ff. and 411 ff.). The hero is assisted by his son Ascanius who, as Virgil narrates, cries, and his divine mother Aphrodite who bears in flight a tuft of Cretan medical herbs collected on Mount Ida. The picture belonged to a 4th style wall datable to the Neronian or Flavian period. The presence of this subject in the triclinium of the house was possibly meant as a display of reverence for the myth of the origins of Rome.

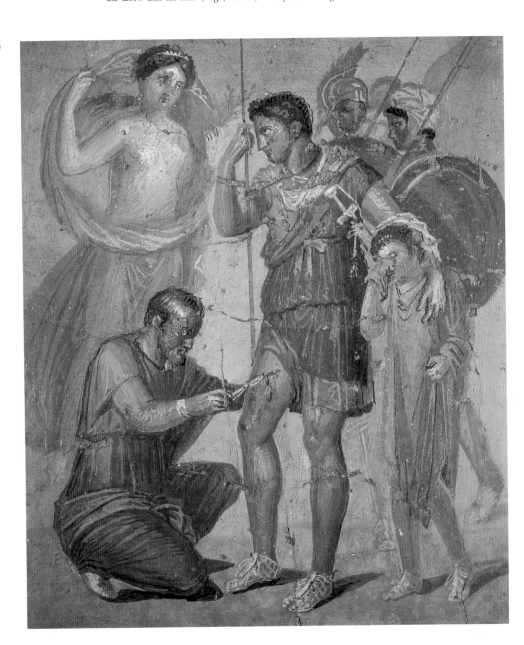

Rattle in the shape of a gladiator, from Herculaneum
inv. 27853
This grotesque figure of a gladiator belongs to a class of figured ityphallic rattles certainly imbued with apotropaic powers. They were probably suspended as lucky charms in the doorways of houses and shops, somewhat like the figure of Priapus at the entrance of the House of the Vettii.
Here, the motif of the phallus is transformed into a panther against which the gladiator is fighting.

Glass vase in the shape of a Negro's head, from Pompeii
inv. 129404

The invention of the technique of glass-blowing in the second half of the 1st century B.C. was one of the greatest discoveries of ancient industry (Rostovzev). When combined with the use of moulds, it enabled craftsmen to produce mechanically in great quantities vases of any shape at a cheap price. The industry of perfume soon availed itself of the seductive forms and transparencies of these new bottles as containers for its luxury products.

These vases shaped as the head of an Ethiopian slave, a model already attested in Attic ceramics, were themselves certainly used as perfume containers. Juvenal reports the traditionalists' criticism of the excessive use of perfume: "among luxury objects... perfume is the most superfluous of all. Pearls and gems can be left as an heirloom, cloth lasts for a certain time, but perfumes, instead, evaporate instantly and, so to speak, die at birth... They are sold at more than 40 denari per pound. And this is the price of other people's pleasure, as he who uses it cannot smell it."

266

"Blue vase", from Pompeii
inv. 13521

The technique of cameo-glass consisted of superimposing on glass of a very intense colour, generally cobalt-blue, a layer of dull white glass which was then partially removed according to a design, as in the technique used for cameos on hard stones, so that the white design contrasted with the dark background. In this famous "blue vase", the glass, before being incised, was shaped in the form of a wine-amphora. In keeping with this shape, the decoration represents the Dionysiac theme of grape harvesting carried out by cupids under vine stalks harmoniously winding around the body of the vase (the elaborate vegetal motif of the secondary side), while others cupids play music on a *kline* under a bower.

The discovery of this precious object in 1834, in a tomb near the Villa of the Mosaic Columns along the *Via dei Sepolcri*, has aroused a lot of discussion, but an analogous case is known, viz. that of the rock-crystal cup from a tomb in Capua (see description on p. 234).

Cameo-glass panels, from Pompeii, area of the insula Occidentalis
inv. 153651-2

These two panels, found as sporadic material in the area outside the so-called House of Fabius Rufus, are the only known examples of glass panels made with this technique. They were possibly used to decorate a small closet, in lieu of ivory inlays. The decoration is, once again, a Dionysiac theme. On the first panel, Dionysus appears to the sleeping Ariadne, accompanied by a Satyr and Cupids alluding to the imminent amorous epilogue.

On the other is a scene possibly alluding to Ariadne's initiation; a Maenad is pouring wine into her cup in the presence of a dancing Satyr, among trees from whose branches symbols of the cult of Dionysus are suspended.

Portrait on glass, from Pompeii
inv. 132424
The thoughtful expression and delicate colours of this fine head painted on glass, probably originally part of a double medallion, calls to mind the Fayyum portraits, and is probably an Alexandrine product, as a comparison with a similar specimen from Hawara, datable to the first half of the 1st century B.C., bears out.

**Plaquette with a figured frieze,
of unknown provenance**
inv. 13638
Here glass is used for a small element of
a frieze featuring alternating heads and
lotus flowers, certainly imitating the
simae, the earthenware architectural
friezes crowning the most important
buildings. The style is strongly archaistic
and pervaded with exotism. The object
possibly belonged to the decoration of a
shrine-shaped chest.

Fictile statuette of Aeneas, Anchises and Ascanius, from Pompeii
inv. 110338

Its well-planned triangular composition indicates that it may derive from a traditional pictorial pattern. Aeneas, bearded and wearing a cuirass, advances in wide strides towards the right, his cloak flapping; on his left arm he carries Anchises, wrapped in his cloak and holding the reliquary containing the Penates; with his right hand he leads the little Ascanius, a child with a Phrygian hat and a shepherd's staff (*pedum*) in his hand, the same iconography as Attis. The figurine, rather plain, but enlivened by its intense polichromy, may have been a trinket, or even an element of the lararium of a Pompeian cherishing the ideological traditions of the Julio-Claudian period (cf. the helmet on p. 124).

Statuette representing two slaves
carrying a litter, from Pompeii,
House of the Marbles (VII, 2, 20)
inv. 110340
The form of the two elderly bearers,
staggering under the weight of the litter,
is barely sketched, the details being
mainly rendered by gaudy colours.
Litters were a status symbol of the well-
to-do classes rather than a means of
transportation of women and sick people.

Juvenal caricatures their use in his first
satire, and this Pompeian statuette reminds us of his "overloaded litter of
Matho the Causidic" (*causidici nova
cum veniat lectica Mathonis plena
ipso*).
A similar figurine was found in the
kitchen quarter of the house of M.
Lucretius (inv. 20255), where it is
thought that the owner kept a collection
of statuettes.

272

Bone pin with female head,
from Pompeii
inv. 77441

This hairpin bears at the top a representation of a female bust on a base. The coiffure, featuring two fan-shaped rows of locks framing the forehead, dates the object to the Flavian period. The fashions for female coiffures changed greatly during the Imperial period, and are extremely useful for the dating of portraits (see the portrait of Terentia from Herculaneum).

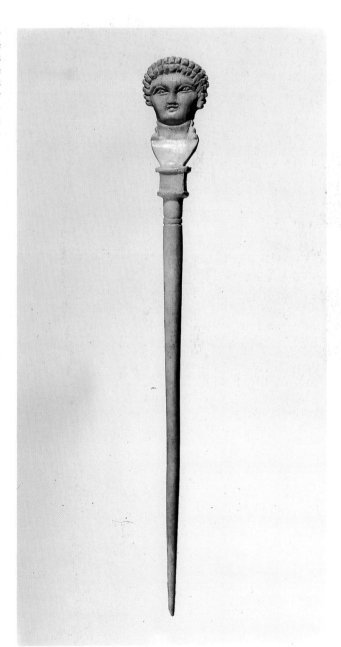

Ivory statuette of the goddess Laksmi, from Pompeii
inv. 149425

This ivory statuette, found in a house on the *Via dell'Abbondanza*, along with Puteolan records of Nabatean cults and pearls and precious stones from India, is the most eloquent testimony of the existence of commercial routes leading through Alexandria, the Nubian desert, the Red Sea and the Indian Ocean, allowing Roman merchants – graffitoed names found in the desert wadis could very well belong to Puteolans or Pompeians – to reach the fabulous Indian lands. The statuette represents, in the characteristic Indian style of the time, the Hindu Aphrodite, the goddess of beauty and fertility, Laksmi, bride of Vishnu, naked and flanked by two handmaids.

Ivory statuette of Venus, from Pompeii, House VI, 1, 18
inv. 110924
This small ivory figurine reproduces the celebrated Hellenistic statue-type of Aphrodite emerging from her bath (*anadiomene*), wringing her hair in a graceful gesture that serves as a pretext to display the beauty of her naked body. In spite of its small scale, the statuette has lost nothing of the soft contours of the original. The dolphin at her side alludes to the sea from which the goddess was born.

Comb with figured decoration,
from Pompeii, House IX, 5, 18
inv. 118729
The incised decoration of this comb is
especially interesting. It features two
peacocks standing either side of a basket
full of fruit from which grapes hang
down.

276

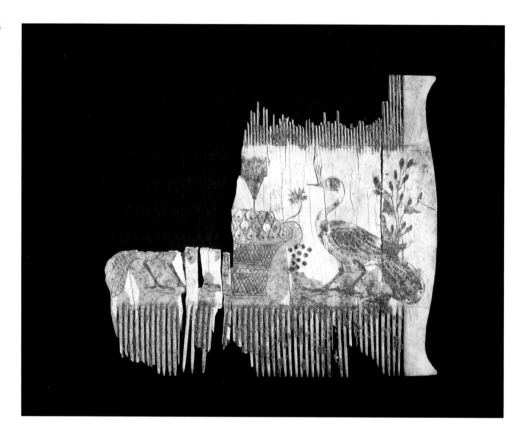

Silver mirror of Phaedra, from Pompeii inv. 25490

The scene decorating this mirror back certainly derives from a painted original. The theme, an appropriate one for an instrument of Aphrodite, is that of the fatal love of Phaedra, who is consumed by her passion for Hippolytus. In the Imperial period, the theme of the mirror also became the subject of displays of rhetoric, such as the following one by Apuleius (*Apol.*, 14): "nothing is more pleasing to the eye of man than his own likeness [...] in the mirror one sees the wonderfully reproduced image, identical and moving, obedient to each motion of the head [...] that artistic polish of the mirror and its creating shine surpass the arts of portraiture".

Silver mirror with a figured emblem, from Pompeii, House of the Menander
inv. 145524

The back of this mirror, adorned with elaborate openwork, is decorated with a bust probably representing Apollo, considering that it is identical to the one depicted in the carnelian intaglio inv. 26145 from Pompeii (see description on p. 284), where the god is identified by his cithara. On mirrors, a female instrument, the image of Apollo possibly alluded to the Graces, inseparable companions, with the *Horai*, of the god.

Bulla from Pompeii, House of the Menander (I, 10, 4)
inv. 145490
Pliny says (*N.H.*, XXXII, 4): "Golden objects are placed on newborn babies to protect them from curses". These objects probably included the *bullae*, amulets in the shape of small round cases of Etruscan origin. Besides having this apotropaic value, the *bullae* soon became a distinctive sign of free birth.
The ceremony of laying down the *bulla* and putting on the virile toga was an important turning point in life.
This specimen, from the treasure of the House of the Menander, presents a remarkable gold thread decoration.

Necklace of gold, mother-of-pearl and emeralds, from Pompeii
inv. 113576

This necklace, found in a villa in the area of the port of Pompeii, documents very well some of the main materials used in Roman jewellery from this period: gold, pearls (*margarita*, *unio*), emerald (*smaragdos*), here combined in an ensemble of lively colours. The Roman jewels from Pompeii and Herculaneum rarely attain the great technical quality of the products of the Hellenistic goldsmiths. It should be kept in mind, however, that the use of jewels had increased greatly, due to its extension to new social categories. Thus, the Pompeian evidence, which gives us a more or less complete overview of the jewels of members of all social classes, is much less selective than, say, that of the Apulian tombs.

The passion of Roman ladies for jewellery had become out of control. It is Juvenal once again who echoes the vain protests of the traditionalists (*Satires*, VI, 457-59): "there is nothing that a woman thinks she cannot do, nothing she deems unworthy, when she can adorn her neck with gems, when she can hang from her ears jewels so large that they deform the lobes".

Snake-shaped golden bracelets, probably from Pompeii
invv. 24824-85
The motif of the serpent, used in all of the Roman world for bracelets such as these and for gold and silver rings, derives from a type of jewel already very common in Hellenistic times. The quality of the workmanship is especially evident in the fine incision of the scales and the geometrical rendering of the head, originally provided with inlaid eyes, probably made of glaze. The serpent, besides being sacred to Asclepius and Isis, was itself an "agathodaimon", i.e. a bringer of good-luck. Thus, a snakeskin sealed by a golden lamina was worn by Nero as a bracelet (Suaetonius, *Nero*, VI).

Ring with mask, from Pompeii
inv. 25181
This ring is famous for having been worn by Charles III of Bourbon and given back to the Museum when this king left Naples for Spain. The cameo decoration of the sardonyx bezel represents a theatrical mask of the New Comedy (the poor and crapulous old man), a philosophical allusion to the theme of the "theatre of life" derived from Hellenistic philosophy.

Female bust with a branch, agate-onyx cameo, from Stabiae
inv. 26775
This somewhat cold, but skilfully executed figure is probably an Aphrodite, as the myrtle in her hand and her slightly sensual attitude seem to indicate. Comparisons with other sculptures date it to the Julio-Claudian period.

Octavianus, sardonyx-onyx cameo, from Herculaneum
inv. 25876
This is a magnificent portrait of the young Augustus, represented with great finesse according to the canons of early Imperial portraiture, combining a celebrative intention with realism. The latter trend is evident in the curve of the forehead and the lines of the chin and mouth.
The rendering of the locks of hair in the style of Polycletus and the general abstract appearance of the profile connote the figure as that of a hero, soon to become a god, as the Doryphorus that official sculpture looked to for inspiration.
The use of a portrait of the *princeps* for such a personal object (gems are first and foremost a symbol of their owner) evidently is intended as a display of loyalism, typical of the new regime issued from the civil wars.

Apollo citharedus, carnelian intaglio, from Pompeii (?)
inv. 26145
The bust of the young god, identified by the very low relief cithara in front of him, has the exquisite and somewhat cold elegance of the bronze busts of the Doryphorus and the Amazon of the *Villa dei Papiri*. It is in the classicist style of the Augustan and Julio-Claudian periods.

284

Alexander the Great as Achilles, glaze intaglio, from Pompeii
invv. 129432, 158837

The theme of Alexander the Great who, represented as Achilles, contemplates the latter's weapons, is the subject of a famous gem, presently in the Naples Museum and formerly probably in the Orsini collection (inv. 26092), signed by the celebrated Dioskourides, an Alexandrine artist who accompanied Caesar to Rome and became Augustus' favourite *gemmarius*. The pre-sence of two glaze intagli with the same subject from Pompeii show how rapidly the iconographies adopted by court artists became diffused in Roman society. The presence of workshops of *gemmarii* in Pompeii is well documented. One of them, *Pinarius Cerialis*, lived in house III, 4, b, where, in one of the cubicula, his tool chest was found. It contained some burins and 114 precious stones, 28 of which had been worked, while 79 were unworked or merely polished.

The Villa of the Pisones

This villa was initially investigated in the first generation of excavations in Herculaneum and Pompeii (1750-1761) by the tunnelling method. Recently new probes have been carried out below the impervious stratum of lava and debris left by the eruptions of 79 A.D. and 1631 which covers it to a depth of more than 20 metres.

The original exploration of the villa provided the newly created Museo Ercolanense in Portici with a rich haul of extraordinary works of art, above all sculptures (no less than fifty in bronze and twenty-one in marble). They comprised the sumptuous decor of the villa, which continues to be the best known example of those havens of *otium* which members of the Roman aristocracy had built for themselves on the shores of the Bay of Naples. The importance of the villa itself is matched by that of the extensive library of papyrus scrolls found inside (a grand total of 1,758 scrolls). The library comprised mainly Greek works of Epicurean philosophy written in the first century B.C. by Philodemus of Gadara and some Latin texts, including the anonymous poem *de bello Actiaco* recounting the war that saw Mark Anthony and Cleopatra opposed to Octavian.

A villa with such contents could only have belonged to someone possessing a refined Hellenising culture, and various hypotheses have been made as to the owner's identity. Since he must clearly have been a member of the Roman *nobilitas* with Epicurean leanings, the choice fell on L. Calpurnius Piso Cesoninus, Caesar's father-in-law and consul in 58 B.C., who as we know from Cicero's oration *In Pisonem* had close ties with the philosopher Philodemus, or possibly his son, who was consul in 15 B.C. On the basis of this identification Pandermalis analysed the villa's corpus of sculptures in terms of a scheme which alluded to the Epicurean principles of the passive and the active life. Another scholar, Sauron, interprets the sculptures as an illustration of the Elysian Fields of the greatest Latin poet, Virgil, whose name has recently been discovered in one of the scrolls from the villa. One weakness of the Piso hypothesis is that we have no epigraphical evidence for the presence of this family in Herculaneum (although the villas were to some extent a separate entity with respect to the cities: no reference to Cicero is found in inscriptions from Pompeii, but we know that he owned his *Pompeianum),* while such evidence has recently suggested another hypothesis, linking the villa to Appius Claudius Pulcher. This man was consul in 38 B.C. and the brother-in-law of Lucullus. He was famous for his Hellenistic sympathies, and contributed to the erection of the "small Propilei" at Eleusis. His name occurs in the dedication of a statue put up in his honour in the theatre by the citizens of Herculaneum.

The villa stood on a hill overlooking the sea on the other side of the stream that marked the western boundary of Herculaneum. Built on a series of terraces which gave every opportunity for the achievement of *amoenitas,* to our knowledge it measured 250 metres from end to end. In the visitor's itinerary through the Museum the villa will come as the culmination of the section dedicated to Greek culture in Campania and serve as an introduction to the decoration and furnishing of the houses and villas in the Vesuvian area, of which it remains the outstanding example.

Marble portrait of Pyrrhus
inv. 6150

The identification of this portrait, from the great peristyle of the villa, with the famous king of Epirus, is based on solid grounds. First of all, the chronology of the portrait, which is inspired by the Lysippean portraits of Alexander the Great; then the oak-leaf wreath adorning the helmet, evidently alluding to the most renowned place of Epirus, the sanctuary of Zeus at Dodona where oracles were entrusted to the leaves of the sacred oak. Plutarch tells us that, during the revolt of Argos in which the king was killed, he tore the wreath (possibly the golden one presented to him in Catane) from his helmet to avoid recognition; it was evidently a very distinctive sign, and nothing would have been more distinctive of the King of Epirus than the wreath of Dodona.

Marble portrait of Archidamus III
inv. 6156

The great peristyle of the villa was decorated by several portrait-herms of illustrious Greek kings, military leaders, philosophers and men of letters. This portrait in military attire depicts an Archidamus, as the Greek inscription painted on the right shoulder tells us, certainly to be identified with the Spartan general Archidamus, who led a campaign in Italy alongside the Tarentines against the Lucanian and Messapian barbarians. Another group of portraits of Hellenistic rulers, in bronze, was set up in the atrium.

Bronze portrait, so-called
pseudo-Seneca
inv. 5616

The identification of the character represented here with Seneca goes back to Fulvio Orsini and his studies of the portraits of illustrious men.

It was accepted by antiquarians and was the reason for this type's great popularity, until the real portrait of the Roman philosopher was discovered in 1813 on a double herm with Socrates.

This head from the great peristyle of the villa, whose original is datable to the end of the 3rd-2nd century B.C., certainly portrays a great poet, as the ivy crown he is wearing and the great number of copies, about forty, that have reached us bear out.

His identification, however, is still doubtful. The names of Hesiod, Callimachus, Philemon, Apollonius Rhodius etc., and, more recently, Ennius have been proposed.

Bronze statue of a drunken satyr
inv. 5628

The garden of the great peristyle of the villa, besides being the seat of a thiasus of illustrious men, was also the kingdom of Dionysus, as real nature was thought to be. The drunken satyr is a typical character of the cortege of the god. In the representation of the exasperated and manifold expressions of drunkenness, Hellenism found an ideal subject for its hyperrealistic taste and its penchant for genre themes. The satyr is lying back on a lion-skin covering a rock, shaking in an unbridled laugh, one arm outstretched and his body wine-heavy yet still majestic with its mature athletic forms.

Marble group of Pan and goat
inv. 27709
Its bidimensional composition, virtually enclosed in the shape of a parallelepiped, the pruriency of its erotic theme, relieved by the humorism of the play of glances between the languorous goat and the small Pan, and its Rococò pastoral taste date this small garden sculpture (from the great peristyle, where it was perfectly in character with the Dionysiac theme) to the 2nd century B.C.

Bronze statues of Hermes at rest
inv. 5625

This is an eclectic work, inspired by motifs of the Lysippean school (such as the seated Hercules, Hermes unlacing a sandal, a Hermes from Vienna), re-elaborated according to the taste of a local workshop that produced many such bronzes (no replicas of the present specimen are known). The presence of Hermes in a garden – the statue comes from the great peristyle – is perfectly conceivable when we think that the god was the guardian of the gymnasium, and that this garden is explicitly identified as such (see following object).

292

Statues of runners

invv. 5626-27

The theme of the gymnasium, introduced by the Hermes at rest, becomes explicit in this pair of runners, twin replicas of the same sculpture of the end of the 4th century B.C., probably the honorary image of a victorious athlete in one of the great Panhellenic games. The best source for these *ornamenta gymnasiode* is a letter of Atticus to Cicero (1, 6) in which the orator beseeches his learned friend to procure a Hercules and a Hermathena for the garden of his villa, to give it the allure of a gymnasium.

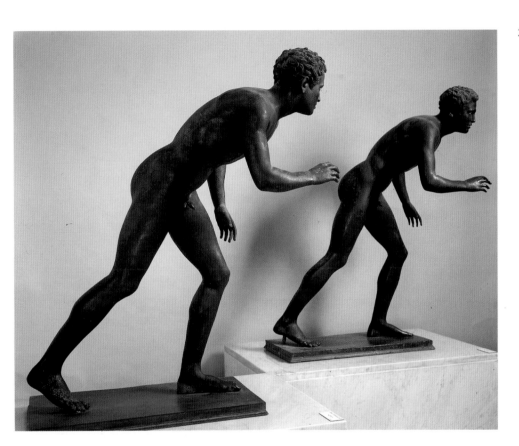

Statues of peplophorai
invv. 5604-05, 5619-20-21

These five bronze statues in various attitudes, thought by Winckelmann to be "dancers", have recently been recognised as "water-carriers" (*hydrophorai*) and hence identified with the Danaids, the fifty daughters of Danaus condemned to the endless drawing of water. The theme was popular in the Augustan age because it decorated the portico surrounding the temple of Apollo on the Palatine, dedicated by Augustus in 36 at Naulocus and inaugurated in 28 B.C. An illustrious contemporary, Propertius, describes the event thus: "our great Caesar has opened the golden portico of Phebus; it is immense in its splendour, with rows of columns of Punic marble, between which stand the numerous daughters of old Danaus!" The decoration of the small peristyle of the villa, comprising statues of *peplophorai* lying near the water basin, classicist works influenced by the great "stern style" 5th century sculpture, possibly alluded to this Apollinean sphere.

Marble statue of Athena promachos
inv. 6007

This fine statue of Athena *promachos* (i.e. proceeding to battle) decorated the tablinum of the villa. It is a re-elaboration of the great figure that decorated the Acropolis of Athens.

The visitor of the villa thus was under the impression of having entered a small Athens, a place of refined culture, an allusion reinforced by the busts of Demosthenes and Epicurus placed in the same room.

The statue seems to derive from the figures on Panathenaic amphorae. In keeping with the archaistic style of which it is an example, it presents an exquisite imitation, from a completely bidimensional point of view, of the decorative play of the drapery typical of the Archaic style. Augustan-age replica of a 2nd century type.

Bronze herm of an Amazon
inv. 4889

Pliny the Elder narrates a competition between five great artists of the 5th century B.C., Phidias, Polycletus, Phradmon, Cresila and Kydon, for the consecration of the statue of an Amazon in the temple of Artemis in Ephesos.

The truth of this story, in spite of its fabulous allure, is confirmed by the presence, in the figurative tradition of Roman copies of Greek originals, of a group of statues of Amazons from the same period traceable to at least four different prototypes. One of these sculptures was used as a caryatid in the theatre of Ephesos, an unquestionable proof that this famous 440 B.C. competition actually took place.

The bronze herm from Herculaneum has been recognised as a copy of the statue attributed to Phidias (one of the best replicas is the one in the Villa Adriana), who was defeated, on this occasion, by Polycletus. In the Villa dei Papiri, the head was a *pendant* to a bronze head of Polycletus' Doryphoros (see the marble statue from Pompeii described on p. 114).

Bust of Dionysus

inv. 5618

This fine bust representing the bearded Dionysus was found in a peripheral room of the villa. It has been recognised as a copy, dating approximately from the middle of the 1st century B.C., of a Hellenistic original.

The figure, with its thoughtful expression, its handsome beard growing down to its chest, and its finely incised hair held by a headband, obviously derives from a Hellenistic type of Dionysus like the one depicted in the *theoxenia* from the Borgia collection (see description p. 376).

Bronze bust of Epicurus
inv. 546

Portraits of Epicurus, the renowned philosopher from Samos who lived in Athens until his death in 271 B.C., are preserved in about thirty replicas of the Roman age. Only two of them, this one from the villa dei Papiri and a herm of Epicurus and Metrodoros at the Capitoline Museums, still bear the inscriptions identifying him. These copies of the portraits of Epicurus are thought to go back to an original of the first half of the 3rd century B.C. Cicero mentions that images of the philosopher were very common in the Roman age, appearing even on dishes and rings. One of the skeletons on the silver glass from Pompeii, kept in the Naples Museum, bears Epicurus' name. The presence of this bust of the Master of the "Garden" in the Villa dei Papiri, a cenacle of Epicurean philosophy, is of course no surprise.

Herm of a Greek Cynic philosopher
inv. 6154
Dishevelled hair is an iconographic *topos* characterising philosophers of the Cynic school (see the description of the earthenware Antisthenes from Pompeii). One has therefore proposed to identify the figure with Menippus, the philosopher from Gadara who lived in the 3rd century B.C. The original should date from the middle of that century.

Still life with roedeer

inv. 8759

The motif of the hunt, already exemplified in the earlier fine painting of hares and fish on the wall of the *insula Occidentalis* in Pompeii (see description on p. 149), returns in this fragment of a 2nd style wall with a painting of ducks and roedeer captured alive, possibly with nets. The motif is perfectly attuned to the character of the house, as the pastime of hunting was part of the ideal of life cultivated by the owners of *otium* villas. The sources inform us that many of these villas included in their parks *leporaria, therotrophia* and *avaria* in which hares, wild animals and birds were raised for the pleasures of the hunt. A replica of the same picture, evidently of Hellenistic origin, appears in the peristyle of the house of the Dioscuri in Pompeii a few decades later.

300

Other residential sites in Roman times: Baiae, villas of the Phlegrean Fields, Sorrento, the Bay of Gaeta

While the corpus of decorative sculptures from the Villa of the Papyrus scrolls has come down to us virtually intact, the Museum also contains statues and reliefs from other villas round the Bay of Naples and beyond which add significantly to our knowledge of the Roman villa culture. We have already referred to Baiae, the most famous resort, whose name is almost synonymous with the "villa way of life". The sculptures found there, regrettably more often than not by chance, are of the highest quality: the works chosen to be copied by the artisans working for the court and its *entourage* were, as we see from the casts found in Baiae, the greatest masterpieces of Greek art in the classical age.

Around Baiae the coastline was covered with villas, from Miseno to Bacoli (*Bauli*), along the *ripa puteolana*, where Cicero had one of his villas, and beyond Pozzuoli to Nisida (the villa of Marcus Brutus) and Posillipo, which we have already described. The correspondence of Cicero, Tacitus or Suetonius reveals just how cultured and refined life was in these aristocratic residences, but also not without its fair share of intrigues, conspiracies, pacts, torbid rivalries and tormented love affairs. Here Brutus and Cicero met in the former's villa on Nisida to discuss future action following the assassination of Caesar, and here too Nero plotted the murder of his mother Agrippina.

In addition to the Phlegrean villas we should recall those on the Sorrento peninsula, as far round as Amalfi, and those along the northern reaches of the Campanian coast, from Sinuessa to Sperlonga and Gaeta. The latter were connected to the large *praedia* or farmsteads which the Roman aristocracy and the Imperial court possessed in that area. From the Augustan age onwards, it is no exaggeration to say that every site on the shores of the sea and lakes of Campania which offered the promise of *amoenitas* was duly occupied by a villa of *otium* with its rich artistic decor.

Head of Apollo, from Baiae
inv. 153640

This head belongs to a statue type known from a series of replicas, the best and most famous of which was found in Athens near an *omphalos* on which it may have stood (hence the name of "Apollo of the omphalos" used by archaeologists for this type).

The sculpture, dating from ca. 470 B.C., is attributed to one or other of the major artists of the stern style, from Calamis to Myron. It was certainly a votive bronze in the style of the *kouroi*, and the pronounced bending of its powerful body gave it a very special allure.

This Baiae copy is of especially fine workmanship. It still echoes in its marble the vibrant quality of bronze sculpture, and maintains the delicate psychological characterisation of the eyes and mouth of the original.

Aphrodite Sosandra, from Baiae
inv. 153654

It is generally accepted that the prototype of this sculpture was a work in the stern style of ca. 470-460 B.C., viz. the Aphrodite Sosandra ("saviour of men"), one of Calamis' masterpieces. The writer Lucian tells us that this celebrated statue was veiled and had a "pure and venerable smile", and none of the few extant veiled statues displays a comparable majesty. The popularity of this original is attested by the over twenty replicas that have reached us, some reworked as portraits. The figure is constructed from the contrast between the ample luminous surfaces of the heavy cloak and the face, and the play of shadows under the outstretched hand and the hair. For works of this kind, one rightly speaks of "architectural drapery", of which Sosandra is doubtlessly the most refined example. The Neapolitan copy comes from the Thermae of Baiae.

Statue of the Borghese Hera type, from Baiae

inv. 150383

The style of the Attic school of the gene-ration following that of Phidias can be recognised in the virtuoso rendering of the "wet" drapery, endowing with sen-suality and grace this majestic figure of a goddess (Hera, Hygeia or Aphrodite, according to different hypotheses). The name of Agoracritus of Paros, a pupil of the great master, has been suggested for the creator of the type, certainly a famous work of the Classic age, as the numerous surviving copies bear out. The signature on the lower left hem of the cloak has preserved the name of the copyist, Aphrodisios of Athens, who must have been active either in an Athenian workshop or in a Baian branch of the same, to meet the great demand by the rich owners of Roman villas. The copy has been attributed to the Augustan age.

Aphrodite "Pudica", from Sinuessa
no number

This remarkable statue of the bathing Aphrodite was found in 1911 in a Roman villa on the hills overlooking ancient *Sinuessa*. Due to the masterful rendering of the naked female body, devoid of academic coldness, it is thought to be an original creation of 2nd century B.C. Hellenistic art. The "swallow-tail" rendering of the drapery in front is an archaistic mannerism. The sensual gesture of holding between clenched legs (and with the missing left hand) the falling dress, while the other hand attempts to hide the breast in the gesture of the "Pudica", is typical of the Hellenistic taste of that period. A less accomplished variant of the type is the Aphrodite from Pozzuoli (inv. 6295).

Colossal statues of the Dioscuri, from Baiae

inv. 131209

The model for these statues of the sons of Zeus ("*Dioskouroi*") and Leda with their horses (here reduced to mere busts emerging from the ground, as in a statue from the Campana collection, presently in the Louvre) was elaborated in the Hellenistic age on the basis of types created in the 5th century B.C. They are depicted naked, except for the chlamys slung over one shoulder, and armed with a sword. They wear the conical beret (*pilos*) assimilating them to the entities called Cabiri, the guardians of navigation. The parallel with the latter is a consequence of their identification with the constellation of the Twins, Castor and Pollux. The two sculptures were discovered, on separate occasions, in Baiae, in the area of the Thermae and near the so-called "Temple of Venus".

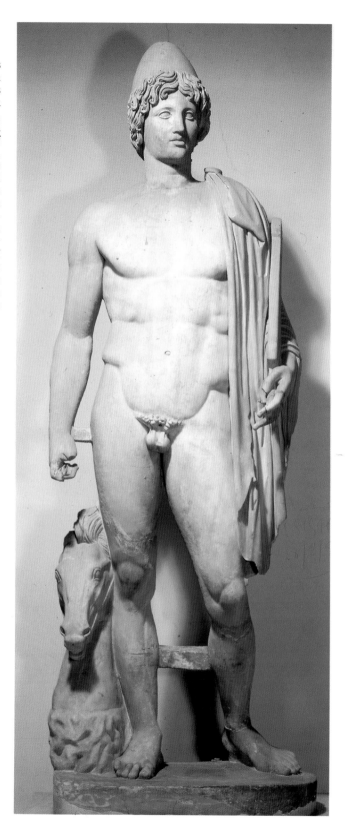

Eleusine marble relief, from Sinuessa
no number

The side-pillars and roof framing the scene identify the monument as a Greek votive relief, while the style of the figures and of the draperies dates it to the first decades of the 4th century B.C. It represents a scene of the cult of Demeter in Eleusis, from which this relief was very probably taken to be displayed, probably as a sign of appreciation of Greek art, in the Sinuessan villa of a Roman aristocrat, where it was found at the beginning of this century. From right to left are Triptolemos sitting on his winged and wheeled throne, then Persephone holding torches and Demeter wearing the *polos* and holding a sceptre. It is not clear who the other characters are. They could be members of a family learning the mysteries for which the sanctuary was renowned.

Marble crater by Salpion, from Gaeta
inv. 6673

The signature "Salpion the Athenian made" (*Salpion Athenaios epoiese*) incised on the body assigns this vase, made of Paros marble, to the Neo-Attic school. The object was famous from the 18th century onwards, being illustrated in the *Museum Carthaceum* by Cassiano dal Pozzo. It presumably comes from a villa on the Formia coast, and was used in the Middle Ages as a bitt in the port of Gaeta, then re-used, after being brutally reworked, as a baptismal font in the cathedral of the same city. In 1805 it finally reached the Museum.

The scene represents Hermes turning over the infant Dionysus, wrapped in a cloth and crowned with ivy, to the nymphs of Nysa who will raise him. Silenus, half-clad and also crowned with ivy, looks on, accompanied by two nymphs.

The peacefulness of this scene is contrasted with the other one on the left, featuring a Bacchic thyasus of dancing and playing Satyrs and Maenads. 1st century B.C.

308

The Farnese collection

The Farnese collection was the most famous of the antiques collections in Renaissance Rome. It was started by Alessandro Farnese, who in 1534 became Pope Paul III. At first he pursued the traditional papal policy of incrementing both the Vatican Museums, which were then taking shape round the courtyard of the Belvedere, and the Musei Capitolini (one of his actions was to transfer the equestrian statue of Marcus Aurelius to Campidoglio). In 1541 he began rebuilding work on a grand scale in his main Roman residence (Palazzo Farnese, nowadays occupied by the French Embassy), and at the same time initiated a new, private fashion for collecting antique works of art. He transferred the statues of the Dacian prisoners from Palazzo Colonna ai Santi Apostoli to his palace, after the defeat of the Colonna family by his son Pier Luigi. In about the same year he issued an edict which, contrary to contemporary legislation and indeed to a previous decree of his intended to benefit the construction of St Peter's, gave his family the right to excavate in order to obtain marble and stone, with an exclusive claim on all statues brought to light, for the construction and decoration of Palazzo Farnese. Thus in 1545 the famous Bull (*Toro Farnese*) was uncovered in the Baths of Caracalla, a year later the *Hercules* by Glykon, and so on for many other outstanding sculptures. One of the tasks of Michelangelo, who in 1546 was put in charge of the building work on the palace, was to design appropriate settings for these masterpieces.

The collection grew considerably through the efforts of the Pope's grandson Alessandro who was made cardinal at the tender age of 14 (and was known as the "great cardinal"). He was one of the leading patrons of the arts of his day. He engaged Vignola to restore the family residence at Caprarola, ordered the building of the Chiesa del Gesu, purchased Villa Chigi, later known as la Farnesina, and commissioned Titian to paint *Danae* and Giulio Clovio to paint the *Farnese Hours*. It was during his lifetime that the Farnese collection reached its maximum size. It benefited from bequests, as in 1587 with the inheritance of Margaret of Austria, "la Madama", formerly the widow of Alessandro dei Medici and subsequently of Ottavio Farnese (her collection included the famous gems once the property of Lorenzo dei Medici, such as the *Tazza Farnese,* and the marble statues from

Pergamon) and also from purchases carried out, between 1566 and 1589, with the judicious collaboration of the greatest antiquarian of the age, Fulvio Orsini. On the latter's death, in 1600, his collection too, comprising above all gems, coins and busts, was left to Odoardo Farnese.

This enormous quantity of marble sculptures, pictures, gems, books and drawings was mainly concentrated in Palazzo Farnese. In the courtyard, framed in the archways, stood the two statues of Hercules (that of Glykon and the so-called *Ercole Latino,* now at the Royal Palace in Caserta), a pair of statues of "*Flora*" and two *Gladiators,* one of them identified as Commodus. The *Bull* stood in the inner courtyard in a special enclosure, while a garden overlooking the Tiber was dedicated to the theme of love, with two statues of *Venus,* a *Pan and Olympus* and *Mercury embracing a Nymph.* Antique statues were distributed through the palace grouped according to subject, in the Great Hall, the Room of the Emperors, the Room of the Philosophers and the Gallery of the Carracci. Other sculptures considered of less value were kept in the other residences such as the Farnesina and in the famous gardens or *Horti Farnesiani* on the Palatine, created by Vignola.

The collection began to be dispersed in 1662 when Ranuccio II, Duke of Parma, took one hundred pictures from Palazzo Farnese and installed them in his residence in Parma, repeating the operation eleven years later with twenty-seven sculptures. In 1720 Duke Francesco undertook excavations on the Palatine Hill and for the first time the finds, including such outstanding colossal works as *Hercules* and *Bacchus* in basalt, were not displayed in Palazzo Farnese but went to the new family capital of Parma.

The dynasty came to an end in 1731, and its inheritance passed to the Bourbons through Elisabetta Farnese, wife of Philip V of Spain. On his arrival in Naples in 1734, Charles transferred the Parma collection to his new capital, and in 1770 his son Ferdinand made an explicit request to the Pope for permission to do the same with the Roman collections. Several years of diplomatic wrangling followed, but in 1787, in spite of the stipulation in the will of Alessandro that the collections were to remain in Rome *in perpetuum* and the vigorous protests of Pietro Ercole Visconti, the Keeper of Papal Antiques, the great removal began. The event was a trauma for Rome and for the world of culture in general. Goethe deprecated it, even though it was being supervised by his good friend Hackert. Today however, with the benefit of hindsight and knowledge of the great sales and depredations to which Roman collections fell victim in the nineteenth century (there is no doubt that, had the whole collection remained at Palazzo Farnese, the last Bourbons would not have spared it, for they showed no scruples about selling off the few pieces still left there), the removal can be considered a fortunate event which allowed the collection to be kept largely intact in Naples, so that we can still admire this remarkable achievement of the culture of Renaissance Italy.

The sculptures

The crowning glory of the Farnese collection are undoubtedly the sculptures, the most famous of which were brought out from the «quarry» opened up in 1545-46 on the Aventine Hill in the complex of the Baths of Caracalla. The same system of excavation had already been adopted by Ippolito d'Este at Villa Adriana in Tivoli and by the Della Valle brothers in the area of the Forum.

The Baths were built in a surprisingly short space of time, between 212 and 216 A.D., but this does not mean that all the sculptures date from the preceding reign of Severius. In fact they date from various periods, and were undoubtedly either purchased or removed from previous buildings and complexes. Their chief characteristic is their architectonic significance: the dimensions, composition and subject matter of the figures and groups were dictated by considerations of the overall appearance of the building.

Another aspect which is of great historical interest concerns the restoration they underwent, which in effect took place on two occasions. In the 1500s, before they were put on display in Palazzo Farnese, the task of cleaning (or refashioning) and integrating the fragments, which is what restoration was taken to mean in that period, was entrusted to various sculptors. In particular G.B. Bianchi worked on the *Bull* and G. Della Porta on the *Hercules*. A new round of restoration was necessary at the end of the 1700s in preparation for the move to Naples, entrusted to Carlo Albacini, but the damage suffered during the transportation made it necessary to carry out further work in Naples, and this was done by Cali, Brunelli and others.

Wounded hero
inv. 6410

The cloak hanging lightly over the right leg indicates that this sculpture is certainly patterned on a Greek bronze original datable, from the rendering of the anatomy, to the middle of the 5th century B.C. The wound on the thigh from which blood spurts out has often suggested parallels with the so-called *Vulneratus deficiens* (cf. p. 336).

In both cases, a wounded hero is represented, but the numerous possible alternatives (Protesilaos, Theseus, Hippolytus, Telephus etc.) make it impossible to identify him.

Aphrodite Callipygos

inv. 6020

The artistic quality of this sculpture, found in the area of the *Domus Aurea*, is observable in its ancient part, the lower one, while the head and shoulders are integrations by Albacini. The correctness of the restoration is at all events confirmed by comparisons with gems and bronzes, also indicating that it must have been a renowned work. Since Praxiteles, with his Cnidia, first unveiled the body of the goddess of beauty in the 4th century B.C., Hellenistic art explored every nuance of the theme of the naked female figure. The motif is here treated with the mischievous and light taste of the so-called Hellenistic "rococò" of the 2nd century B.C., and the idyllic theme of the fountain becomes a pretext for the goddess' nudity. Aphrodite, about to bathe, raises her dress and turns her head back to admire the reflection on the water of her splendid posterior nudity, justifying perhaps the modern name of *kallipygos* ("of the beautiful buttocks") erroneously attributed to this statue while it actually refers to a famous statue in a temple in Syracuse.

314

Statue of a fallen giant
inv. 6013
All the numerous replicas of the figures of Amazons, Giants, Persians and Galatians forming the group known as "Small Pergamene Donary" are made of Asiatic marble.
The original was erected on the Acropolis of Athens (on the balustrade on the side overlooking the Theatre of Dionysus) by Attalus II of Pergamon after his victorious war against the Gauls in 165 B.C., and copies were placed near the Pergamon altar.
The sculpture celebrated the glory of the Attalides in the baroque language of the Pergamene style, but with hints of classicism.

Kneeling Persian
inv. 6115
Its trousers (*anassirides*), mitra and long- sleeved tunic characterise this figure as a Persian prisoner, kneeling down to serve as a telamon and symbolising the Roman victories over the Parthians. The use of coloured marble is typical of figures of exotic characters and alludes to the remote countries where this exotic stone was quarried.
One of the two twin statues was in the Del Bufalo collection.
Age of Trajan.

316

Bust of Homer
inv. 6023

Portraits of Homer naturally belong to the category of reconstructed portraits. This means that the artist, or rather, the many artists who measured themselves with this theme, strove to project in the portrait what tradition had for centuries built up around the mythical figure of this venerable blind bard. Since the Homeric poes were the foundation of Greek education, the portrait of the poet was one of the most popular of the Classic period, and was displayed in sanctuaries and libraries, such as the celebrated *Homereion* of Alexandria, a key centre for the cult and studies of Homer in the Hellenistic age. Widely circulating products such as coins, gems and, presumably, illustrations of the volumes of Homeric works, lost to us, also contributed to its diffusion.

This Farnesian portrait is one of the most perfect examples of a Hellenistic type of the 2nd century B.C. Its emphasis on the most realistic aspects, such as the hollow cheeks, the parched skin and the unkempt hair and beard, indicate that it probably was a creation of the Rhodian school.

Portrait of Euripides
inv. 6135

Its inscription identifies this herm as a portrait of the Greek tragedian of the 5th century B.C. Its prototype, a seated statue, as a replica in Istanbul bears out, dates from the second half of the 4th century B.C. In this period, Lysippus and his followers created a trend aiming at a psychologic and spiritual interpretation of the portrayed subject. Another portrait of the tragedian, called "Rieti", is identified by the Euripidean verses inscribed on its base, and is possibly a replica of the statue erected by Lycurgus in the theatre of Dionysus in Athens. It is more realistic and has a more fleshy face, and dates from a slightly earlier period.

318

Herm of Socrates
inv. 6415

According to the descriptions of Xenophon, Socrates was rather stocky, with broad shoulders and a protruding belly, a massive face with a squat nose and a wide mouth with thick lips. All in all, not what one would call an elegant physique; the philosopher himself would joke on his appearance, defining it "Silenic". Diogenes Laertius reports that, long after his death, the Athenians entrusted Lysippus with the fabrication of a bronze seated statue of the philosopher, and placed it in the *Pompeion*. Lysippus allegedly emphasised this rather coarse appearance, projecting onto it the new significance that the Dionysiac cultural trend was taking on in contemporary Athens.

This Farnesian herm is a replica of this Lysippean type (another, a standing statue, existed).

On its pillar it bears an ancient quotation from Plato's *Cratilus*: "not today for the first time, but always it has been my custom to submit my will to nothing else of myself but the force of what seems to me to be the best reasoning".

Athena

inv. 6024

This sculpture, formerly in the Albani
collection, derives from a prototype of
the second half of the 4th century B.C.
The majesty of the figure and its serene
face have led some scholars to attribute
it to Phidias' pupil Agoracritus of Paros.

So-called Agrippina
inv. 6029

The type derives from a female statuette of a goddess, probably an Aphrodite of the middle of the 5th century B.C. attributed to Phidias or Alcamenes. In spite of its rigidity, this Roman copy recalls the seated figure of the pediment of the Parthenon. A portrait head of the Flavian period, recognisable from its typical curly-haired coiffure, has been imposed on the Classic type.

Claudius
inv. 6060
The bust is modern. The intensely pathetic head belongs to the main type adopted for portraits of this emperor, with the civic wreath ideologically alluding to the legacy of Augustus.

Flavian lady
inv. 6062
The high coiffure with snail-shaped curls, contrasting with the polished female face, well expresses the colourful taste of the Flavian age.

6062
DAMA ROMANA
ГАВНЕЦ

Roman lady
inv. 6085
This bust of a lady of the Severian age (first half of the 3rd century A.D.) is a precious example of coloured marble sculpture. The draped bust is of "cotognino" alabaster, imported from Egypt. The head, presenting the typical coiffure of the period, is delicately inclined to one side.

324

The cooking of the boar
inv. 6218

The scene of the cooking of the boar, placed whole in the great cauldron, evidently belongs to the "genre" repertory of middle Hellenism (2nd century B.C.). In Roman times, such compositions (like the dogs attacking the boar from Pompeii) were highly appreciated as garden ornaments.

Artemis Ephesia
inv. 6286

Callimachus, in his *Hymn to Diana*, narrates that it was the Amazons who instituted the cult of Artemis in Ephesos. Indeed, since the time of the ancient kings of Lydia, this cult enjoyed great favour in Asia, and its sanctuary still flourished in the Roman Imperial period. The cult image of the goddess, of which countless replicas of every conceivable format and material exist, is only known to us from the Hellenistic age, especially through images on coins minted in Ephesos. The goddess wears the *kalathos*, sometimes temple-shaped. The drapery hanging around this headdress is folded back on the head to form a sort of circular nimbus, sometimes decorated on the sides with gryphon protomae. The dress of the goddess teems with ornaments: on the breast, she wears a necklace, under which several rows of breasts protrude, an evident symbol of fecundity (they have also been identified as the scrotums of sacrificial bulls), while the lower part, clinging to the body, is decorated by rows of animal protomai and bees, flowers, sphinxes and nymphs. The arms are stretched forward, and held a ribbon falling vertically. Although the general type of the figure recalls the geometrism of Archaic female statues, the symbolism of the ornaments is typical of the Hellenistic period, when the ancient cult statue was probably re-elaborated.

Kneeling Aphrodite with Eros
inv. 6293

In the 4th century B.C., the image of female beauty embodied in the figure of Aphrodite left the Olympus of the gods to take on a sensual and languorous humanity. The theme of the naked goddess at her bath, inaugurated by Praxiteles' Cnidia, acquires a more realistic and earthly allure in the kneeling figure of Aphrodite executed by Doedalsas, a sculptor from Bithinia, for the king Nicomedes. The statue was brought to Rome, where it became famous, and was often copied to decorate gardens and, of course, thermae.

Dionysus

inv. 6318

Its thoughtful attitude, recalling Praxiteles' manner, has suggested a date in the 4th century B.C. for the original of this sculpture. The number of known replicas indicates it was a famous type. This statue belonged to Lorenzo the Magnificent, and was later placed in the celebrated Gallery of the Carracci in Palazzo Farnese.

Pan and Daphnis (or Olympus)
inv. 6329

The erotic-idyllic theme places the original of this work in the middle Hellenistic period. This date is to some extent supported by the Plinian mention of a Pan and Olympus sculpted by Heliodorus, who was active in Rome in Pliny's time. That work was, however, a *symplegma* or erotic struggle, while this is a peaceful scene of *paideia*, like the *Achilles and Chiron* from Herculaneum (p. 119).

Atlas

inv. 6374

Of the surviving ancient representations of the Zodiac, this is one of the most complete. It depicts the vault of heaven on the shoulders of the Farnesian Atlas, and probably was originally part of the decoration of the library of the Forum of Trajan. Several replicas exist, indicating that the original was a famous Hellenistic statue.

We may imagine that it was created in a great Hellenistic scientific centre, like the Museum of Alexandria.

Antinous
inv. 6030

Antinous was the Bithynian youth loved by Hadrian. His death in Egypt in 130 A.D. was followed, especially in the Oriental provinces, by his heroisation and cult. His birthday, on November 27, was honoured with a feast. For the needs of this ephemerous cult, which did not survive the reign of Hadrian, the classicist sculptors of the imperial court, especially those of the school of Aphrodisia, produced a number of ephebic statuettes inspired by Apollo and Dionysus types of the 5th century B.C. The Farnesian specimen from Naples, whose provenance is unknown, is certainly one of the best for the extraordinary softness of its contours and the romantic allure of the contrast between the terse lustre of the body and the chiaroscuro of the hair, falling in thick hooked locks.

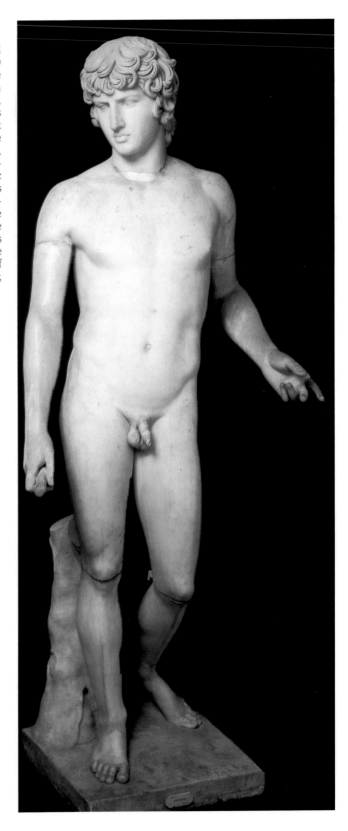

331

The province of Parthia
inv. 6757

A year after the death of Hadrian in 138 A.D., Antoninus Pius had the ashes of his predecessor taken from Puteoli, where he had been buried, to the Mausoleum of Hadrian (Castel Sant'Angelo). Six years later, in 145, he dedicated the temple of the divine Hadrian in the Campus Martius. The building was in the classicist style of the age of Hadrian.

Its architectural order and the decoration of the cella were of Proconnesian marble quarried in the island of Marmara in Crimea (Propontis), used in Rome for the first time in the temple of Venus and Rome, under Hadrian. A series of plinths with personifications of the provinces decorated the podium or the interior of the cella. Of the 38 original figures, only 16 remain, in several collections.

The new conception of the provinces is especially remarkable: no longer afflicted *captivae*, they are majestic and solemn, as they now enjoy equal status within the Empire, an anticipation of the full citizenship soon to be granted to all provincials.

332

Farnesian Hercules, from Rome, Baths of Caracalla
inv. 6001

A work of the Athenian sculptor Glykon, whose signature (*Glykon Athenaios epoiesen*; "Glykon of Athens made") can be read on the rock under the club, this statue is a gigantic replica of a bronze sculpture by Lysippus, one of the masters of the 4th century B.C.

The thoughtful, almost melancholy figure of the hero, after his latest labour, that of the apples of the Hesperides (which he is holding in his right hand behind his back), contrasts with the tradition of the Archaic and Classic period, in which the hero was active, triumphing in his strength. The lively and colourful style of the copyist suggests he dates from the Severian period.

When the statue was found, its left arm was missing (the present one is a plaster restoration), as were its legs, which were redone by Guglielmo della Porta. When the original legs were found, some time after, those by della Porta were reputed superior to them, and the work was left as it was until Albacini's restoration. Della Porta's legs are now on exhibit near the original ones. This sculpture was paired in the Baths, and later in the court of the Palazzo Farnese, with another replica of the same type, the so-called *Latin Hercules*, sent in 1788 to the Reggia di Caserta.

Farnesian Bull, from Rome, Baths of Caracalla
inv. 6002

This group, found in the gymnasium of the thermae, represents the punishment of Dirce who, having inflicted several torments on Antiope, is punished by the latter's sons, Amphion and Zethus, who tie her to the legs of the mad bull which is about to mangle her. A famous work representing this subject is mentioned in the sources as a masterpiece of the Rhodian sculptors Apollonius and Tauriscus of the end of the 2nd century B.C. Asinius Pollio brought it from Rhodes to Rome. The Farnesian group has been interpreted in various ways, as the original, as a replica of the Julio-Claudian period, more recently and, in my opinion, more convincingly, as a replica of the Severian period. A comparison with painted replicas shows, at all events, that this copy maintains the pyramidal composition of the original, although accessory figures have been added, such as Antiope and a shepherd personifying Mount Cithaeron, where the event takes place. The group underwent substantial restoration in the 16th century, when Michelangelo planned to use it for a fountain to be installed at the centre of a garden between Palazzo Farnese and the Farnesina villa. In Naples, the group was placed on the Real Passeggio of Chiaia, before being moved, with the other sculptures, to the Museum in 1826.

Group of a warrior with a child, from Rome, Baths of Caracalla
inv. 5999
The statue, much restored in the 16th century, bears a modern head of the emperor Commodus erroneously imposed upon it by restorers. It originally represented a heroic theme, a warrior in the act of hurling away a wounded youth, held by the foot.

There are several possible interpretations: Neoptolemos killing the little Astyanax (see description on p. 25), Achilles and Troilus, Athamas and Leander.
In Palazzo Farnese, it stood in the courtyard. Having reached Naples in 1787, it was exhibited on the Real Passeggio of Chiaia (the present-day Villa Comunale) before being moved to the Museum in 1826. Severian age.

Vulneratus deficiens, from Rome, Baths of Caracalla

inv. 6416

The rendering of the naked figure of this statue, formerly in the Della Valle collection, is of exquisite quality. There are considerable difficulties in identifying the type of the sculpture and attributing it. Its identification with the *vulneratus deficiens*, in its turn identified with the statue of the strategus Ditrephes, has been rejected, but no better one has been put forward. It is evidently a figure of a wounded warrior (as indicated by the blood streaming out of the wound), about to collapse on his already shaky knees. The original is datable to ca. 460 B.C.

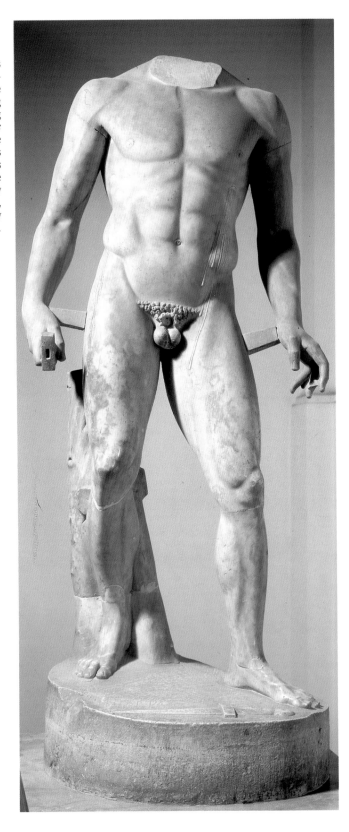

Flora Farnese, so-called Flora Maggiore

inv. 6409

A drawing by Marten van Heemskerck, a Dutch artist who worked in Rome between 1532 and 1536, reproduces the two Florae (this one and the following one) before restoration. We are hence sure that they do not come – as is often said – from the Baths of Caracalla, whose excavation only began in 1545.

The statue, whose provenance is unknown, is a Roman re-elaboration of Hellenistic statue-types, traceable, in their turn, to an Athenian Aphrodite of the end of the 5th century B.C.

It was restored as Flora to pair it with the following sculpture. The 16th century restoration equipped it with a garland, which was replaced in the 19th century by a bouquet.

The head is of plasters, and is inspired by other ancient female heads in Roman collections.

Farnese Flora (or Pomona)
inv. 5978
This sculpture, whose provenance is
unknown, is inspired by Greek models of
the second half of the 5th century B.C. It
was restored as Flora, due to the flowers
it wears on its cloak. It was a *pendant*
to the more famous sculpture of the preceding page in Palazzo Farnese.

The gems of the Farnese collection

Gems were among the first ancient objects to re-emerge from antiquity, thanks to the interest of collectors, and were featured, from the Middle Ages onwards, in the main royal and ecclesiastic treasures. They were often collected as talismans, and became the object of renewed worship. Their ancient iconographies were re-elaborated from a Christian religious perspective, according to peculiar blessing formulas, and their mythical figures were reinterpreted as Christian subjects, with *Poseidon and Athena* as Adam and Eve, *Caracalla* as the Baptist, the scene of *Leda and the Swan* (an onyx cameo formerly in the Barbo collection) as the Annunciation, *Perseus and Andromeda* as David and Goliath. The passion for ancient gems became a conspicuous cultural phenomenon in the Renaissance. One of the largest collections, later to be incorporated in the Farnese corpus, was put together by the Venetian Pietro Barbo, Cardinal of St. Mark, and Pope from 1464 onwards with the name of Paul II, an enthusiastic collector. His corpus was displayed in the Palazzo San Marco in Rome, later to be called Palazzo Venezia. Later on, part of it entered the papal collections, while another part was donated to the Medici by Sixtus V. On the death of the latter, a rumour went around that he had been strangled by one of the demons contained in the bezels of his rings, obviously to stigmatise the immense sums of money he spent to satisfy his passion for ancient gems, which were thought to possess diabolical powers, according to an enduring Medieval belief. The Medici collection, started by Cosimo the Elder, was also renowned. We owe the first testimony of its existence to Lorenzo Ghiberti, the Florentine sculptor, who reports having made a setting for the carnelian of *Apollo, Marsyas and Olympus*, presently in Naples. His interesting description epitomises Humanist culture: "these three figures...were certainly by the hand of Pyrgotiles or Polychretus; they were as perfect as any intaglio work I ever saw". If Cosimo's passion for gems was great, that of his nephew Lorenzo was possibly even greater. In his autobiography he writes that when, at the age of twenty-two, he went to Rome on an embassy, gems were foremost among the trophies he procured "...furthermore, I brought our engraved chalcedony bowl [the Farnese cup] with many other cameos and medals

that were bought at that time, including the chalcedony... [*Diomedes stealing the Palladion*]". The most prestigious works of the treasure of Lorenzo de' Medici were inscribed with a proud *ex gemmis LAVR. MED*. Of course, these Renaissance collections were put together to serve as treasures, as well as repositories of culture and prestige. When finances were low, credit could surely be obtained from banks at favourable conditions by pawning precious stones, especially since their value kept going up – indeed, the cameo with *Poseidon and Athena*, estimated at 180 florins in 1465, only 27 years later was worth 800. The collection of Fulvio Orsini (1528-1600) is one of the most remarkable of the corpuses later to be incorporated by the Farnesian collection and by other nuclei now in foreign museums. This renowned scholar, who was the librarian of Paolo III Farnese, bequeathed to the family his personal collection, mainly composed of incised gems and medals bought from other collectors (de Marii, San Marsale, the Bishop of Spoleto), from the Roman goldsmiths of via del Pellegrino, or directly at the market of Campo de' Fiori, where peasants sold the antiquities they happened to discover in the bountiful soil of Rome and its surroundings. Orsini's collection, besides including some especially remarkable pieces (*The torch-bearing Artemis, Hercules*), is of great historiographical significance, as its gems, coupled with other categories of monuments, notably statues and coins, were used as a source for the reconstruction of the features of the most celebrated men of antiquity. In fact, Orsini is rightfully remembered as the founder of iconography, through his works *Illustrium imagines ex antiquis marmoribus ex bibliotheca Fulvii Ursini* and *Familiae romanae in antiquis numismatibus...* Another interesting feature of the Farnese collection are the gems imitating ancient models. The great demand for gems stimulated a new production of pieces in the style of the ancients and, of course, the creation of many forgeries. We are familiar with the names of some Roman engravers of the time, such as Cesare, Domenico, Ludovico, all called "de' cammei" ("of the cameos"). These works are very faithful imitations of their prototypes, and it is often quite difficult to tell an ancient gem from a well-made Renaissance one.

Agate-sardonyx cameo, so-called
Farnesian Cup, from the Medici
collection
inv. 27611

This is certainly the most celebrated cameo
to have come down to us from antiquity.
On the outside of the cup, obtained from a
single great stone, is an exquisite relief
image of the Medusa. Inside eight characters are grouped to form an allegorical
scene set in Egypt, as revealed by the
presence at the bottom of a sphinx seen in
profile on which an Isis is seated. According to the most widely approved interpretation, which goes back to Ennio
Quirino Visconti and then to Furtwängler,
the scene is a celebration of the fertility of
the Nile.

The main character, the old man sitting
on the throne on the left, draped and
holding the cornucopia, is thought to be
the river itself. He is greeting Triptolemos,
the first to cultivate grain, thanks to the
teachings of Demeter. The *Horai* and the
Etesian winds flying overhead complete
the scene. The chronology is no less
problematic, and varies according to the
proposed identification of the historical
characters, the various Lagide rulers who
succeeded one another on the throne of
Alexandria, thought to lie behind the
allegories of the mythological figures. At
all events, it is certain that this exceptional
object, whose value was estimated at the
enormous sum of 10,000 florins as early
as the 15th century, was made to order for

the royal Ptolemaic court between the 2nd and 1st century B.C. The object must have subsequently entered the Roman imperial treasure. Its traces are then lost in the darkness of the Middle Ages, before re-emerging in Rome, where Lorenzo the Magnificent acquired it in 1471.

From a Persian drawing of the 15th century reproducing it, it seems it must have been in the Orient at this time, possibly in Herat or Samarcanda, but some recently rediscovered documents indicate that, in the 12th century, the cup was very probably in Italy, where it was bought by the Emperor Frederick II.

Athens and Poseidon, sardonyx-onyx cameo, from the Medici collection
inv. 25837

The letters *Py* incised at the bottom suggests that this work could be attributed to a *Pyrgoteles* of the late Hellenistic age. This famous cameo depicts the scene of the competition between Poseidon and Athena for the rule of Athens at the time of the mythical king Cecrops. Poseidon created a salt-water fountain, the "sea of Erechtheus", while the gift of Athena was an olive tree. A version of the myth narrates that the Athenians, thanks to womens' participation in the vote, chose the goddess' gift, and the city was named after her. Between the two deities there is the olive tree and a snake (in which Cecrops or the child Erichthonius became incarnate), both kept in the Erechtheum in the Classic age.

Head of Hercules, sardonyx-onyx cameo, from the Medici collection inv. 25851
On the grounds of its exquisite craftsmanship, its style and the iconographic motif of the isolated head seen in profile, this work has been attributed to *Gnaios*, an engraver of the Alexandrine school of the Augustan age. It is a magnificent three-layer cameo in which the two colours of the stone are used to highlight the white profile of the face of the hero on the dark background and the dark, white-bordered *leonté* on his hair.

Centaur, sardonyx cameo, from the
Medici collection
inv. 25889
This splendid gem bears the amber- and
honey-coloured figure of a centaur carrying a crater on his shoulder, silhouetted
against a white background. It has been
attributed to the Roman classicist trend of
the 2nd century B.C. through the comparison with some representations of centaurs such as those of Aristeas and Papias
in the Capitoline Museums.

Apollo, Marsyas and Olympus, carnelian intaglio, from the Medici collection
inv. 26051
This intaglio (unfortunately broken in 1972) has been attributed to the famous Dioskourides, Augustus' favourite engraver and the author of Caesar's portrait.

The quality of the stone and of its workmanship make it one of the best pieces in the Medici collection.
It represents the myth of the famous competition between Apollo and Marsyas, that ended in the satyr's torture and death, in spite of young Olympus's pleading.

344

Satyr with the child Dionysus, sardonyx-agate cameo
inv. 25880

The child Dionysus playing with the Satyrs on the hills of Nysa where the Nymphs raised him became one of the favourite themes of Classic art from the 4th century B.C. onwards. A renowned example is Praxiteles' Hermes with the child Dionysus in Olympia. In the Augustan classicist revival, the theme became popular once again, as many decorative objects of this period bear out.

The syrinx and shepherd's crook laid on the stone allude to the rural nature of the divine being.

One of the signs of the fortune of this gem in the Renaissance is its faithful reproduction on a marble medallion in the courtyard of the Palazzo Medici Riccardi in Firenze, made by Donatello's workshop. 1st century B.C.

Zeus on his quadriga striking the Giants with lightning, niccolite cameo, from the Orsini collection
inv. 25848

The engraver Athenion, whose signature appears on this cameo, also signed another one with a similar Athena on a quadriga. Its vigorous and baroque style, as well as its Hellenistic political propagandistic motifs, suggest a date between the 3rd and 2nd century B.C.

346

Artemis with torches, amethyst intaglio, from the Orsini collection inv. 26070

It is a moot point whether the Apollonios whose signature appears on this magnificent gem, depicting Artemis dressed as a hunter, with lowered torches, is also the author of a granate from Kerc, in Crimea, with a portrait of Asandros, a king of Ponto of the second half of the 1st century B.C. As the letters are somewhat different and rather worn, it might be another artist.

At all events, this work, in which the softness of the Hellenistic contours harmonises with the terse language of the Augustan age, is probably to be dated in the same period as the other one, which it resembles in style as well.

347

Antoninus Pius, from the Orsini collection
inv. 26088
The emperor is here represented in his maturity, in the attitude of a Greek philosopher. The soft and very fine rendering of the beard and hair of the emperor is typical of the pictorial style of the period. Gems with imperial protraits were one of the favourite themes of the Orsini collections, and still provide important chronological landmarks for the study of the artistic evolution of Roman glyptics.

The epigraphic collection

Although the most recent museographic tendency is to reconstruct the original archaeological contexts of the objects on exhibition, the epigraphic collection of the Naples Museum still deserves to be maintained and displayed as a whole, due to the crucial role it played in the history of epigraphy (one has only to think of the exemplary value of Theodor Mommsen's *Inscriptiones Regni Neapolitani*) and the significance of its documents. In fact, it is one of the most important Greek and Roman epigraphic collections in the world. Its original nucleus is the Farnese corpus, mainly consisting of the collection put together by Fulvio Orsini, the Farnese's librarian, a scholar of repute in the field of antiquarian studies and ancient iconography. After the Farnese collection was brought to Naples, it was joined by other important corpuses of inscriptions, some from private collections, e.g. the Borgia collection, mainly formed of objects found in Latium and Umbria (including an especially remarkable group of Etruscan inscriptions), the collection of the 18th century scholar Francesco Daniele (1740-1820) with a special interest in numismatics and Campanian epigraphs, of which he collected several specimens (this Museo Casertano, visited by many foreign scholars, possessed over one thousand *"marmi letterati"* from Capua, Telese, Sant'Agata dei Goti, Calvi, Teano etc., besides vases and various other ancient objects), and the collection of the great antiquarian *monsignor* Carlo Maria Rosini (1748-1836). The Museum also acquired the corpuses of De Jorio, Castaldi, Crisci, Bruschi, Piscopo, Novi, Barone (the latter also gave the Museum the epigraphic collection of the College of Jesuits), Arditi, Fusco, Sangiorgio. Most of the inscriptions, however, come from the numerous excavations and occasional finds made from the 18th century to the present day in Campania and in the regions of Southern Italy belonging to the Reign of the Two Sicilies. A large number of inscriptions were found in the excavation of the Vesuvian sites, providing a thorough picture of the essential function of written documents in the public and private life of Roman cities. Some of these documents are especially rare, e.g. the wax tablets with the registration of loans from the archive of the Pompeian banker L.

Caecilius Iocundus, providing us with a view of the micro-economical life of the city. Many more written texts came to light in the Vesuvian cities, e.g. the electoral "posters" and the announcements of gladiator games. These graffiti painted on plaster document aspects of public and private life rarely attested elsewhere. The epigraphs in the pre-Roman languages of central-southern Italy, including inscriptions in Etruscan, Oscan (many from Pompeii), Vestine, Volscan etc., are also of extreme importance, as are the numerous Greek inscriptions from the colonies of Southern Italy, bearing witness to the variety of the dialects and alphabets that the colonists brought over from the different regions of their homeland, and to the long duration of the Hellenisation of the peninsula (in Naples, Greek remained the official language to the end of the Roman Empire).

Epigraphs give us extremely accurate knowledge of the most disparate aspects of ancient societies. Especially valuable information is provided by inscribed laws, decrees, and public and private documents in general, direct reflections of the forms of political and administrative organization of the different communities that succeeded one another in Italy and in the ancient world. The Naples Museum has one of the most significant corpuses of this kind, including the renowned epigraphs known as the "Heraclea tablets", the *Tabula Bantina*, the *Lex Acilia repetundarum* and the *Lex agraria* of 111 B.C., written on the two sides of the same bronze slab, the *Lex Cornelia de XX Quaestoribus* of 81 B.C. on the composition of the Senate, the *Lex Antonia de Termessibus* of 71 B.C. on fiscal privileges granted to the city of *Termessos maior* in Asia Minor. Further documents containing interesting data on the political, administrative and religious structure of the Roman state include sacred dedications, calendars (a famous specimen is the Farnesian *Menologium rusticum Colotianum*), military diplomata, milestones and centuriation cippi (famous examples of the latter include the Gracchan cippi and the one for the colony of Capua founded by Caesar in 58 B.C.). Even the simpler funerary inscriptions provide clues to the understanding of major social phenomena, reflected in the form and structure of proper names.

Palaeosabellic inscription, from
Bellante (Teramo)
inv. 111434
This funerary stele, an ovoid cippus, was
found in 1875. It depicts the deceased in
the pose of the famous warrior of Cape-
strano (Chieti Museum), even in the stylised
rendering of the legs. It is therefore datable
to the middle of the 6th century B.C. The
text spiralling around the figure is one of
the most ancient written documents in the
Sabellic language.

350

Terracotta stele, from San Mauro Forte
inv. 112880

This small earthenware pyramid, bearing on its four sides a metrical inscription in Achaean characters, is one of the most ancient documents of Metapontum. The text is a dedication of a ceramist to Hercules (525-500 B.C.).

The artisan Nicomachus writes in elegiac distichs: *"chaire, wanax Erakles, o toi kerameus m'anetheke, Nikomachos m'epoe dos d'e w'in anthropis doxan echen agathan"*, i.e. "Hail, Hercules, lord, the ceramist dedicated me. Nicomachus made me. Let him enjoy fame among men".

The text is all the more interesting because, in recent years, excavations have revealed the site of the Kerameikos (the vase-making quarter) of the city, documenting the lively activity of these and others artisans.

351 Votive cippus, from Locri
inv. 2482

The inscription, which can be dated to the first half of the 5th century B.C. (475-450), contains the name of the dedicators (*Oiniadas kai Eukelados kai Xeimaros*) and an offering formula to the goddess (*anethekan tai theoi*). It doubtlessly comes from the sanctuary of Persephone. The cult of the goddess in Locri was extremely popular, as Diodorus Siculus tells us (XXVII,4,3) and as famous Locrian *pinakes* bear out.

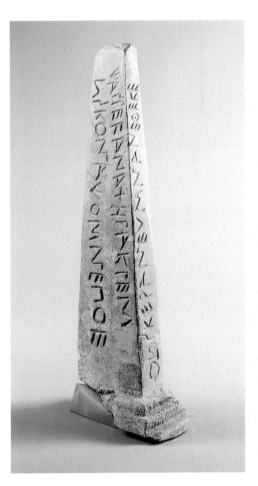

Heraclea tablets

inv. 2481

These two bronze tablets were found on the bed of a creek between 1732 and 1735 in present-day Acinapura, between Heraclea and Metapontum in Basilicata, and eventually came into the possession of Charles III of Bourbon. They bear two inscriptions from the end of the 4th or beginning of the 3rd century B.C. concerning the delimitation and location of some lands, the property of the sanctuaries of Dionysus and Athena Polias in the territory (*chora*) of Heraclea. These plots had been illegally occupied by privates, and then reedeemed. The texts, written in a Doric dialect with strong Attic influences, contain information of all kinds. The wealth of data on the rural economy of the Greek colonies of Ionian Lucania is especially remarkable. Thus, we learn that farmers practiced a five-year rotation, and that the main crops included emmer, wheat, barley, grapes and olives (the latter are also documented by archaeological excavations). Barley was especially important, as the tablets show that rents were paid in measures of barley instead of money. Thus the city had a currency independent of the oscillations of the market.

On the following page:

Orphic laminae from Thurii

invv. 111623, 111624, 111625 from Timpone Piccolo; 111463, 11464 from Timpone Grande (in Favella della Corte).

These two groups of inscribed gold laminae from 4th century B.C. burials found in the territory of *Thurii* belong to a class of Greek inscriptions found in the tombs of Great Greece, in Crete and in Thessaly, containing instructions whose purpose was to lead the souls of the deceased, initiates of a mysteric doctrine going back to Orpheus, to their final promised destiny of eternal blessing at the end of their cycle of reincarnations. These *Thurii* texts belong to a plebeian mysteric sect which had some knowledge of the Orphic-Pythagoric orthodoxy. The text of the longest of the inscriptions kept in Naples (inv. 111625) recites: "I come among the pure (*katharoi*), o pure queen of the Nether world (Persephone), Eukles [Ades] and Eubuleus [Dionysus] and you other immortal numens; in fact I declare myself to belong to your blessed lineage. But Destiny (*Moira*) and the thunderbolt-throwing celestial Bowman (*Asterobleta*) tamed me. I flew away from the painful cycle,

heavy with care, and ascended to the coveted crown with quick feet. I plunged into the lap of the queen of the Nether world, I descended from the coveted crown with quick feet. Oh, you happy and very blessed one, you shall be a numen instead of a mortal (*theòs d'esei antì brotoio*). Like a kid, I rushed toward the milk".

Volscan inscription, from Velletri, Borgia collection

inv. 2522

This inscription on bronze lamina, possibly to be dated to the 4th century B.C., before the battle of Astura in 338 B.C., was found in 1784, and is still the main document of the language of the Volscans. The text, which presents analogies with Umbrian, contains ritual prescriptions for sacrifices to a goddess named *Declona* issued by two local *meddices* whose names would sound thus in Latin: *Egnatius, Cossutius* the son of *Sextus*, and *Maras Tafanius*, the son of *Caius*. The inscription doubtlessly comes from a sanctuary in the Volscan centre of *Velcester* (later *Velitrae*).

Tabula Bantina, from Oppido Lucano
(Potenza)
inv. 2554
This tablet, found in 1793, contains on
one side an Oscan law of the 1st century
B.C., thought to be the statute of the city of
Bantia, and on the other, passages of a
Latin law, possibly a *"lex repetundarum"*
of the time of the Gracchi.

Solar clock, from Pompeii

inv. 2541

This meridian, found in the Stabian Thermae, bears an Oscan inscription on its base commemorating the circumstances of its installation:

"Maras Atinis, the son of Maras, a quaestor (*kvaisstur*) erected by decree of the assembly (*kumbennis*) with the money from fines". Solar clocks, a Greek invention, were a novelty in the Italic world. The first one was brought to Rome from Catane in 263 B.C., but it was only in 164 B.C. that the censor Marcius Philippus commissioned the first *horologium* calibrated for the latitude of Rome.

Lex parieti faciendo, from Pozzuoli
inv. 3231
This inscription is the first document of the relations between Campania and Ptolemaic Egypt and of the presence in Italy of Egyptian cults. It is dated to 105 B.C. (*ab colonia deducta anno XC*, as the first line of the text specifies, a date

confirmed by the mention of the consuls *P. Rutilius* and *Cn. Mallius* in the third line). It explicitly attests the presence, in this period, of a temple of Serapis (*in area quae est ante aedem Serapi...*) in the Phlegraean city, which had become the most important port in the Western Mediterranean.

Bembine tablet, bronze, Farnese collection
inv. Fiorelli 78
Other pieces of this great *tabula*, recomposed from seven fragments possibly found in Rome before 1521, were dispersed all over Europe. On the recto is a text, a "lost-wax" casting, of the *lex agraria* of 111 B.C., on the verso the *lex Acilia pecuniarum repetendarum* of 110 or 123/122 B.C., against peculation.

Military diploma, from Stabiae
inv. Fiorelli 1149

This inscription, dated by the mention of the consul of the year and of the Imperial titles of the time of Claudius to 49 A.D., is a diploma of *honesta missio*, i.e. certifying honourable military service, in this case issued to sea-captains (*trierarchae*) and to the sailors who had done their service on the *classis praetoria* in Miseno at the orders of *Ti. Iulius Optatus*. Through the service,

these people, most of them foreigners from the provinces of the Mediterranean coasts (Egyptian, Syrians, Illyrians etc.; those mentioned in this diploma are from Durazzo), earned Roman citizenship and the *ius connubi*, i.e. the right to contract a legal wedding the children of which would enjoy citizenship. The inscription was an extract of an original placed on the Campidoglio, on the right side of the temple of the *Fides populi Romani*.

Calendar of festivals, from Santa Maria Capua Vetere

inv. 3954

This inscription, found in the excavation of the Campanian amphitheatre in 1829, is incised on the top of an altar with dosserets decorated by an elegant flower motif. The text, certainly much later than the altar itself, is dated to 387 A.D. by the mention of the third consulate of Valentinianus, and contains a list of the main religious festivals of late Roman Capua, or possibly of the province of Campania. It is remarkable that, only a few years after the edict of Costantinus, all the feasts of pagan gods have already been cancelled. On January 3, one makes solemn vows for the health of the Emperor (*vota*); on February 11, the *Genialia* are celebrated; on May 1, a purification ceremony on the Volturnum takes place at *Casilinum (lustratio ad flumen)* and, on July 25, another *ad iter Dianae (Tifatinae)*; on May 13, the *Rosaria* (for the dead) in the amphitheatre; on the 27th of the same month a ceremony for the deceased, the *profectio ad iter Averni*, on the road to the lake where the celebrated oracle of the dead had resided; finally, on October 15, the *Vindemiae*.

358

The Medal Collection

The Medal Collection is one of the richest in Italy and the world (about 20,000 specimens). Its original nucleus is the ancient Farnesian collection, whose numismatic section was put together by Orsini, mainly as a data base for his research on the iconography of Roman emperors (the so-called Imperial series). This corpus was later augmented in Naples by the copious finds of the Bourbonic period in the Vesuvian cities (about 15,000 specimens, especially valuable for the study of monetary circulation through the examination of hoards found in the houses and on the bodies of the Pompeian fugitives), in Great Greece and Sicily. Much of the material (about 42,000 specimens) of the great Santangelo corpus, which was added in 1864 to the important collections already in the Neapolitan Museum, comes from the latter two regions. No less important than the coins of the Classical period is the nucleus of Byzantine, Medieval, Renaissance and modern coins, especially those documenting the activity of mints that succeeded one another in the Kingdom of Naples up to the Bourbonic mint of the Kingdom of the Two Sicilies.

The coin collection of Great Greece and Sicily is naturally extremely rich. Coinage (in silver, the main metal for ancient coins) began in the West among the Achaean colonies of the Gulf of Taranto, possibly at Sybaris or Metapontum, in the latter half of the 6th century B.C. Sybaris is an especially likely candidate, as it had access to the inland silver mines of the Sila, and was a city of legendary power and wealth. The first coins minted in this area are characterised by a special technique called *incusa*, i.e. they bear the same image in relief on the recto and impressed on the verso; this technique later extended to almost all of Great Greece. The basis of this system, called "Achaean", was the tridram of Corinthian origin (8 grams).

Another monetary area comprised the colonies of the straits of Messina (Naxos, Zankle-Messana, Rhegion) and other cities founded by Euboean colonists (Cumae, Himera); here, the Chalcidean system was adopted, based on a dram of ca. 5.70 grams.

Velia (*Hyele*), Poseidonia and later on all the cities of Campania adopted another system, called "Phocaean" or "Campanian", based on a didram of about 7.50 grams. It was adopted, in the last quarter of the 6th cen-

tury B.C., by Massalia as well, although at inferior values, not over one hemidram.

South-western Sicily (Selinus, Agrigentum, Gela), connected via the Punic world to the Iberian silver mines, adopted coinage very soon, possibly as early as the middle of the 6th century, like the Achaean colonies, coining a didram of about 8.70 grams, a prestige coin and an aggressive political instrument from the beginning.

Besides being a very effective means for economic exchange, coins were also an extraordinary instrument of political power, and as such they preserve, in the impressed images they bear, the traces of political events with a vividness sometimes unknown to the literary sources themselves. One only has to think of the "imperial coins" from Sybaris, whose bull looking backwards − a motif adopted by other communities as well who merely added their ethnical name − was almost the banner of the expansion of the city, which came to rule, according to Strabo, over 25 other cities and 4 peoples. Likewise, the extension, after 480 B.C., of the Attic system of the tetradram and of its type, the *quadriga*, from Syracuse to almost all of Sicily and to Cumae is certainly a consequence of the victory over the Carthaginians and the Etruscans at Cumae.

Another distinctive feature of the coinage of Great Greece is the more frequent use of gold, with respect to Greece. Actually, the minting of gold coins by cities such as Tarentum, Metapontum, Heraclea and Locris was induced by the need to pay their wages to mercenaries coming from countries (Macedonia, Epirus) where the currency was in gold.

It was Sicily that first introduced bronze coins, around the middle of the 5th century B.C. The diffusion of money as a universal means of exchange made it necessary to adopt coins made of a metal less precious than silver, whose value was based only on the authority of the state that coined them, to avoid having to mint excessively diminutive silver coins for small commerce.

A great novelty in the history of coinage was the reform proclaimed, in Syracuse, by the tyrant Dionysus I. Inspired by the new tendency to distinguish between fixed-rate money of conventional value for internal circulation and precious metal money for external transactions (asserted by Plato in his *Laws*, V, 742 a-b: "no private individual must be allowed to possess gold or silver, but only coin...that is current locally, but has no value among other peoples..."), Dionysius modified Syracusan coinage radically, creating a bronze coin (1 litra and 5 litrae) for internal circulation, and gold and silver coins (decadrams) for foreign transactions, pieces of very high artistic value made by extremely skilful engravers such as Kimon, Euainetos and Eukleidas.

Another important phase in Greek coinage in the West is the Corinthian monetary policy coinciding with Timoleon's reconquest of Sicily. Syracuse, in fact, suddenly abandoned the Attic system for the Corinthian one, adopting two classical types of its homeland, Pegasus on the recto and Athena wearing the Corinthian helmet on the verso. Its example was followed by many cities of Sicily and Calabria, evidently in the orbit of Syracuse. As it was impossible for these communities, exhausted by the wars, to sustain the costs of coinage, Corinth took this task upon itself, issuing a massive quantity of silver Paegasi, commonly featured in all the *tesoretti* ("hoards") of the second half of the 4th century B.C.

In the Italic world, money was doubtlessly introduced under the influence of the Greek colones. After an initial phase of exchanges in kind, specific weights of metal (bronze) began to be used, first in raw, unworked form (*aes rude*), then smelted into ingots making up an actual ponderal system and bearing symbols (*aes signatum*); the weight unit was the *libra* (first 272.875, later 327.45 grams), on which the earliest Roman system was based. The main unit of the latter was the *as*, a smelted coin (*aes grave*) with the head of two-faced Janus on the recto and a ship's prow on the verso. It was divided into 12 ounces, the *semis* (1/2 *as*, with the sign S), the *triens*, the *quadrans*, the *sextans* and the *uncia*, respectively a third, a quarter, a sixth and a twelfth of an *as*, with four, three, two, and a small globe as marks of value. This system, which remained in use to the end of the Republic, was changed by Augustus in 23 B.C. by introducing copper *asses* and *quadrantes*, and *dupondi* and *sestertii* in orichalc, a brass alloy, according to the following rates: 1 *sestertium* = 2 *dupondi* = 4 *assi* = 16 *quadrants*.

The magistrates in charge of the Roman mint were the *Triumviri monetales A(ere), A(rgento), A(uro) F(lando) F(eriundo)*, whose acronyms appear regularly on coins, unless they were issued by special decree, for example of the Senate, in which case they bear the formula S.C. (*senatus consultu*). The religious iconography of the more ancient types was gradually replaced, in the course of the 2nd century B.C., by that of types alluding to the persons of the monetary magistrates or to their families and, finally, to contemporary political events, thus providing precious information on political competition as well as a useful cross-check with the literary sources. In the course of the 3rd century B.C., Rome began to coin silver (probably using the Naples mint), with the *denarius* as the base unit. At the end of the first century B.C, gold coinage began. Under Augustus, a gold *denarius* and *quinarius* were respectively equivalent to 25 and 12,5 silver *denarii*, while a silver *denarius* and *quinarius* were equivalent to 16 and 8 copper *asses*. During the Empire, besides the Roman mint, many provincial ones were active as well. Coins became more and more an instrument of propaganda. The types bear the portraits of the emperor and the princes of the imperial family, and images alluding to the *princeps's* achievements, including his military successes (images of captive provinces, triumphs, trophies), the construction of temples and other public buildings, and the exalting of his own personified virtues or those of his time (*Concordia, Felicitas* etc.).

Incused "Ami" stater, from Cittanuova
inv. 111315

On the recto, in exergue, the inscription *Ami*; retrorse bull facing left. Above it, a locust; tress-shaped rim. On the verso, same type; the rim is bordered by a fish-spine motif. This silver coin, weighing 7.84 grams, is dated to 540-510 B.C.; the retrorse bull, in this shape, is a type of the Sybarite mint, and identical reproductions are found on the coins of the Achaean colony and of its satellites.

Incused stater from Caulonia
Fig. 3311

On the recto, on the left, is the inscription *Kaul*. In the field, on the right, is a standing figure of Apollo with a branch in his hand and a small running figure on his left arm. In front of the god is his sacred animal, a retrorse deer. On the verso, the same type appears.
The coin dates from 530-510 B.C.

Decadram from Syracuse
Fg. 5122
On the recto, a quadriga is galloping toward the left, and a Nike is crowning the driver. Under the exergue line, a panoplia is represented. On the verso, a head of Kore is depicted, with a wreath of wheat ears on the left and dolphins all around. At the bottom is the signature of the engraver, Euainetos
This is one of the finest known Greek coins. It is dated to ca. 390 B.C.

Didram from Alife
S.G. 410
On the recto, a head of Athena facing right, with her helmet adorned by an owl and an olive branch; on the verso, above, the inscription *Alipha*, in Oscan; below, a human-faced bull, facing left. The coin, datable to the period 400-395 B.C., is modelled on a Nolan coin on its verso, while on the recto it is inspired by the Neapolitan version of the Parthenos of Athens.

Didram of Cora
inv. 124158

On the recto, a head of Apollo, crowned with laurel; on the verso, in exergue, the inscription *Corano*, in Latin; in the field, figure of a rider dressed with a petasus and a chlamys, galloping to the right, his spear in his right hand. Datable to the first half of the 3rd century B.C.

Denarius of Brutus
F.r. 3072

On the recto, the head of Brutus, the assassin of Caesar, with the inscription *Brutus*; on the verso, a head of *C. Servilius Abala*. The coin dates from 54 B.C.; the depiction of Brutus is a fine example of portraiture on Republican coins.

Gold medallion of Augustus, from Pompeii

F.r. 3692

This medallion, coined in the mint of Lyon (*Lugdunum*) in 9-8 B.C., is an *unicum* found in Pompeii in 1759. On the recto, it bears the head of Augustus wearing a laurel wreath; on the verso, the inscription *Imp.(erator) XV* and the statuary figure of an Artemis that must have been popular in Sicily (in exergue is the inscription *Sicil*). The figure may be a replica of the famous statue of Diana of Segesta, holding the bow and in the act of drawing an arrow out of the quiver.

The Egyptian collection

The Egyptian collection of the Naples Museum, the second in importance in Italy, after that of the Egyptian Museum in Turin, was formed from several nuclei. Only one piece belonged to the Farnese collection, viz the naophorous statue called, appropriately, "Farnese", originally displayed in the Roman palace in the room "of the emperors" and, in Naples, in the portico called "de' miscellanei".

The main nucleus of the collection (rooms I-III) was put together in the second half of the 18th century by Cardinal Stefano Borgia. The Cardinal inherited a collection of Roman and Etruscan antiquities found in Rome and in his family's estate in the territory of Velletri. In his capacity as Secretary and later Prefect of the Congregation of Propaganda Fide, he was presented by travellers and missionaries returning from the Orient not only with Coptic manuscripts (the acquisition of which was the main reason for the voyages of many clergymen), but with numerous Egyptian objects as well, enabling him to put together the richest Egyptian collection of his time. His nephew Camillo, having inherited it, repeatedly sought to sell it, first to the King of Denmark, then to Joachim Murat, and finally to Ferdinand IV, who purchased it in 1815. A third nucleus is the collection of Giuseppe Picchianti (rooms IV-V), a Venetian 19th century traveller who, drawn by the fame of the discoveries made in Egypt by Belzoni, a Venetian himself, and by the mirage of treasures to be discovered, set off in 1819 on a voyage that lasted about six years, taking him as far as the Nubian desert. At Giza, Saqqara, Thebes, and in Nubia, he collected a remarkable quantity of objects, mainly from funerary contexts, which he submitted to the great Champollion for examination. He managed to sell a part of it to the British Museum, while another and more conspicuous lot was bought by the Museum of Naples from his widow in 1826.

Of the other, smaller collections that entered the Museum, we still need to mention that of Schnars (room III, showcase 15), a German traveller who had visited many sites of Upper and Lower Egypt, putting together a small collection which he donated to the Museum in 1842. The Museum also acquired a few single objects, such as the so-called *naoforo Casanova* from Pozzuoli (1827), or the mummy donated in 1885 by E. Stevens, to whom it had been presented while he was travelling through Egypt.

The Egyptian objects found in the excavations of the cities of Campania, especially the Vesuvian sites destroyed by the 79 A.D. eruption, are an important component of the Neapolitan collection. As was said elsewhere, relations between Egypt and Campania, which began at the time of Greek colonisation through the intermediation of Phoenician trade (scarabs and faience objects appear in tombs of Pithekoussai, Cumae, and the indigenous communities of the interior), became closer from the Ptolemaic age on, leading, in the 2nd century B.C., to the irradiation of the Isiac cult to Campania (cf. the *lex parieti faciendo* in Pozzuoli) and Rome. Pompeii, Herculaneum and Stabiae, and Naples, Sorrento and Benevento as well, have yielded numerous Egyptian and Egyptianizing sculptures and objects, used both in the ritual of the Isiac sanctuaries (eg. the shabtis, the stela of Samtowetef-nakhte in the temple of Isis in Pompeii, four canopic vases also from Pompeii, the Isis, the naophorous statue and the sphinx from the Iseum in Cumae), and as mere decorative objects, according to the fashion that had spread all over the Roman world after the conquest of Egypt (e.g. the votive offering table with the name of Psammeticus from the House of the Double Lararium in Pompeii, or the male statuettes used as table supports).

This variety of influxes makes the Neapolitan collection especially interesting for the history of Egyptology itself. The Borgian phase, which discovered Egypt without moving from Rome, and focussed on its magical and religious aspects, is contrasted with Picchianti's and Schnars' travels, epitomising the romantic and semiscientific adventure of searchers of antiquities to supply the European museums.

The archaeological aspects of the collection are no less interesting than the historical ones. The recent exhibition presents the sculptures (statues and reliefs) of the Borgia collection in the first room, the funerary and votive objects of the same collection in the second, in the third a group of inscriptions (and 19th century casts) providing a view of the different types of writing used in Egypt from the origins to demotic and Greek, and the Egyptian objects from Campania. In the fourth room are the vases, the funerary stelae and a rich series of shabtis from the Picchianti collection, along with mummies, both human and animal, also forming the main theme of the fifth and last room.

The curiosity of visitors is often drawn to some mummy fragments consisting of human feet under a glass dome. They are a testimony of the very peculiar use of mummies that was made after antiquity. In the process of mummification, a natural bitumen was employed (the *Mumya* or *Mumia persica*), used in Medieval medicine to obtain a drug of allegedly miraculous powers, "the mummy powder", from mummified human bodies. This macabre therapy remained in vogue until the last century, leading to an actual commerce of mummies (and, naturally, to the forging of mummy material as well). In the Neapolitan collection there are mummies from the Pharmacies of the suppressed church of San Francesco di Paola and of the Real Casa Santa dell'Annunziata.

Canopic vases are also well represented in the Neapolitan collection. They contained the internal organs of the deceased, which were removed before mummification and put into these vases, bearing the name of the deceased, and placed alongside the sarcophagus. The name comes from that of Menelaos' helmsman, who died in Egypt and was deified in the form of a vase with human head. The lids of the vases present, in fact, the striking characteristic of being shaped as the heads of the sons of Horus. The human-headed one (Amset) contained the stomach and the intestine, the baboon-headed one (Hapy) the small intestine, the jackal-headed one (Duamutef) the lungs, and the falcon-headed one (Qebehsenuf) the liver and the gall-bladder.

The *shabti* collection is also remarkable. It comprises stone, wood and faience mummy-shaped statuettes embodying entities required to work in the afterworld instead of the deceased (*ushabty*: "he who answers"). Thus, the statuette, bearing the name of the deceased, is inscribed with the formula of the Book of the Dead in which one orders the shabti to work in his stead. They eventually became very numerous, up to 365, one for each day of the year, led by overseers, and were put into boxes placed inside the tomb. The *Harpocratean stelae* are also interesting. They consist of slabs having the function of providing their owner with magical protection against the attack of dangerous animals such as snakes, scorpions etc. On one side of the stelae, Harpocrates (Hor-pa-khered, Horus the Child) was depicted, with the typical tress along the side of his head, trampling over crocodiles and holding dangerous animals in his hands.

On the other side are hieroglyphic formulae reporting episodes of the myth of Horus, protected by his mother Isis against the animals raised against him by Seth, the wicked brother and murderer of Osiris.

Naophorous statue of Uah-ib-ra Mery-neith, so-called "Naoforo Farnese", from Rome (?)
inv. 1068

Egyptian statues differ from Classic ones, in that they were thought to be imbued with life, being animated, through a ritual called the "Opening of the Mouth", by the vital essence of the represented person (this is why the bust did not exist). The function of statues was to act as an intermediary between men and the gods, and to receive the funerary offerings of the living. Their features are conventional, lacking physiognomic characterisation; their identification is entrusted to the inscriptions and outward status signs (the dress, attributes). The Farnese statue, of basalt, belongs to the category of naophorous statues, representing a kneeling official (in later times a standing one as well) holding in his hands a shrine (*naòs*, in Greek) containing the figure of the king, and later on of a god (here, it is the figure of Osiris). The hieroglyphic inscription on the back-pillar of the figure (fantastic interpretations of which were proposed by Father Athanasius Kircher in the 17th century) identifies the official it represents as Uah-ib-ra Mery-neith, son of Ta-qerenet, Royal Seal-Bearer, Director of the House of the Two Crowns, Priest of Horus, Chief of the District of Pe, Superintendent of the Seals; it contains the so-called "formula of Sais". The iconography and the formula date the statue to the XXVI dynasty (664-525 B.C.).

368 This limestone stele, whose colours are rather well preserved, goes back to the beginning of the XIX dynasty (1320-1200 B.C.). It depicts, on three registers, the deceased, Huy, "Scribe of the Offering-table of the Lord of the Two Lands, Guide to the Festivals of Osiris", in the presence of the gods. In the upper register, Huy, on the right, faces an offering table placed in front of a shrine in which Osiris sits, followed by Isis and the falcon-god Horus. In the middle register, Huy gives offerings to his father Pah and his mother Sati. In the lower register the priest Pa-nehu, with shaven head and wearing a panther-skin, libates and burns incense for Huy and his wife Kuy.

Varia

We have gathered under this heading the many other series of objects that entered the Museum under various circumstances, and which it would be difficult to fit into a historical discourse. The main nucleus is, as we hinted earlier on, the Borgia collection, which was purchased by the Museum immediately after the Restoration. Alongside the Egyptian antiquities, the Museo Veliterno (in Velletri) included many Italic, Etruscan and Latin antiquities, and even some important Greek and Oriental objects.

Several single acquisitions were made by the Museum following archaeological discoveries, purchases or testamentary legacies. One of the most significant of the latter is a recently acquired group of sculptures from the Astarita collection, including a splendid head in Pergamene style.

Among the "minor", so to speak, collections, also of great cultural importance, the incised "rami" (etchings) of the Stamperia Reale Borbonica, one of the greatest chalco-graphic collections in Italy, deserve a mention. This collection includes the especially important plates of the *Antichità di Ercolano*, the precious volumes that the Accademia Ercolanese worked on for about a century to publish the ancient monuments of the Vesuvian cities. The etchings and their preparatory drawings, still in part unpublished, are an extremely significant patrimony attesting the evolution both of documenting methods and incision styles from the middle of the 18th century on.

No less important are the documents in the archives of the Soprintendenza di Napoli e Caserta, including drawings, watercolours, models, casts and photographs, as well as correspondence and scientific reports that allow us to reconstruct the dense interplay of historical relationships that surrounds archaeological research and its protagonists and is one of the main reasons for this discipline's appeal.

Melian relief, from Ruvo (?)
inv. Santangelo 361

This relief, datable to ca. 470-460 B.C., belongs to a series of unusual fictile plates, moulded and worked "a giorno", whose centre of production is still discussed by scholars, but somewhere between the Aegean islands (Melos?) and Corinth. It seems that an origin from one of the major Greek artistic centers can be ruled out.

These plates, probably used as *appliqués* for wooden caskets or other pieces of furniture, were decorated with mythological themes. Their repertory is very varied, often revealing a remarkable iconographic autonomy with respect to Attic and Corinthian models.

This specimen represents the ancient myth of Atteon eaten by his own dogs for having offended the goddess Artemis by spying on her as she was bathing in a fountain. The scene is constructed by the opposition between the slender figure of the adolescent goddess with her imperious gesture and proud stride under her transparent clothes, and the athletic body of Atteon, who has collapsed to his knees, a prey to his lean, fierce greyhounds.

The elegant and somewhat angular forms are typical of the end of the stern style.

370

Fictile slab with a chariot-race, from Velletri, Borgia colleciton
inv. 21608

The Archaic terracottas that entered the Borgia collection belonged to the 6th century fictile decoration of the temple under the church of Santa Maria la Neve. By combining them with other slabs from the same building, found in the excavations of 1915, it is possible to reconstruct at least part of the decoration, in purely Etruscan style, of this building of the main city of the Volscans (cortege of chariots, banquet scenes, chariot race, assembly of gods, etc.).

Ionian funerary stele, Borgia collection
inv. 6556

This stele, datable to the years after 480 B.C., is one of a group of funerary monuments from the late Archaic period and the beginning of the stern style, typical of the art of the Greek cities of the Aegean islands and Asiatic Ionia.

The deceased is represented according to the ideological canons of Archaic aristocracy, as an athlete (the *aryballos* contains gymnasium oil) and a hunter (as indicated by the dog at his side). The gesture of holding out a grasshopper to the dog is humoristic and elegant.

Attic lekythos with a white background
inv. 124708 (Canessa purchase)
White-background *lekythoi*, produced in
Athens after the end of the 6th century
B.C., acquired, from the middle of the
following century, an iconography in
keeping with their funerary use as containers of ritual oil and perfumes. Thus, in
the cult scene, the *lekythos* is represented in the hands of the girl sitting
near the tomb. Second half of the 5th
century B.C.

Wild goat from Edessa,
Borgia collection
inv. 24286
The ancient Mesopotamic and Persian tradition of representing animals is well expressed by this goat figure, moving its head with a liveliness and grace that obscure the material value of the gold of which it is made (it is a full fusion). 4th century B.C.

374

The Tyrannicides, from Tivoli,
Villa Adriana
inv. 6009-6010

In 514 B.C. two young Athenians, *Harmodios* and *Aristogeiton*, killed Hipparchos, the younger son of the tyrant Pisistratus, and paid for their act with their lives. The Athenian democratic party later made of their gesture the symbol of liberty itself and, as soon as the Tyrants were banished (510 B.C.), two bronze statues made by the sculptor Antenor (a fragment of the base with the remains of the epigram was found in the excavations) were erected on the Agora. When the Persians occupied the city in 480 B.C., they took the statues as spoils and brought them to Susa (they were given back to the Athenians by the successors of Alexander the Great a century and a half later). After their victory over the Persians, the Athenians decreed that a new bronze statue group of the Tyrannicides should be erected, and entrusted Kritios and Nesiotes with its execution (476 B.C.). Images of this group, by then a symbol of patriotism and of the cult of the ancient Attic virtues, survive on coins, painted vases and reliefs. On the basis of these reproductions, it has been possible to identify these two Neapolitan statues, Roman copies of the 2nd century B.C. found in the Villa Adriana in Tivoli. The figures are an example of the "stern style" at its height. The bodies are wiry and powerful, but devoid of the archaic calligraphisms still found, for example, on the pediments of Aegina. Both figures are portrayed in action: Harmodius, the beardless young man, is attacking with his arm raised, while Aristogeiton stretches his arm forward to shield his friend. The head of Aristogeiton is a cast of a head presently in the Vatican. A splendid ancient cast of the bronze original was found in Baiae and is on display in the Museo dei Campi Flegrei at Baia Castle.

311

So-called "Lar"
inv. 5975

The association of a drawing of this statue with a view of the Baths of Caracalla
in the collection of drawings of the
Dutch M. van Heemskerck led scholars
to presume that the statue originally
came from the Thermae themselves.
The fact that the drawings are earlier
than the excavation later ruled out this
hypothesis. Nevertheless, this colossal
statue certainly comes from a great
urban public complex. The type of the
curly-headed boy with the patera, the
drapery of the dress and the shoes suggest an identification of the figure as the
Genius populi Romani. If this is true,
the left hand possibly held a cornucopia.

312

Acanthus-leaf crown from Falerii,
Borgia collection
inv. 25288
In 1811, three cups, datable to the 2nd
century B.C., were found in *Falerii*,
present-day Civita Castellana. They were
part of an unfortunately dispersed treasure
also including a silver statuette of a
centaur presently in Vienna. They are an
exquisite example of the refinement of
the goldwork of a Hellenistic Asiatic
workshop, either Pergamon or Antiochia.
The cups must have been spoils of war
or products made to satisfy the Roman
aristocracy's need for *luxuria*. They
resemble the toreutic models from
which the humble earthenware containers
known as "megarese" vases derive.

Marble relief with the visit of Dionysus, Borgia collection

inv. 6713

This relief of unknown origin, a product of the Neo-Attic school (other replicas are known in the Louvre and other museums), represents the arrival of Dionysus, portrayed as a drunken elderly man supported by a young Satyr, with his cortege of Satyrs and Maenads, near the house of Ikarios. The latter, lying back on his *kline* in the company of a woman, Antigone, greets the god he has evoked, who is taking off his shoes with the help of another young satyr. In this *theoxenia*, evidently Hellenistic in inspiration, the architectural background of Ikarios' house is especially interesting. Its perspective planes recall the style of a city portrayed on the Boscoreale wall in the Metropolitan Museum of New York. These stylistic elements indicate a date around the middle of the 1st century B.C.

Situla with figures of bathing women
inv. 25289
In spite of its being registered in the inventories of Portici, this cannot have come from Herculaneum.

The architectural background of columns and arches recalls the one found on late Roman sarcophagi, and the style of the figures indicates a date in the 3rd century B.C. The scene, representing Aphrodite at her bath, assisted by handmaids, reveals the function of this refined object used in the female bath and toilette, whose actual provenance we would indeed like to learn.

Head of an Athlete, Astarita collection inv. 205248

The head with its strong chin, the thick lips, the arrangement of the hair in concentric rows of comma-shaped locks are typical of the great bronze statuary of the 5th century B.C. On the other hand, the polished surface of the copy, the precision of its contours, the inclination of its eye, veiling it with a streak of melancholy, are characteristic of the academic purism of the age of Hadrian. This sculpture is a free re-elaboration, although it adheres quite closely to the Classic taste, of the statue of an athlete, similar to Myron's Discobolus.

Glass goblet with Dionysian scenes, from Saepinum
inv. 138739
This vase, decorated with incised Dionysian figures alluding to the millenary theme of the symposium and wine, was found in 1919 in a tomb in the necropolis of *Saepinum*, a centre on the Pescasseroli-Candela droving route, at the foot of the Molisan Matese. It can be dated to the 4th century B.C. The most active workshops of the time were in Egypt, Cologne and Aquileia, and *Puteoli* as well, as we know from the famous souvenir flasks presenting views of the Phlegraean coast. Further fragments of fine incised glass objects were found in Campochiaro, in a sanctuary on a road leading from Campania to Molise; their origin is possibly Puteolan.

Fibula and pair of earrings, gold and hard stones, from Senise
invv. 153621, 153618

The fibula, found with the earrings in a grave in Senise (MT), in the valley of the Sinni, presents refined granulation of the gold and hard stone inserts (the central one is unfortunately missing). The find is dated to the 7th century by the impression on the earrings of a golden coin of the emperors of the East Heraclius and Tiberius (659-668 A.D.) who, at the time, ruled over Basilicata.

These objects are typical products of Byzantine goldsmiths, like the jewels worn by the dames and dignitaries pictured in the Ravenna mosaics.

Bibliography

382   L. Giustiniani, *Memorie storiche critiche della Real Biblioteca Borbonica*, Napoli 1818

G.B. Finati, *Il Regal Museo Borbonico*, I-III, Napoli 1819-1823

M. Gélas, *Catalogue des statues en bronze exposés dans une grande salle du Musée Bourbon à Naples*, Napoli 1820

L. Giustiniani, Fr. de Licteriis, *Guida per lo Real Museo Borbonico*, Napoli 1822

A. Niccolini, *Real Museo Borbonico*, XVI, Napoli 1824-1857; II ed., Roma 1837-1845

E. Gerhard, Th. Panofka, *Neapels antike Bildwerke*, I Teil, Stuttgart und Tübingen 1828

Regolamento pel Museo Reale Borbonico, Napoli 1828

A. Morelli, *Musée Royal Bourbon*, Naples 1835

Fr. Alvino, *Description des Monuments du Musée Royal Bourbon*, Napoli 1841

B. Vulpes, *Illustrazione di tutti gli strumenti chirurgici scavati in Pompei ed Ercolano*, Napoli 1847

C. Ceci, *Museo Nazionale*, Napoli 1854 (II Ed.: *Piccoli bronzi del Real Museo Borbonico*, Napoli 1858)

G. Fiorelli, *Catalogo del Museo Nazionale di Napoli, Raccolta pornografica*, Napoli 1866

G. Fiorelli, *Catalogo del Museo Nazionale di Napoli, Raccolta epigrafica I, Iscrizioni Greche ed Italiche*, Napoli 1867

G. Fiorelli, *Catalogo del Museo Nazionale di Napoli, Armi antiche*, Napoli 1869

G. Fiorelli, *Catalogo del Museo Nazionale di Napoli, Collezione Santangelo, Monete greche*, Napoli 1866

G. Fiorelli, *Catalogo del Museo Nazionale di Napoli, Collezione Santangelo, Monete del Medio Evo*, Napoli 1867

G. Fiorelli, *Catalogo del Museo Nazionale di Napoli, Medagliere, I, Monete greche*, Napoli 1870

G. Fiorelli, *Catalogo del Museo Nazionale di Napoli, Medagliere, II, Monete romane*, Napoli 1870

G. Fiorelli, *Catalogo del Museo Nazionale di Napoli, Medagliere, III, Monete del Medio Evo e moderne*, Napoli 1871

G. Fiorelli, *Catalogo del Museo Nazionale di Napoli, Medagliere, VI, Matrici, punzoni e conii della R. Zecca*, Napoli 1866

Bollettino del Museo Nazionale di Napoli, I, 1864

W. Helbig, *Wandgemälde der vom Vesuvius verschütteten Städte Campaniens*, Leipzig 1868

H. Heydemann, *Die Vasensammlung des Museo Nazionale zu Neapel*, Berlin 1872

D. Monaco, *Guide Général du Musée National de Naples, suivant le Nouvel Arrangement*, Naples 1874

A. Migliozzi, *Nuova Guida Generale del Museo Nazionale di Napoli secondo i più recenti riordinamenti corredata di un'appendice riguardante Pompei e la Certosa di S. Martino*, Napoli 1876

G. Fiorelli, *Documenti inediti per servire alla storia dei Musei d'Italia*, I, Firenze 1878-1879

A. Avena, *La conservazione dei monumenti e lo scalone del Museo Nazionale di Napoli*, Napoli 1897

B. Croce, *Un nuovo scandalo al Museo di Napoli*, in «Napoli Nobilissima», vol. IX, 1900, p. 145-148

G. De Petra, *Intorno al Museo Nazionale di Napoli. Autodifesa*, Napoli 1901

N. Breglia, E. Martini, B. Croce, *Relazione della Commissione per la sistemazione dei lavori del Museo e della Biblioteca di Napoli*, in «Napoli Nobilissima», vol. XI, issue VI, 1902, p. 92

G. Ceci, *Il Palazzo degli Studi (I-III)*, in «Napoli Nobilissima», vol. XIII-XV, 1904-06

B. Croce, *Il Museo sotto i Borboni*, in «Napoli Nobilissima», vol. XV, issue II, 1906

A. Ruesch, *Guida illustrata del Museo Nazionale di Napoli*, Napoli 1908

A. Ruesch, *Compendio della guida illustrata del Museo Nazionale di Napoli*, Napoli 1925, 1928

G. Consoli Fiego-A. Maiuri, *Museo Nazionale di Napoli. Salone degli Arazzi*, Napoli 1927

V. Spinazzola, *Le arti decorative in Pompei e nel Museo Nazionale di Napoli*, Milano 1928

A. Maiuri, *Aspetti e problemi dell'archeologia campana*, in «Historia», IV, 1930

G. Pesce, *Il Museo Nazionale di Napoli*, Roma 1932

O. Elia, *Pitture murali e mosaici nel Museo Nazionale di Napoli*, Roma 1932

G. Pesce, *Oreficeria, Toreutica, Glittica, Vitraria, Ceramica*, in «Itinerari dei Musei e Monumenti», 19, Roma 1934

A. Maiuri, *Gli studi di Antichità a Napoli nel Sette e Ottocento*, in «Rendiconti della Reale Accademia di Archeologia, Lettere e Belle Arti di Napoli», XVII, 1937

E. Pernice, *Gefässe und Geräte aus Bronze (Die hellenistische Kunst in Pompeji, VI)*, Berlin 1938

L. Breglia, *Catalogo delle oreficerie del Museo Nazionale di Napoli*, Napoli 1941

A. de Franciscis, *Per la storia del Museo Nazionale di Napoli*, in «Archivio Storico per le Province Napoletane», N.S., XXX, 1944-46, p. 169-200

A. de Franciscis, *Restauri di Carlo Albacini a statue del Museo Nazionale di Napoli*, in «Samnium», XIX, 1946, pp. 96-102

A. Adriani, *Vasi di stile attico a figure nere*, C.V.A., Italia, issue XX, Museo Nazionale di Napoli, I, 1950

A. Rocco, *Ceramiche delle fabbriche tarde*, in C.V.A., Italia, issue XXII, Museo Nazionale di Napoli, 1953

Eadem, *Ceramiche a decorazione sovradipinta*, in C.V.S.A., Italia, issue XXIV, Museo Nazionale di Napoli, III, 1954

Siviero, *Gli ori e le ambre del Museo Nazionale di Napoli*, Napoli 1954

B. Maiuri, *Museo Nazionale di Napoli*, Novara 1957

I. Donsì, *Uno dei fondi recuperati dell'Archivio di Stato di Napoli*, in *Studi in onore di R. Filangieri*, Napoli 1959, p. 54.

A. de Franciscis, *Il Museo Nazionale di Napoli*, Cava dei Tirreni-Napoli 1963

A. de Franciscis, *Musaici antichi del Museo Nazionale di Napoli*, Cava dei Tirreni-Napoli 1963

G. E. Rubino, *La sistemazione del Museo Borbonico di Napoli nei disegni di Fuga e Schiantarelli*, in «Napoli Nobilissima», vol. XII, issue IV, 1973, pp. 126.

M. Grant, A. Mulas, *Eros a Pompei, il gabinetto segreto del Museo di Napoli*, Milano 1964

P.G. Guzzo, *Le gemme a scarabeo del Museo Nazionale di Napoli*, in «MEFRA», 83, 1971, pp. 325-366

AA.VV., *Da Palazzo degli Studi a Museo Archeologico. Catalogo della Mostra storico-documentaria del Museo Nazionale di Napoli*, Napoli 1977

AA. VV., *Atti del II Incontro di studi sull'»Instrumentum domesticum» di Pompei ed Ercolano nella prima età imperiale*, in «Quaderni di Cultura materiale», I, Roma 1977

A. González-Palacios, *Il trasporto delle statue farnesiane da Roma a Napoli*, in «Antologia di Belle Arti», 1978, pp. 168-174

A. Giuliano, *Documenti per servire alla storia del Museo di Napoli*, in «Rendiconti dell'Accademia di Arch., Lettere e B. Arti di Napoli», n.s., LIV, 1979, p. 93.

E. Pozzi, *Per un riordinamento delle collezioni del Museo Archeologico Nazionale di Napoli*, in «Immagine del Museo negli anni '80», *Bollettino d'Arte*, 1982

AA.VV., *Itinerario Farnesiano. Le sculture Farnese del Museo di Napoli*, Catalogo della Mostra, Napoli 1982

A. Allroggen-Bedel, H. Kammerer-Grothaus, *Il Museum ercolanese di Portici*, in *Cronache Ercolanesi*, 13, 1983

N. Valenza Mele, *Museo Nazionale di Napoli. Catalogo delle lucerne in bronzo*, Napoli 1983

L. A. Scatozza Hoericht, *Restauri alle collezioni del Museo Ercolanese di Portici alla luce di documenti inediti*, in «Atti Accademia Pontaniana», 21, 1983, p. 495.

U. Pannuti, *Museo Archeologico Nazionale di Napoli. Catalogo della collezione glittica*, I, Roma, 1983

A. Ferri Messano, *Il funzionamento dei Musei napoletani in età borbonica. Alcune novità*, in «Museologia», 16, 1984

Il Museo Archeologico Nazionale. Napoli «Guide pratiche Garolla», Milano 1984

J. Papadopoulos, *Museo Archeologico Nazionale di Napoli, Le sculture della Collezione Astarita*, Napoli 1984

E. Pozzi, *Il percorso della Mostra tra il museo di ieri e il Museo di domani*, in *Napoli Antica*, exhibition catalogue, Napoli 1985

G. Hölbl, *Museo Archeologico Nazionale di Napoli. Le stele funerarie della collezione egizia*, Roma 1985

AA. VV., *La cultura classica a Napoli nell'Ottocento*, Napoli 1987, pp. 815-902 (*Gli studi archeologici: dall'antiquaria alla storia; Francesco Maria Avellino, Giulio Minervini, Giuseppe Fiorelli, Giulio De Petra*)

AA. VV., *Classicismo di età romana. La collezione Farnese*, Napoli 1988

AA. VV., *Le collezioni del Museo Nazionale di Napoli*, Roma, I 1986, II 1989

AA. VV., *La collezione egiziana del Museo Archeologico Nazionale di Napoli*, Napoli 1989

AA. VV., *Il Toro Farnese. La «montagna di marmo» tra Roma e Napoli*, Napoli 1991

M.R. Borriello, *Collezione Spinelli*, in C.V.A., Italia, issue LXVI, Museo Nazionale di Napoli, IV, 1991

AA. VV., *Alla ricerca di Iside. Analisi, studi e restauri dell'Iseo pompeiano nel Museo di Napoli*, Napoli 1992

C. Gasparri, *Le Gemme Farnese*, Napoli 1994

I Greci in Occidente: La Magna Grecia nelle collezioni del Museo Archeologico di Napoli, exhibition catalogue, Napoli 1996

The Western Greeks, Napoli 1996

Published by Electa Napoli
in September 1996

Typeset by Photocomp 2000, Naples
Photolithos by SAMA, Naples
Photo-engraving by Centro dms, Naples
Printed by Incisivo, Salerno
Bound by Legatoria S. Tonti, Mugnano, Naples